Learn, Teach...
Succeed...

With **REA's TExES™ English as a Second Language Supplemental (154)** test prep, you'll be in a class all your own.

WE'D LIKE TO HEAR FROM YOU!
Visit **www.rea.com** to send us your comments

TExES™ ESL SUPPLEMENTAL (154)

TEXAS EXAMINATIONS OF EDUCATOR STANDARDS™

Beatrice Mendez Newman, Ph.D.
The University of Texas Rio Grande Valley

Research & Education Association
www.rea.com

Research & Education Association
258 Prospect Plains Road
Cranbury, New Jersey 08512
Email: info@rea.com

TExES™ English as a Second Language Supplemental (154) with Online Practice Tests, 2nd Edition

Published 2022

Printed in the United States of America

Library of Congress Control Number 2020914978

ISBN-13: 978-0-7386-1267-6
ISBN-10: 0-7386-1267-7

The competencies presented in this book were created and implemented by the Texas Education Agency and Pearson Education, Inc., or its affiliates. Texas Examinations of Educator Standards and TExES are trademarks of the Texas Education Agency. All other trademarks cited in this publication are the property of their respective owners.

Cover image: © iStockphoto.com/Wavebreakmedia

REA® is a registered trademark of Research & Education Association.

Contents

About the Author

Beatrice Mendez Newman

Dr. Beatrice Mendez Newman is Professor of Rhetoric and Composition in the Writing and Language Studies Department at The University of Texas Rio Grande Valley. Her research has been published in collections on teaching writing at Hispanic-Serving Institutions and writing center pedagogy; her work has appeared in the *English Journal*, *Voices from the Middle*, *HETS Online Journal*, and the *Writing Center Journal*. She has published REA guides in PPR and ESL as well as an Allyn & Bacon guide for English teacher certification in Texas. She recently received UTRGV's award for Excellence in Online and Hybrid Teaching. Dr. Newman is very active in the National Council of Teachers of English, serving as a certification program reviewer, a member of the award-winning *English Journal* Editorial Review Board, and national judge for the NCTE Achievement Awards in Writing. She has also served as a board member of the Washington-based Council for the Accreditation of Educator Preparation. She can be reached at *beatrice.newman@utrgv.edu.*

About REA

Founded in 1959, Research & Education Association (REA) is dedicated to publishing the finest and most effective educational materials—including study guides and test preps—for students of all ages.

Today, REA's wide-ranging catalog is a leading resource for students, teachers, and other professionals. Visit *www.rea.com* to see a complete listing of all our titles.

REA Acknowledgments

We would like to thank Pam Weston, Publisher, for setting the quality standards for production integrity and managing the publication to completion; John Paul Cording, Technology Director, for coordinating the design and development of the REA Study Center; Heidi Gagnon for digital content preparation: Larry B. Kling, Editorial Director, for his overall direction; Karen Lamoreux for copyediting; Fiona Hallowell for proofreading; Caragraphics for typesetting; and Jennifer Calhoun for book file prep.

Foreword

This REA test guide "met and surpassed my expectations,"
writes Dr. Luis Rosado, the award-winning founding
director of the Center for Bilingual and ESL Education at
the University of Texas at Arlington.

The state of Texas has a very demanding testing-driven process to certify teachers. Teacher candidates are required to pass two exams to receive the Core Subjects certification in elementary education or to earn secondary content-based certification. Teachers take one or two additional certification exams to add supplemental certification to their existing teaching certificate. To become certified to teach English as a Second Language (ESL), teacher candidates take one additional exam—the ESL Supplemental (154) test.

To prepare candidates to take the ESL supplemental certification, Dr. Beatrice Mendez Newman, from The University of Texas Rio Grande Valley, wrote this fully revised and updated comprehensive guide to the TExES ESL Supplemental test. As part of REA's quality assurance process to produce these kinds of publications, I was invited to review the book. To review someone's work is always a challenging task, especially with a book designed to help teacher candidates meet certification requirements. It is important to be fair to the author but at the same time ascertain that the work meets its purpose and addresses the needs of teacher candidates. With this in mind, I undertook the task of reviewing Dr. Newman's book.

After reviewing the test-taking strategies in Chapter 1 and the content of Chapters 2 and 3, any skepticism that I may have had disappeared. This book met and surpassed my expectations. From that point on, I continued reading the book to learn more about the concepts I thought I knew well.

What makes this test guide different?

To develop this book, Dr. Newman went directly to the sources of the test—the ESL Educator Standards, the three domains of the test, and the 10 competencies and their accompanying descriptive statements. Understanding the connection among these components is vital for teacher candidates to master the content and skills required to be successful in state certification exams. Consequently, the author undertook an extensive analysis of each element and its role on the exam. From the descriptive statements, the author extracted a list of vocabulary words or core ideas for each competency. The use of these core ideas affords candidates valuable exposure to the nomenclature and concepts needed to master the exam.

The narrative of the chapters traces the contours of each competency, emphasizing the key concepts and detailing the competency descriptors. The author presents the information in an easy-to-read-and-understand narrative. She provides school-based examples for each of the key concepts linked to the competencies to ensure readers are able to grasp the core concepts. At the end of each chapter, there is a "chapter wrap-up" to guide students to identify key elements of the chapter. Each chapter also features a "self-check" section with a series of questions to conduct self-assessment of the relevant content.

The author presents sample multiple-choice questions in the chapters to highlight how the content can be expected to be presented on the actual test. When readers complete the "chapter wrap-up" and the follow-up activities, they should thus be equipped with a better understanding of each chapter's major takeaways.

Another major feature of the book (and the corresponding online REA Study Center) is the inclusion of two 80-question practice tests to assess your readiness for test day. Questions are carefully aligned with the 10 competencies covered on the test. This alignment enables students to see the connection between the content covered in each competency and the kinds of questions the test is most likely to ask. The REA practice tests are diagnostic in nature and designed to determine your test-readiness by identifying areas where you need further development.

Candidates should take each practice test and then check the answers and the explanations given for each test item. Importantly, the explanations serve a dual purpose: to both identify the rationale for the answers and to add additional information to get students ready for the official test. When candidates read these detailed explanations, they are encouraged to examine the concepts and vocabulary used in the explanation to determine whether they have a working knowledge of the ESL Supplemental exam's core concepts. Additionally, students are encouraged to develop a list of statements summarizing the ideas learned from the questions and the explanations given. In preparation for the actual exam, students should drill down to the level of the competency descriptive statements that detail discrete skills assessed on the test.

Most of the questions in the exam use the traditional four-option multiple-choice item; however, this test also contains a new question type that requires test-takers to select more than one correct answer. Such questions typically accommodate multiple responses by presenting up to an additional three responses. Thus, the options might run from A to G, and the question might require you to identify two or three answers instead of just one. This type of question is relatively new for these exams, and it requires a deep understanding of the competencies of the test.

As an award-winning author with over 35 years' experience in preparing bilingual/ESL teachers, I can tell you that this ESL Supplemental (154) test guide is a remarkable academic work—in fact, one of the best of its kind. Teacher candidates who pair the content covered in their teacher preparation program with the content and strategies discussed in this book will put themselves in an excellent position to pass the ESL Supplemental certification exam.

I endorse this book as a companion to a textbook for a course designed to prepare teacher candidates for the ESL supplemental exam. I also want to commend Dr. Newman and the staff of REA for developing this much-needed publication.

Dr. Luis A. Rosado
Professor of Bilingual/ESL Education
Founding Director of the Center for
 Bilingual Education
The University of Texas at Arlington

INTRODUCTION
Getting Started

Getting Started

Congratulations! By taking the TExES English as a Second Language (ESL) Supplemental (154) test, you are on your way to a rewarding career teaching English learners. Our book and the online tools that come with it provide abundant resources for succeeding on this important exam, bringing you one step closer to being certified to teach ESL in Texas.

Our *ESL Supplemental (154)* Book + Online Prep package includes these key features:

- An overview of the ESL Supplemental test

- Comprehensive explanation of the ESL domains and 10 competencies

- Two full-length practice tests, both in the book and online

- Detailed response explanations for the practice test items that connect correct answers to relevant terms and concepts from the associated competency and explain why the other responses are incorrect.

There are many different ways to prepare for the TExES ESL Supplemental exam. What is best for you depends on how much time you have to study and how familiar you are with the subject matter. Our Book + Online Prep has a plan that you can customize to fit both your lifestyle and study style.

How to Use This Book + Online Prep

The review chapters in this book are designed to help you sharpen your command of content and pedagogical skills so you can pass the ESL Supplemental test. The test requires specialized skills contextualized within your knowledge of general pedagogy. The ESL skills and knowledge required for all 10 competencies are defined, discussed, illustrated, and exemplified in the designated chapters.

Our targeted review chapters are grouped in three major sections according to the domains and cover fundamental content for each competency. Each chapter outlines a specific competency, identifies core concepts for the competency, provides definitions and explanations of concepts relevant to the competency, and presents review questions in the context of the competency. Each chapter is designed to strengthen your knowledge of ESL concepts and pedagogy connected to that competency and to present specific strategies to prepare for the exam.

About the REA Study Center

We know your time is valuable and you want an efficient study experience. At the online REA Study Center (*www.rea.com/studycenter*), you will get feedback right from the start on what you know and what you need to learn.

Here's what you will find at the REA Study Center to prepare for the TExES ESL Supplemental Exam (154):

- **Two full-length practice tests**—These practice tests, also printed in this book, will enable you to assess your strengths and weaknesses in ESL content and pedagogy.

Each online test comes with:

- **Automatic scoring**—find out how you did on your test instantly.

- **Diagnostic score reports**—get a specific score on each competency so you can focus on the areas that challenge you the most.

- **Detailed answer explanations**—see why the correct answer is right, why the other choices are incorrect, and how the item stem offers clues about how to approach the test item.

- **Timed testing**—learn to manage your time as you practice, so you'll feel confident on test day.

All Texas Examinations of Educator Standards (TExES) tests are **computer-administered tests (CATs).** You register for the exam through the test vendor site run by Pearson Education at *https://www.tx.nesinc.com.* The exam registration site includes a link to find a testing center in your area. Although the exams are CATs, you will need to take the exam at a designated testing center where you will need to provide identification information and then be guided to a testing carrel.

Overview of the Test

Full, current information about the ESL exam is available at the TExES website, which can be accessed through the **Texas Education Agency** menu tab labeled Texas Educators.

Here is an overview of the exam:

- The exam is based on 10 competencies presented in three domains.

- The domains and competencies address holistic areas of ESL knowledge and content expected of entry-level educators in Texas.

- Each competency is subdivided into descriptive statements that detail the range, breadth, and specific content of the competency.

- The exam is 4 hours and 45 minutes long and consists of 80 selected-response items.

- The score is reported as a scaled score from 0 to 300 with 240 as the passing score.

- The exam may include items that are not scored; the final scaled score is based only on the scored items.

- The 80 items are divided as follows: approximately 25% for Domain I, 45% for Domain II, and 30% for Domain III.

- All test items are selected-response items.

- A web-based preparation manual is available for this exam.

(Pearson, 2019a, 2019b)

According to the Texas Educator Certification Examination Program website, there are several types of questions and question formats in the exam (Pearson, 2019a):

- Single-correct response items—there is only one correct response.

- Multiple-correct response items—there are several correct responses, so you need to select all of the correct responses. These items are likely to have more than the traditional four responses, and you will be prompted to select all items that are correct.

- Clustered items—a scenario is presented with several questions related to the scenario.

- "Unfamiliar question formats"—the test preparation materials explain that variable formats (charts, graphics, reading passages) or interactive items may be included.

A total of five hours is allotted for the exam appointment, but you need to factor in a short exam tutorial and other initial activities, leaving the actual testing time as 4 hours and 45 minutes. This may seem like a lot of time, but think of it as 285 test-taking minutes for 80 test items, which is about 3.5 minutes per item. You may be able to read and respond to some items quickly, perhaps in a matter of seconds, but others will require slow, careful reading and rereading because of the complexity of the item stem or the scenario. We advise you not to rush through the test. Our practice tests will help you learn how to pace yourself so you go into the real test feeling confident about working within the allotted testing period.

In addition, the official exam website includes a lengthy section on preparing for the exam, including advice on how to process the test items as you read them, what to do if you do not know the answer, and how to set up a study plan (Pearson, 2019a). You should look thoroughly through these materials, created by the Texas Education Agency, either before you work through our book or in tandem as reinforcement of the guidance we provide.

Overview of ESL Pedagogy and Practice

In Texas, students are designated as **English learners (EL)** when their main language is a language other than English and their scores on a state-approved English proficiency exam indicate that their proficiency level will impede the likelihood of academic success (TAC, 2018, §89.1203. Definitions). EL students in Texas comprise 18.8% of the total public school student population, thus indicating the profound impact that ESL teaching has in the overall pedagogical landscape in this state (TEA, 2017, Pocket Edition). In academic and pedagogical discussions, the terms EL/ELs and ESL are frequently used interchangeably. In our book, we will refer to *students* as ELs, since that is the designated term used by the state and the federal government to identify students who need special language programs, and we will use the term ESL to refer to theory and practice. The term **Limited English Proficiency (LEP)** is used in federal and state documents to classify students who need language support to succeed in school. We will use the term LEP only in reference to state and federal materials.

In Texas, EL students can be channeled into two specialized language programs: **bilingual programs**, in which students receive instruction in English and another language and **English as a second language (ESL)** programs, in which students learn academic content in English while they are also developing **English language proficiency**. While ESL programs are implemented within school districts and specific schools, ESL and bilingual programs at individual schools must conform to expectations, regulations, definitions, and requirements mandated by federal and state laws.

Teaching ESL creates opportunities for prolific teaching, student-centered instruction, and inclusive pedagogy. The 10 competencies assessed on the ESL Supplemental exam illustrate the breadth of possibilities for working with students who are learning English, ranging from learners who are new to formal education to students who have attended American schools but have limited English proficiency.

ESL Supplemental Exam Study Plan

To prepare effectively for the ESL Supplemental exam, even though you are using our book, you need a well-conceived study plan that enables you to proceed logically and purposefully toward success on the exam. Consider the following strategies:

1: Organize your study tools

Even in our age of electronic convenience, using "traditional" study tools might be the best route to reinforce your knowledge of ESL content.

- Use a dedicated spiral or notebook to take notes as you read through the book.

- Organize all of your ESL study documents from TEA and other websites in a ring binder.

- Get a variety of index cards to create flash cards to record definitions of key terms.

- Use highlighters, flags, and annotations in your printed documents, including our book.

2: TEA materials

Before you work through this book, you need to check the **Texas Education Agency** website for the latest information on the TExES English as a Second Language (ESL) Supplemental (154) exam with links to the exam vendor. Websites that disseminate test information change periodically, so you need to be proactive in ensuring that you have the most up-to-date information on the test by checking the TEA website regularly. Access these necessary test preparation materials from the links provided on the TEA website:

- **ESL Supplemental (154) Preparation Materials** (Pearson, 2019a). These materials are fully web-based, with interactive links to the 10 competencies and descriptive statements that will be tested on the ESL Supplemental exam. This test prep manual also includes test-taking advice directly from TEA, sample test items explained from the perspective of item design, and the full list of Educator Standards and the ESL test competencies. Our book does not replicate the information in the test bulletins or the preparation manual, so it is vital that you access the preparation materials as a necessary companion document as you work through our book. TEA includes a link to the current test provider under the Texas Educators tab.

- The **English as a Second Language (ESL) Standards** (State Board for Educator Certification, 2001), the approved educator standards for this test. The TExES examination framework is based on the educator standards for each exam area. The standards reinforce the content of the test competencies by presenting ESL core content as teacher knowledge (what beginning teachers should know) and application (what beginning teachers should be able to do). There are seven ESL educator standards, each presented as coordinated lists of teacher knowledge (k) and application (s). Each domain of the ESL (154) exam is aligned to one or more of the standards.

- The **English Language Proficiency Standards (ELPS)** which are central to a full understanding of ESL teacher responsibilities and expectations for learners. This document represents the required curriculum for ESL under the Texas Administrative Code and the Texas Education Agency. ELPS are available through a link on the TEA website (TAC, 2007).

ELPS will be critical for a full understanding of many of the competencies and associated descriptive statements. ELPS includes levels of proficiency—beginning, intermediate, advanced, and advanced high—for instructional levels K–12, with specific characteristics in listening, speaking, writing, and reading. Additionally, ELPS include requirements for supporting students' proficiency in content areas, presented as cross-curricular knowledge and skills. ELPS are complex and detailed and should be examined carefully with the intention of learning the characteristics assigned to the various proficiency levels. You should expect numerous test items focused on ELPS, on characteristics for specific proficiency levels, and on integrating ESL pedagogy into content-area instruction.

3: ESL/bilingual education books and articles

If you went through a university-sponsored ESL or bilingual education program, you should have a good collection of books, articles, professor notes, your own notes, class materials (tests, reviews, papers, PowerPoint slideshows, bibliographies, etc.) to refer to as you work through our book. Have these handy as you study. When you start reading our chapters, you should be disciplined enough to look up terms, concepts, and strategies that we mention. In some chapters, we will recommend specific books as major resources for the content of that chapter; you should be ready to check those books out from your university or local library. Remember that our book is a *study guide*, not a first-time, comprehensive presentation of all ESL content. So, having your class materials at hand will reinforce what we cover in our book.

4: From competencies to descriptive statements to ESL content

If you have had even a little bit of training or classroom study of ESL or bilingual education, looking through the competencies and descriptive statements will remind you of terms and concepts from those courses. If you are new to ESL pedagogy, there will be a steep learning curve, but not insurmountable. Here are some strategies you should use as you study for the test:

- Set up a study plan that ideally includes a chunk of study time every day as you work toward the target test date.

- As you work through each chapter, reinforce your study by jotting down terms and definitions. At the end of each chapter, do the self-assessment to ensure that you have a holistic understanding of the overall topic of the competency, the core ideas relevant to the competency as presented in the descriptive statements, and the definitions of key terms for that competency.

- Allow yourself to do web breadcrumb searches of terms you encounter in the chapters. If you have some basic ESL resources at hand, check the indexes of books to get further insight on these terms.

- Take time to study some of the resources suggested at the end of each chapter. The content of each competency includes specialized information about teaching ESL. The suggested resources have been selected because they include chapters or overall coverage on key aspects of the competency content.

5: Response strategies for test items

A key strategy for successfully negotiating the ESL exam is figuring out how to "decode" test items efficiently and accurately. Regardless of the type of question (stand-alone or clustered), each individual item reflects a *specific* competency and descriptive statement. Recognizing what competency is reflected in the item stem is the single most important strategy for selecting the correct response. None of the items reflects multiple competencies. And there are no "trick" questions or obvious responses. The items are challenging and require concerted attentiveness to the way the item is presented in the stem.

Our book includes practice items in each chapter that are easy to link to the relevant competency. In our two 80-item practice tests, as on the actual test, you will not know what competency pertains to each item, but you can rely on clues and limiters in the item stem to figure out the domain and competency addressed by the item. Picking the correct response depends on your ability to connect the competency implied in the item stem to the response that matches the parameters established in the stem. Throughout our study guide, we will consistently remind you to *learn the competencies and associated key terms*. This will be your best strategy for recognizing the competency relevant to each test item.

In many cases, all of the responses will seem to be viable choices for dealing with the situation or question presented in the stem. In a real classroom, you might find yourself effectively using all of the strategies presented as the response options, so none of them will seem overtly "wrong." Picking the correct response does not mean eliminating responses that represent abjectly poor teaching actions or are obviously wrong responses (or what test developers call "distractors"). The test items are not set up to present obviously wrong responses. Instead, you need to consider which choice *best* fits the conditions established by the stem. In other words, the correct response will be the one that best reflects the competency-based scenario, situation, or question presented in the stem.

Here are some strategies for responding effectively to ESL Supplemental test items as you take the practice tests in preparation for the real test:

1. Read the item stem slowly and carefully. Do not do a rushed reading. You need to pay attention to *every word* of the item stem. In fact, you should read the item stem over several times, asking yourself, "What is the question asking or seeking?" and "Which of the 10 competencies is suggested by the wording of the stem?" You want to find yourself thinking, "Oh . . . the stem is obviously about using technology in ESL teaching so it's about 003," or, "The stem is about fostering parent-teacher collaboration, so I need to pick the response that focuses on that."

2. Figure out, from the wording of the item stem, which specific competency is being assessed by the item. This connection between the stem and the targeted competency is your prime strategy in answering the item correctly. No item will merge several competencies in the stem or in the responses. For each item, you can expect distinct, obvious connection to a specific competency. So a crucial test-taking strategy you need to cultivate is to know fully and confidently what the overall topic of each competency is, as well as the associated terms and concepts.

3. Pay attention to limiters such as *initial, best, most, first* which establish clear restrictions for the right response.

4. Identify key words in the stem that reflect a specific competency. The chapters on the competencies in the rest of our book will guide you in associating relevant terms, concepts, and practices with each competency.

5. Read each response item carefully. This is not a time for skimming. Do not select your response choice until you have carefully evaluated all of the choices. For challenging items (those for which the correct response isn't obvious to you immediately), you will have to do a critical analysis of the responses, working to find the best match between the content of the item stem and content of the correct response.

6. Do not pick your response too quickly. Ask yourself, "What is the rationale for picking this response?" Your response to this self-check question should be based on knowledge of the competencies.

7. Self-assess your knowledge as you work through each practice item in our book. Once you have read the explanation of the item, develop statements describing what you learned from the question and the explanation of the answer. These can serve as a quick study guide for the test. You might also develop a list of key terms and concepts used in each item to be sure you know their meaning and determine how they can help you pass the test.

A Practice-Test Item

Let's put these strategies into action in this annotated practice item.

Table 1.1.
Annotated Practice ESL Test Item

Practice ESL Item	Analysis using response strategies
Students in a grade 4 English language arts class are in a unit on narrative writing. About half of the students are English learners, most at the beginning and intermediate levels. At this point in the unit, the students have read several short books to understand narrative structure and are now working on short drafts of a personal story about a favorite toy. Which of the following instructional strategies would effectively address the teacher's objective to promote the ESL students' communicative competence?	Competency 004 focuses on *communicative language development*, which targets listening and speaking proficiencies. Holistically, Competency 004 and the descriptors address affect and classroom environment as contributors to ESL students' ability to demonstrate communicative proficiency. Thus, a good strategy for selecting the correct response is to look for a response that clearly shows the teacher focusing on listening or speaking skills.
A. The teacher has students work collaboratively to identify verb form errors in each other's drafts.	A is incorrect because, while the activity might reinforce students' syntactic skills, there is no direct connection to the teacher's objective to focus on promoting communicative competence.
B. The teacher administers a quiz requiring students to list the key parts of a well-constructed narrative.	B is incorrect because this activity is better as a preliminary activity when the narrative assignment was being introduced. Additionally, this is an independent activity that is not primarily aimed at promoting communicative competence.
C. The teacher has students read their narrative drafts aloud to the class.	C is incorrect because the oral reading of the drafts would likely cause anxiety for the students since most are at the beginning and intermediate level. While oral reading is a typical activity in ELA classrooms as a fluency and comprehension strategy, in ESL classrooms, oral reading might exacerbate learners' anxiety about their developing proficiency. The anxiety caused by the oral reading is very likely to inhibit communicative competence rather than promote it.
D. The teacher has students work in pairs to identify their favorite sentences from their partners' drafts and explain in a whole-class share session why they like the sentence.	D is correct because it is scaffolded in the productive pair-share activity that allows collaboration, sharing, and then whole-class presentation. D allows learners to interact in a low-stress setting with partners and then use their speaking skills to demonstrate their appreciation of the partner's writing. The strategy described in D most closely connects to the parameters of the item stem.

Let's practice self-assessing what we abstracted from this sample item:

- The stem includes some qualifiers: the class is an elementary-level class with a substantive number of beginning and intermediate ELs. This class configuration suggests that the teacher will need to implement appropriate scaffolding to ensure all learners are meeting the learning goals and to use activities targeted at the grade level of these young learners.

- Because the stem mentions beginning and intermediate ELs, this is a good time to consult the ELPS and jot down some notes on expectations for beginning and intermediate performance levels in speaking and listening.

- The activity involves understanding of narrative format; however, the stem clearly indicates that the activity is not a writing activity. The upshot is that this item focuses not on writing but on communicative competence.

- The term *communicative competence*, used in the focal question, should trigger connections to listening and speaking as detailed in Competency 004, which focuses on communicative language development.

- The responses all are viable classroom activities, so selecting the correct response does not mean eliminating activities that seem inherently problematic. Instead, finding the activity that best promotes communicative competence is the key to answering correctly.

Recap: This practice-item analysis is intended to show you how to use the parameters of the item stem to evaluate the item responses and confidently select the correct response.

Given the competency-based foundation of each test item, it is crucial that you thoroughly learn the concepts, terms, and pedagogical principles associated with each competency. One of our prime study suggestions will be to create notecards or flash cards to reinforce the core content of each competency so that you can adeptly recognize the "hints" and overt terminology in item stems that link the test item to a specific competency.

Summary, Action Plan, and Introduction Wrap-Up

The 10 chapters in our book address each of the ESL competencies, with each chapter structured for optimum study with the following components:

- A summary overview of the competency

- Core content for each competency

- Targeted explanations of the core content relevant to the competency

- A self-check to assess your understanding of key terms and concepts from the competency

- Suggested targeted resources for further study

- A few practice items with explanations

Our study guide also includes a glossary of important terms which you should use in creating the suggested flash cards for core competency terms. The 10 competency chapters are followed with two 80-item practice tests with detailed explanations of the responses (also available online at *www.rea.com/studycenter*).

Study Plan

- Before you move to the first competency chapter, have ready access to your ESL (154) exam materials: the website for the preparation materials, the educator standards, and the ELPS, all available through links on the TEA website.

- Organize your study approach with a spiral notebook, ring binder, index cards, and other traditional study aids. And be diligent about taking notes. Don't trust yourself to remember details. Write things down.

- Assemble any ESL books, articles, and notes you may have from courses in which you may have studied ESL or bilingual education issues.

- Check the exam registration information on the Texas Educator Certification Examination Program website, including the nearest testing center, dates, procedures, test cost, and general information to ensure you are all set to take the actual test when you complete our study guide.

TExES
ESL SUPPLEMENTAL (154)

Domain Reviews

PART I: DOMAIN I

Language Concepts and Language Acquisition

Language Concepts and Language Acquisition

■ Overview of Domain I

Competencies 001 and 002 of Domain I primarily address linguistic content that affects teaching and learning in ESL environments.

Domain I Competencies

Competency 001: The ESL teacher understands fundamental language concepts and knows the structure and conventions of the English language.

Competency 002: The ESL teacher understands the processes of first-language (L1) and second-language (L2) acquisition and the interrelatedness of L1 and L2 development.

(Pearson, 2019a)

Core Content from Domain I Competencies

To get started in your study of the Domain I competencies, you should zoom in on the basic terms and concepts articulated and suggested by the descriptions for each competency.

Domain I is aligned with Standard I and Standard III of the English as a Second Language (ESL) Standards (SBEC, 2001, pp. 1, 3):

- **Standard I:** The ESL teacher understands fundamental language concepts and knows the structure of the English language.

- **Standard III:** The ESL teacher understands the processes of first- and second-language acquisition and uses this knowledge to promote students' language development in English.

- As you look through the chart below, refer to the English as a Second Language Supplemental (154) Preparation Materials, the educator standards, and ELPS.

Table D1.1.
Core Content from ESL (154) Domain I

Domain I	Language Concepts and Language Acquisition
Competency # and General Topic	**Core Ideas from Descriptive Statements**
001 Linguistic content (4 descriptive statements)	• Basic linguistic content (phonology, morphology, syntax, semantics, pragmatics) • Language registers • Interrelatedness of listening, speaking, writing, and reading • Using linguistic knowledge to promote learning as described and defined by the English Language Proficiency Standards (ELPS)
002 Language acquisition (5 descriptive statements)	• Language acquisition (relevant theories, concepts, and research) • Connecting knowledge of acquisition theories to instructional methods and strategies • Interrelatedness of L1 and L2 • Common difficulties in L2 acquisition

According to the ESL Supplemental (154) Preparation Materials website, Domain I items compose 25% percent of the 80-item test (Pearson, 2019a).

CHAPTER

Competency 001

1

Competency 001: Fundamental Linguistic Knowledge

The ESL teacher understands fundamental language concepts and knows the structure and conventions of the English language (Pearson, 2019a).

Competency 001, which is focused on **linguistic knowledge** ESL teachers should have, is presented in four descriptive statements that cover the following general topics:

- Major areas of linguistics: **phonology**, **morphology**, **syntax**, **semantics**, **lexicon, discourse, pragmatics**

- **Registers** of language

- **Interrelatedness** of listening, speaking, reading, and writing

- Ability to align morphological and syntactic knowledge with ELPS

For ESL teachers, foundational knowledge of linguistics allows for adept assessment of learner progress. ESL teachers should be able to recognize attempts at new constructions, innovative **transfer** of L1 to L2, and crossovers that demonstrate a learner's **translingualism**. To recognize how learners are progressing in their journey toward English proficiency, ESL teachers have to know and be able to apply understandings about the major areas of linguistics.

Competency 001 Core Content

The following terms reflect the content of Competency 001 and Standard I and Standard III, which are aligned with Domain I.

Table 1.1.
Competency 001 Core Content

conventions	language systems	phonology	morphology	syntax
lexicon	semantics	discourse	pragmatics	registers
proficiency	structure of English	mechanics	content-based instruction	ELPS
error	academic language	interrelatedness	sentence patterns	modifications
common difficulties	transfer	functions of language	grammar	idioms

This is the first competency of the ESL exam, and it references the English Language Proficiency Standards, affording a powerful indication of the importance of ELPS in preparing for this exam. Ideally, you should have a printout of ELPS so that you can annotate and highlight connections to Competency 001. ELPS will be referenced throughout the 10 competencies, so it is a great study strategy to have your copy of ELPS nearby. Reminder: you can access ELPS at the TEA website by going to the "Academics" tab. Then follow the link to "Curriculum Standards" and then to "Texas Essential Knowledge and Skills."

Competency 001 introduces basic terms used in discussion of English as a second language: SLA to denote **Second Language Acquisition**, **L1** to denote the speaker's first or native language, and **L2** for the second or **target language**.

ESL, Linguistics, and Second Language Acquisition

As an ESL teacher, you will be guiding learners in acquiring a second language. Second language acquisition theories are predicated on understandings and adjustments relevant to first language acquisition, which most experts agree happens intuitively and "naturally" as learners interact with caregivers as they are learning language. Second language acquisition, however, often is modulated and directed through formal instruction in schools which may or may not be supported outside the educational context. ESL instruction is not just about learning the grammar of a second language. Acquisition of a second language necessarily involves rhetorical, cultural, political, social, economic, and environmental factors. The content of Competency 001 focuses on basics of linguistics as a platform for formal

ESL instruction in the classroom. Later chapters explore exigencies that impact learners' affective, cognitive, social, and psychological responses in the acquisition process.

Areas of Linguistics

Competency 001.A identifies seven areas of basic linguistics as knowledge that a beginning ESL teacher should have: phonology, morphology, syntax, lexicon, semantics, discourse, and pragmatics. These areas cover technical aspects of English, explaining how everything from sounds to conversations are formed by applying interrelated linguistic knowledge. To help students develop proficiency in listening, speaking, reading, and writing, ESL teachers must have a robust understanding of the language systems of English.

Phonology

Phonology is the study of the sound system of a specific language. Each language has a different phonological system that reflects the specific sounds used in that language. Unless an ESL teacher is working with very young learners (K or early elementary), direct instruction in phonology is not likely. In traditional classrooms, phonology, presented as phonics, is addressed when young learners are being introduced to the alphabet and English sound patterns. However, for students with interrupted or non-existent education in L1, ESL teachers may have to integrate phonics instruction to support ELs at the beginning ELPS level.

For an ESL teacher, a strong foundation in phonology contributes to helping learners recognize and use distinct sounds and orthography of English. You could anticipate situations in which you have to decipher or interpret a student's language output. Unless you are working with learners who have never had formal phonics training in traditional school settings, your ESL learners should have operational knowledge of sounds in their L1. Your task will be to help them recognize distinct English sounds and to negotiate areas where crossover or interference from L1 sounds may create aberrant pronunciations or spellings.

At its most basic level, English is comprised of individual, meaning-making sounds, or **phonemes**. A phoneme is the smallest unit of spoken language that makes a difference in a word's meaning. For example, the first phoneme in *cap* is /k/. Changing the phoneme /k/ to the phoneme /m/ creates a word with a different meaning: *map*. Learning to distinguish among the phonemes in a language and using those perceived distinctions to construct words is a fundamental learning milestone in second language acquisition. Phonemes are combined into clusters and syllables to form words. In ESL instruction, teachers must remember that EL students may have trouble hearing the distinctive sounds in L2, especially if some sounds from L2 do not exist in L1 phonology.

Letters and Sounds

The International Phonetic Alphabet is a chart that uses both letters of the Roman alphabet and specialized symbols for the sounds that linguists have identified as existing in spoken languages throughout the world (Fromkin, Rodman, & Hyams, 2017, p. 187). In our discussion of phonology, we will not use those technical symbols, but instead, when we discuss vowels, we will use English alphabet symbols with diacritical marks to designate long and short sounds to reflect the typical classroom presentation of sound-letter correspondence.

The consonants and vowels of English are distinguished by the way they are produced in the vocal tract. Vowels are produced by air flowing through the vocal cords and the vocal tract with little restriction. Consonants are produced when parts of the vocal tract come together with friction, restriction, or obstruction (Pei & Gaynor, 1954, pp. 46, 229; Fromkin, Rodman, & Hyams, 2017, p. 189). ESL teachers need to know some fundamentals of sounds in order to help EL students produce challenging sounds, perhaps by having them produce related sounds and being aware of how the sounds are produced. It would be a good study strategy in your ESL exam preparation to consult a classic linguistics textbook such as *An Introduction to Language* (Fromkin, Rodman, & Hyams, 2017) to look at diagrams of the vocal tract (p. 190).

Consider "practicing" making vowel and consonant sounds and noticing how the air is flowing through your vocal tract or how parts of the vocal tract feel when you pronounce similar sounds such as *pet* and *bet* or *ant* and *ain't*. Simply opening or closing the larynx or relaxing or tensing parts of the vocal tract completely changes the sounds we produce. Such knowledge will be helpful for guiding EL students in understanding differences between L1 and L2 sounds. Additionally, it would be a good study strategy to look at a chart of the International Phonetic Alphabet showing the phonetic symbols for sounds that are found in numerous languages (International Phonetic Association, 2015). Knowing that EL students may have sounds in their L1 that are not in English or that English includes sounds not in the learner's L1 will offer significant clarification for you as you work with EL students. *InternationalPhoneticAlphabet.org* offers an *interactive* IPA chart that you can click on to hear the sounds (InternationalPhoneticAlphabet.org, 2020).

Consonants

Linguists do not agree on the precise number of phonemes in English. General estimates are between 42 and 44, depending on variables such as dialect and changes in stress. There are about 25 consonant phonemes in English. Eighteen are represented by a single letter such as /n/. Seven consonant phonemes are orthographically represented by two letters such as /sh/ or /th/ or /ng/. These two consonant sounds are known as *digraphs*. Digraphs do not represent a logical blending of two phonemic sounds but instead a new, created sound. For example, /ch/ is not a phonetic blending of /c/ and /h/ but is instead an entirely different sound. (Parker & Riley, 2010, pp. 99–109)

Consonants can be classified according to how they are produced. Remember that consonants are produced through friction in parts of the vocal tract and restriction of airflow.

- Place of Articulation—the specific part of the vocal tract where air is restricted. Restriction of airflow can occur at the lips, teeth, tongue, palate, or glottis (the vocal cords and the larynx);

- Manner of Articulation—how the air flow is restricted as parts of the vocal tract touch or are tensed or shaped to form the sound;

- Voiced or Unvoiced—whether the vocal cords are open for free airflow or closed for restricted airflow.

Other distinctions in consonant sounds include nasals, stops, liquids, glides, trills, and fricatives which allow us to produce an amazing variety of sounds.

(Fromkin, Rodman, & Hyams, 2017, pp. 189–197)

Vowels

Standard American English has 15 vowel phonemes represented by the letters /a/, /e/, /i/, /o/, and /u/ individually and in combination as diphthongs. The 15 vowels include 12 that represent single phonemes such as the /e/ in *pet* or the /u/ in *but*, and three *diphthongs* which are vowel sounds created by smoothly joining two separate vowel sounds as in *boy* which combines /o/ and /e/ sounds (Fromkin, Rodman, & Hyams, 2017, pp. 201, 207).

Vowel phonemes are primarily produced by varying the tongue position, tensing or relaxing the tongue, and rounding or spreading the lips (Fromkin, Rodman, & Hyams, 2017, pp. 189–202).

Phonology and SLA

For ESL teachers, this technical knowledge of how phonemes are produced is valuable in helping learners negotiate problematic areas of acquisition. Some sounds may be difficult for second language learners to produce because they are not in the repertoire of sounds in their native language. For example, the trilled *r* of Spanish is notoriously difficult for English speakers to produce because no consonants in English involve the configuration of the vocal tract required to say *rico* or *perro* in Spanish with a *trill* produced by vibrating the tongue. Similarly, moving from various L1 phonological systems to L2 English, learners have to contend with vowels and consonant configurations that don't exist in their L1. Knowledge of phonology enables ESL teachers to recognize learners' pronunciation "errors" as evidence of attempts at producing L2 sounds rather than as deficient pronunciation.

For speakers of only one language, it is difficult to imagine what trying to hear the sounds of a different language in meaning-making contexts might be like. Consider what a different language *sounds* like when you have limited or no knowledge of the language and cannot distinguish sounds or words or hear meaningful sentences. If you have never tried to listen to a television or radio program in a different language, take some time to do that, particularly a language with which you have no experience. It may sound like gibberish, but if you know even a bit about the way the sound system of language works, you can start to recognize distinct sounds and eventually words. While English may not sound like gibberish to an EL student, ESL teachers do need to know how to use their phonological knowledge to help learners negotiate the meaning-making sounds of English.

Simple, basic knowledge of phonology can help ESL teachers see and hear the structures that learners are approximating, recognizing the effort and attempt within the context of phonology, instead of marking it as a superficial error. ESL teachers should be aware that vowel sounds and the accompanying orthographic symbols vary significantly among languages and these variations can be a source of phonetic difficulty for EL students. Teachers also need to recognize *invented spellings*, systematic but unconventional spellings that indicate the sounds a learner "hears" (McGee & Richgels, 2012, pp. 91, 96). Even in the writing of more advanced EL students, invented spellings are evidence of syntactic growth and experimentation, not orthographic deficiency. For example, in a geometry class, a beginning or intermediate EL student might write the following sentence in the exit slip about the day's learning: *We learn that silendors has volym calculate with lent and radiz from the top.* The teacher should be able to recognize the crossovers from the students' L1 phonological knowledge and see the "misspellings" as approximations of the content-area words *cylinder* and *radius* and other content-area terms, recognizing the aberrant spellings as laudable attempts to join the conversation of the discipline. Knowledge of phonology gives ESL teachers a powerful tool for interpreting the linguistic efforts of EL students and for explaining how to move from error to achievement.

Phonology matters as an ESL teaching resource because English is not a phonetic language, meaning that there is no reliable correspondence between orthography and pronunciation. ESL teachers need to understand the source of apparent errors in spelling caused by mishearing or by inappropriate transfer of L1 sounds to L2 **orthography**. Take the English word *pie*, for example. Phonetically, the /e/ is silent and /i/ is long, and native English speakers know that. However, a beginning or intermediate EL with Spanish as a first language, a phonetic language where there is a closer correspondence between sound symbols and pronunciation, might apply L1 phonetic knowledge to pronounce *pie* as /pēĕ/, long /e/ sound and short /e/ sound. A Spanish speaker would recognize *pie* as the Spanish word for *foot* and possibly apply L1 phonological knowledge to pronounce the word. In contrast, in Spanish orthography, a word pronounced /pī/, the English pronunciation for *pie*, would be spelled /p-a-y/ because /ay/ is a Spanish diphthong sounded as –/ī/. These sorts of mismatches between L1 and L2 sounds and orthography can be a source of confusion and error for EL students. However, "errors" such as these actually show how ELs **transfer** knowledge from L1 to create L2 utterances.

For ESL teachers, technical knowledge of phonology can be a huge advantage in helping EL students negotiate transfer of alphabetic and phonetic competencies from L1 into L2. Teachers with a good foundation in phonology can mentor EL students in understanding why alphabetic representations of L2 and L1 can designate different sounds.

Morphology

Morphology is the science of words and parts of words.

Morphemes are the combinations of phonemes into meaningful units represented by graphemes and recognizable, meaning-bearing sounds to form words and parts of words. A morpheme may be an entire word like *play* or part of a word like *–ful*. A short word, *undo*, for example, can be made up of two meaningful units: *un + do*. On the other hand, a longer word, *establish*, for example, can represent a single morpheme because it cannot be broken down into smaller, meaning-making units. Make sure not to equate morphemes to syllables. (There's a discussion of this distinction later in this chapter.) Morphemes are the building blocks of English words. We construct new words by combining morphemes into new words. Native speakers of English learn these word parts quickly and intuitively, but EL students generally need help in transferring L1 knowledge into L2 morphology.

There are two basic types of morphemes: free and bound. Free morphemes can stand alone as words. Bound morphemes must be attached to other morphemes to make words. Anglo-Saxon root words, or base words, are free morphemes. They are the short, common words used in everyday speech such as *help, night, dog, work, house, love, spell*. They can stand alone, be combined into compound words (*doghouse*), or have prefixes and suffixes added to them (*misspell*, *spelling*).

Roots with etymologies in Latin or Greek have to be combined in order to create meaningful English words. For example, *struct* is part of the affixed English word *construction*. The prefix *con-* and the suffix *-ion* were added to the root to make a complete word. Another example: *microscope* is made up of the two roots, *micro* and *scope*, each of which can be combined with other roots or affixes to create new words.

Suffixes and prefixes are a special type of bound morpheme. Two types of suffixes are added to Anglo-Saxon root words—derivational and inflectional morphemes. Derivational morphemes allow us to *derive* new words by adding meaning-bearing morphemes as suffixes or prefixes. For example, we can derive nouns by adding *–ment* or *–ion* to root words. We can create adverbs by adding *–ly*. Derivational suffixes often change the root word's part of speech (*playful*, *lovely*). They may also alter the base word's meaning (*loveless*), pronunciation, or spelling. Similarly, prefixes added at the beginning of the word can substantively change the meaning, as in turning *true* to *untrue* by adding a prefix. Knowledge of derivational prefixes and suffixes enables ELs to experiment with L2 structures and in some cases create inventive "new" words.

Inflectional suffixes do not change a word's part of speech. Inflectional morphemes signal grammatical qualities such as possession (*child's*), number (box*es*), verb tense (help*ed*), and comparison (*louder*). Table 1.2 offers examples of English inflectional morphemes.

Table 1.2.
English Inflectional Morphemes

Morpheme	Grammatical Function	Examples
-s	Marker for present tense verbs used with third person subjects	My cat meows when she is hungry.
-ed	Marker for simple past tense and past participle forms with regular verbs	The ball bounced around the court. The ball had bounced all over the court before Jaime grabbed it.
-ing	Marker for creating progressive tense	Our team is winning by a large margin. My dad was waiting for us after the game.

Morpheme	Grammatical Function	Examples
-en	Marker for creating past participle verb forms of irregular verbs	My friends have eaten everything in the refrigerator. The teacher's favorite coffee cup was broken when someone bumped into her desk.
-s	Marker for regular plurals	My friends enjoy gathering at my house.
-'s	Marker for regular possessive for proper and common nouns	The girl's story made everyone cry. Jaime's free throw clinched the team's victory.
-er	Marker to show regular comparison	The taller boys were immediately chosen for the team.
-est	Marker to indicate regular superlative	The quickest way to get in trouble is to ignore rules.

Morphemic Analysis in Teaching ESL

It would be a good idea to review basic information about English prefixes, suffixes, and roots before you attempt the ESL 154 exam. Find an internet list of common prefixes and suffixes. Consider how easy it is for EL students to confuse prefixes that have similar meanings, like *un-, dis-, non-, anti-, ex-*. Or how easy it is to confuse a part of a morpheme for a prefix, as in *exam* or *undulate* or *discipline*.

Another study strategy, especially in light of the emphasis on content-area learning in the context of ESL teaching, is to find a list of roots common in your content area. Perhaps the most significant application of an ESL teacher's knowledge of morphology is in content-area vocabulary. For each content area, we can identify vocabulary that is distinct to the discipline with etymologies that require deep knowledge of structures of the discipline. Consider this chart that shows sample, specialized vocabulary from key content areas:

Table 1.3.
Comparative Chart of Content-Area Vocabulary

Math	Science	Social Studies	English Language Arts
symmetry	hypothesis	chronology	simile
hypotenuse	photosynthesis	heritage	metonymy
numerator	kinetic	environment	synecdoche
rhombus	metamorphic	consumption	hyperbole

The limited example of Table 1.3 points to the confluence of phonological and morphological knowledge as an ESL teacher resource in helping learners function within the discourse of the discipline. Content-area teachers must be able to "deconstruct" discipline-specific terms using knowledge of roots, affixes, phonology, and orthography to help EL students understand the discipline-specific connections of content-area vocabulary.

One last point in our discussion of morphology: syllables and morphemes are not equivalent linguistic structures. Syllables are vowel-sound combinations that reflect the patterns of a specific language. In English, syllables must contain a vowel, even if it's a barely detectable vowel as in the *–ble* of *able*. Syllabic combinations of sounds contribute significantly to the sound of a language because syllables clearly reflect the "allowed" sounds and sound combinations in a language. In English, for example, *ng* at the beginning of a word does not reflect English speech patterns but there are many *–ng* occurrences at the end of words or syllables as in *bringing*.

If you have never read Lewis Carroll's poem "Jabberwocky," you should take a look at it. Carroll's poem is a tour-de-force of English syllabication. Because he constructs "nonsense" words in English sound patterns and arranges them as parts of speech in correct syntactic patterns, we can make linguistic sense of the poem. Here are the first two lines: 'Twas brillig, and the slithy toves/ Did gyre and gimble in the wabe" (Poetry Foundation, 2020). We can read the poem because the sound, morphemic, and syntactic patterns are familiar even though some of the words are not actual English words.

Syntax

Syntax refers to the rules of grammar that govern how sentences are formed based on word-order patterns. Syntax can be considered separately from meaning in order to help students understand how speakers of a language know how to put words together to form meaningful sentences. Consider Noam Chomsky's famous "nonsense" sentence: *Colorless green ideas sleep furiously* (1957; 2002, p. 15). The sentence correctly strings together adjectives, noun, verb, and adverb in an English syntactic pattern, but it doesn't make semantic sense. A vital aspect of linguistic knowledge is knowing how to construct meaningful utterances in a language by putting words together in the conventional syntactic patterns of the language.

Understanding how words, phrases, and clauses are combined into meaningful sentences requires a great deal of knowledge—from sentence types and sentence structures to parts of speech function and the mechanics of written language. "Syntax" is the root of most grammar instruction—the "rules" associated with writing and speaking are mostly traced to syntactic patterns and expectations.

What ESL Teachers Should Know About Syntax

A *sentence* is a group of words that expresses a complete thought. Linguists often refer to *utterances* rather than *sentences* because a complete thought can be expressed without following traditional grammatical expectations for a "complete" sentence. Traditionally, in the context of didactic or prescriptive grammar, every sentence has a *subject* (whom or what the sentence is about) and a *predicate* (what the subject is, has, or does). However, there are abundant exceptions when writers use non-conventional patterns to make a point, as in this passage from a student's essay about winning a hard-fought basketball game against a rival team known for cheating and referee favoritism:

> The fourth period was over and the buzzer sounded. The final score was 67–53. Our entire school went crazy. We finally beat Juan Diego! Fair. And. Square.

Technically, the writer "broke" sentence-construction rules in the three one-word sentences. But, he did it to create a rhetorical impact (which we will discuss in the pragmatics section of this chapter). That the writer chose to ignore the rules of English syntax to create this passage is a testimony to the creativity possible when we know what we can do with language.

To help EL students understand basic English syntax, ESL teachers need to have firm, fundamental knowledge of structural and functional possibilities for creating and combining utterances we typically call *sentences*.

English grammar generally presents four sentence *functions*:

Declarative. A straightforward statement. Examples: Israel read *One Hundred Years of Solitude*. He thought the original Spanish version was better than the English translation.

Interrogative. A question, usually marked typographically with a question mark, and in terms of pragmatics, inflection changes when a question is being expressed. Examples: Are we going to have to read *One Hundred Years of Solitude*? Is *One Hundred Years of Solitude* based on a true story?

Exclamatory. Surprise, outrage, anger, or any other emotive utterance. Usually marked with at least one exclamation point. Orally, an exclamation can be louder or can demonstrate the intended affect. Examples: No way! 600 pages! You gotta be kidding! Not happening!

Imperative. Usually an explicit or implicit command. Examples: For Tuesday, read the first 100 pages of *One Hundred Years of Solitude*. Do not show up without your book.

Sentences are also classified according to structure based on the configuration of independent and dependent clauses. Independent clauses can function as stand-alone sentences, but they can also be linked to other independent clauses or to dependent clauses. Dependent clauses are minor (dependent) structures that must be syntactically and semantically linked to the major (independent) clause. Reminder: a clause is a subject-verb combination.

A *compound sentence* has two independent clauses that are joined with a coordinating conjunction such as *for, or, and, nor, yet, so,* or *but*, or with a semicolon. Example: Jaime was late to class, but Ms. Petok did not mark him tardy.

Compound sentences can also be joined with a semicolon. Example: Jaime was late to class again today; he did not have an excuse.

A *complex sentence* has one independent clause and one or more dependent clauses. Example with an independent clause and one dependent clause: Jaime was late to class because his P.E. teacher assigned extra laps today.

A *compound complex sentence* combines a compound and complex structure. Example: Although Jaime was late to class, Ms. Petok did not mark him tardy, but she warned him that this was the last time.

An important aspect of syntactic knowledge is that sentence structure can be used to modulate meaning. Syntactic density contributes to the simplicity or complexity of the message. For EL students, the dual literacy tasks of reading and trying to learn content-area knowledge in L2 creates a learning challenge that ESL teachers must address.

Syntax in Academic Texts

In order to read and respond to content-area texts, English learners need to be guided in unpacking the meaning of dense, complex discipline-specific sentences. This is why ESL teachers in all disciplines need to know how to talk about sentences, how to explain the relationships among simple, coordinate, and complex structures, and even how to demonstrate how punctuation choices impact meaning. Let's look at this passage from a social studies nonfiction text for late elementary to middle schoolers. The book presents the historical circumstances of the 1793 yellow fever outbreak in Philadelphia (the sentences are numbered for clarity in our discussion):

(1) ***Sunday, August 25.*** (2) The spread of the disease and of fear among the citizens had one immediate consequence: people began leaving the city. (3) Clothes were packed in haste, windows slammed and shuttered, doors locked tight. (4) Sometimes servants were ordered to stay behind to guard the house against thieves; sometimes everyone living under a roof fled. (5) Printer and publisher Mathew Carey watched sadly as "almost every hour in the day, carts, waggons, coaches, and chairs, were to be seen transporting families & furniture to the country in every direction." (Murphy, 2003, p. 21)

What a social studies teacher should notice in the sentences and explain to students:

- The "announcement" of the day in boldface as a lead-in to the paragraph. Sentence (1).

- The use of a colon and a semicolon in the passage, two punctuation marks that significantly impact the writer's directions about how a passage should be read. Sentences (2) and (4).

- The use of parallel s-v-o structures in Sentence (3) with an understood *were* in the second and third strings.

- The use of a direct quote from a contemporaneous document with the spelling and punctuation of the original preserved "waggons."

Every discipline has distinct expectations for syntactic patterns. Content-area teachers need to demonstrate to students the discipline-specific structures and linguistic cadences of the content area. Students need to know that reading a novel in English is different from reading a math problem and different in turn from reading a historical document. And they need direct instruction in knowing how to make adjustments for reading and writing in different content areas. This type of knowledge moves into content-area literacies that are the responsibility not of the English teacher or ESL specialist but of the content-area teacher.

Semantics

Semantics is the study of meaning. Meaning does not reside in individual words but in the speaker/user's intent within designated contexts. Semantics is a complex study of how we use words to affect action on the world, to get things done, to express ourselves. Words also have variable meanings depending on circumstance, audience, tone, figurative use, idiomatic expressions, and idiosyncratic inventiveness. And words have denotations and connotations which add "extra" meaning to the simple word.

For example, consider the word *family*. Most people would think it's a straightforward word that denotes blood relationships. But look at all these semantic variations of the word:

Table 1.4.
Semantic Variation Examples

The Garza family is growing.	The Garzas are some "family."	The Corleones redefined how we think of family.
The family of man	The Addams Family	Our new SUV changes the way we family.
Family time	Family man	Family vacation
We are family.	All in the family	Family tree

Let's consider a simple example from the TNT film *The Ron Clark Story* (Haines, 2006), a fictionalized presentation of the experiences of real teacher Ron Clark. On the first day of class, Clark clips a poster on the board: "We are family." One student dismisses it, saying, "But you don't look nothing like me." The other kids roll their eyes at Clark's attempts to get them to buy into the "family" metaphor. There is a semantic roadblock in this scene: Clark considers the word *family* a positive word; the kids see only negative associations because of their problematic family environments. Thus, his poster fails to have the community-forging impact that he wanted. In the context of semantics, this scene illustrates how easily meaning can be derailed when listeners and speakers don't agree on the meaning of a word.

Words have semantic features that we can metaphorically designate with + or − labels: some words seem positive, some seem negative. The word *sit* may seem to be neutral, but what about *plop* or *slump* or *perch*? In the "We are family" poster example from *The Ron Clark Story*, we clearly see the clash between + and − features of the word *family*.

Connotations are suggested meanings beyond the literal meaning of a word or expression. Denotation generally refers to an objective meaning (but it is difficult to absolutely declare that any given word has a completely objective meaning). Connotation is a meaning suggested by a word. Consider how often young people are told not to call anyone "stupid." The root of this advice is that "stupid" has very negative, ambiguous connotations. No one tells anyone not to say "wow, you're brilliant!" That's because "brilliant" has highly positive connotations, unless it's being used ironically as when someone makes a mistake and someone else says, "Well, that was brilliant!"

Some words clearly carry negative connotations. Take for example, the word *homework*. Think of all the other ways that teachers refer to things that have to be done out of class in order to avoid the negativity suggested by *homework*: *projects*, *assignments*, *opportunities*, *problems*, *entrance tickets*, *practice*.

These "extra" meanings give rise to euphemisms, words that are used to soften harsher meanings or to gloss over painful denotations. Think of all the different ways we can say *die*: *passed away*, *expired*, *passed on*, *kicked the bucket*, *is in a better place*, *lights out*, *didn't make it*, *sleeps with the fish*.

Rhetoric and intentionality affect the way meaning is contextualized and interpreted. Let's consider a word as simple as *gardener*. We can say a *gardener* is someone who tends to plants, lawns, shrubs, and trees in a garden. That seems objective, right? But let's consider a scenario where Jaime and his mother are arguing because Jaime brought home a report card of mostly C's and D's and he spends more time watching Netflix than doing school assignments. His mother yells at him, "Ten years from now, do you want to be a gardener, pushing a lawnmower, working in 99-degree heat, getting $40 for two hours of work on some rich person's huge yard?" All of a sudden, *gardener* becomes a negative term because of the contextualized rhetoric of the mother's usage.

Beyond the specific, situational use of distinct words, as in the examples we've just looked at, we have *collections* of words we know and use in general and highly contextualized situations. A lexicon is generally a collection of words associated with specific usage or users. More expansively, however, each language has a lexicon that includes all the words and relevant knowledge associated with the language. Clearly, no individual speaker could know the entire lexicon of a specific language. In the context of SLA, each learner constructs an idiosyncratic, individual collection of all the words he/she knows in L2. A lexicon is not just vocabulary; it includes understanding of cognitive recognition of words as well as operational use such as we describe in this chapter. Lexicons can be expansive, applying to vast numbers of users, or far more specific, related to an environment that requires specialized knowledge. For example, students with an affinity for sports have lexicons that reflect their knowledge and experience not just in their specific sport but in sports in general. Words included in specific lexicons may take on meanings that they don't have in other contexts. In tennis and volleyball, for example, a *serve* has a very different meaning from *serve* in a culinary lexicon or *serve* in a political context. *Nets* in sports have different denotations from *nets* in hunting.

One of the most difficult aspects of EL experience is figurative language, especially idioms. Idioms are expressions that cannot be processed through literal meaning; historically, through creative invention and usage, idioms have acquired figurative meanings that can sometimes be traced to a logical origin but sometimes cannot, thus, the meaning cannot be lexically explained. Because of the lack of literal meaning, idioms are difficult for EL students to understand. Let's consider some idioms:

Table 1.5.
Some Examples of Idioms

Dog eat dog world	Heavy hitter	Spilled the beans
Rings a bell	Grass is greener on the other side	Piece of cake
Straight from the horse's mouth	Over the moon	Hit the road
The other side of the tracks	Water under the bridge	Crying over spilt milk
Egg on your face	Hit it out of the park	Starting from scratch

Idioms can be very difficult for EL students to understand because all of the traditional context cues and semantic clues we rely on in a lot of communication are absent with idioms. A college teacher tells the story of a recent immigrant from Asia who was working in a service industry. She told her boss that she was taking a quick lunch break and would be going to the cafeteria to get a sandwich. The boss said, "Okay, but step on it." The student told her college teacher that she could not fathom why her boss wanted her to step on her sandwich.

All languages have idioms. A fun, learner-centered ESL activity would be to have EL students share idioms from their native language and explain and illustrate the meaning by trying to translate them into English.

Promoting Semantic Growth in EL Students

Semantics is far more than vocabulary but in classroom contexts, students' semantic growth is strongly promoted through attention to vocabulary. In fact, throughout ELPS, vocabulary is cited as a marker of proficiency in English. Teachers can promote semantic growth in traditional and creative ways. Word walls maintained by learners are aimed at promoting semantic growth. Word walls in content-area classes can help learners master the lexicon of a specific discipline, a competency that is vital to mastery of content-area concepts. Traditional vocabulary quizzes can be direct, albeit not very creative, ways to assess students' semantic growth. On-the-spot, just-in-time opportunities during class can show students how word choice works powerfully to operationalize meaning and intention in our language choices.

Semantic growth is modulated by communicative interactions. Words don't have user-specific meaning until they can be used in authentic communicative contexts.

Pragmatics

Pragmatics pulls together a language user's literal knowledge of language structures in deliberate efforts to act upon the world. Pragmatics is the study of how we use language to do things and to get others to do things. Pragmatics looks at the real, practical intentions operationalized by our linguistic choices. Pragmatics sometimes reveals power relationships. Let's look at a simple, typical exchange of classroom discourse:

Student: "What do we have to do for homework?"

Teacher: "You don't *have* to do anything. I just make the assignment and you can make the choice to do it or not do it."

Pragmatics allows us to look at this very simple exchange from several perspectives. Perhaps the student was simply, innocently asking for objective information, but if the question was uttered indifferently or aggressively, the teacher's response would show a reaction to the student's tone, which is an element of pragmatics. However, if the student simply wanted basic information and the teacher responded the way we see here, the teacher is highlighting a power relationship: "homework" may be something that can be completed or not, but choosing not to complete it will have negative consequences for the student. All of that is implied in the teacher's comment that goes way beyond a simple, objective, informative response. Let's consider an alternative teacher response: "Just do the three questions I put on the board. Shouldn't take you more than about 5 minutes since we spent so much time on the story in class today." The pragmatics are starkly different. In the alternative teacher response, we see a friendly, student-centered, equitable tone but *pragmatically* the intent is identical to the first response: both responses are aimed at getting the student to do the homework.

In EL situations, pragmatics offers opportunities to show learners the power of simple linguistic choice and the power of linguistic growth. Saying "My *Mámi* said I couldn't go to the concert tonight" is very different from saying, "*She* [uttered in a sneering tone] is forbidding me from going." Referring to the mother in the affectionate name in the first sentence softens the tone and modulates the tenor of the utterance: the speaker seems to accept the mother's restriction without rancor whereas the generic, emphasized pronoun in the second sentence coupled with the powerful *forbidding* creates an aggressive situation with the mother as warden and the young person as prisoner. This is what pragmatics is all about: adding tone, modulation, and rhetorical context to enhance meaning and support intentionality.

Discourse

Discourse is boundaried communication. A lot of our talk is presented and enacted in circumstances that are defined by rhetorical, situational, and community boundaries. James Paul Gee, a prime authority in discussion of discourse analysis, suggests that individuals choose to be in discourse communities, which involves deciding to join a group identified by language, interactions, objects, symbols, tools, and beliefs (2001). In rhetorical and general communicative contexts, discourse shows intentionality, control, expertise, community, and authenticity. Discourse, in the most expansive definition, defines a communicative transaction controlled in time and space, with a definite creator and designated recipients.

In the context of ESL teaching and learning, discourse analysis helps learners understand how to be actors and agents in specific communicative interactions. An adept user of language can control what happens in a constructed discourse. A lot of the discourse that is analyzed in classes is content-area discourse. For example, in a math class, a simple word problem can be considered a discourse because it is a specific communicative transaction, mostly presented in declarative and imperative sentences, possibly with an ending interrogative utterance that could also be seen as a directive, imperative speech act:

> Linda has 10 problems for math homework in her third grade class. The problems are simple multiplication of double-digit numbers, like 24×47. Linda's best friend, Amy, is coming over to watch their favorite show at 5:00 p.m. School gets out at 2:45; it takes Linda 30 minutes to get home. Usually she spends 15 minutes changing into comfy clothes and getting a snack. How much time per problem will Linda have before Amy arrives?

In the context of ESL teaching and content-area expectations for ELPS, an EL learner needs to recognize how to "read" this problem, how to identify the required operations, how to rule out extraneous information which may be included in the problem, and how to shape a response within the boundaries of the expectations for the content-area discourse. There may be instructions elsewhere regarding expectations such as "show your work," "use a pencil to present your response in case you have to erase," "use the problem-solution paradigm we practiced in class," "write legibly." The learner's response both extends and completes the discourse created by this communicative transaction.

A discourse can also be spontaneous but still controlled, as when friends are collectively participating in a sporting event, or concert or movie viewing and there is ongoing commentary on the event or there is a post-event commentary.

In the school setting, every class session is a discourse which can be segmented into smaller discourses if the teacher is using demonstrations, guided practice, collaborative opportunities, and independent work. In a discourse, the players/actors/participants usually know their roles and the extent of their expected or possible participation. Those expectations could be deemed to be restrictive but they are also indicative of understanding communicative roles. For example, it's usually not deemed "okay" for a student to blurt out, right after a teacher has made a homework assignment, "Geez! Are you kidding me?! This is such a dumb assignment." But, the discourse boundaries would allow for an intrepid student to say, "Ma'am, most of us are going to the basketball game tonight. Could we do this tomorrow night?"

Understanding the boundaries of discourse is vital for success in content-area classes. Reading an assigned chapter in a science text should trigger acts of metacognitive agency in a learner, such as making sure that the whole chapter is read, taking notes, looking up challenging words, creating graphic organizers, highlighting new words that reflect new content, and anticipating what might be asked in class the next day. In ESL teaching and learning contexts, learners need to be reminded of these content-area expectations.

An ESL teacher who wants to promote students' understanding of how linguistic skills contribute to agency in communicative transactions could do in-class fishbowls or group scenarios to allow students to demonstrate linguistic agency and integral use of basic linguistic knowledge.

Registers

Register refers to the variety of language appropriate in a given situation. Everyone, including ESL students, somewhat intuitively knows that different rhetorical situations require different, appropriate uses of style, tone, vocabulary, and other linguistic elements. Simplistically stated, registers explain why we speak differently to authority figures, our friends, our family, and strangers. Registers also extend to expectations for certain kinds of linguistic acts that don't carry over from one environment to another. Consider something as ordinary as the environment of an elevator. The appropriate register for interactions with strangers in an elevator might include avoiding eye contact or making meaningless, phatic small talk. This would not work in a classroom or in an afterschool band practice session or in a conference with a teacher.

Most fluent speakers are able to communicate in a variety of registers: *formal* with strangers, *informal* with friends, *technical* in the workplace, and *colloquial* to *slang* with the closest discourse group. Most English learners understand the concept of adapting language as a sign of respect for older family members, adults, and authority figures in their culture, but it may be difficult to transition that knowledge of L1 registers to L2. Consider how L1 learners have to concentrate on simply expressing what they want to express in L2. The registers requirement adds a layer of linguistic self-consciousness and filtering that may impede communication. Registers also require adept assessment of the social context, and second language speakers may be so focused on fundamental linguistic concerns (like pronunciation, using the right words, the sentence structure) that the register becomes almost an irrelevant concern—but registers do matter. Using the wrong register can be a marker and can segregate the speaker from being a member of a discourse community.

Although English learners may understand the concept of registers, they do not have the same intuitive sense as native speakers about the appropriateness of specific English words and grammatical structures in distinct communicative settings.

English Language Proficiency Standards

The Texas Administrative Code presents the English Language Proficiency Standards as descriptive statements of student performance levels and student expectations in four proficiency levels, stipulating that school districts must implement ELPS "as an integral part of each subject in the required curriculum" (TAC, 2007). ELPS clearly shows the cross-curricular responsibility for promoting English proficiency in EL students and the integration of proficiencies in listening, speaking, reading, and writing. Additionally, ELPS specifies criteria for assessing students as beginning, intermediate, advanced, and advanced high EL proficiency levels.

ELPS presents responsibility for ESL instruction as collective and collaborative among all subject areas. In the context of Competency 001, which focuses on language concepts and the structure and convention of English, this suggests needed **accommodations** to support learners as they move toward higher levels of language proficiency. "Accommodation" means learner-centered modification not simplification. ELPS specifically mentions communication, sequencing, and scaffolding as types of accommodation. As operationalized in classroom activities, accommodation means creating learning activities that do not single out EL students but that provide holistic, equitable participation for all learners while providing language support to EL students. Cross-curricular modifications include the following classroom teaching activities:

- using more visuals in lessons

- creating opportunities for interactive class work that relies on collaboration

- creating whole-class discussions that include community-building activities so that EL students are able to participate

- integrating kinesthetic activities

- providing succinct summaries of class lessons at the end and beginning of class

- allowing time for all learners to copy important lesson information in their notebooks.

Furthermore, content-area teachers have special responsibilities to guide EL students in recognizing distinct terminology, discipline-specific syntactic structures, and discourse boundaries relevant to the discipline.

Competency 001 should trigger your immediate attention to ELPS. Make a substantive effort to carefully read and annotate ELPS, taking note of how the explanations of proficiency levels consistently integrate vocabulary, language structures, communicative intent, disciplinary content, syntactic complexity, comprehensible writing, discourse varieties, and meaningful output.

Interrelatedness of Communicative Skills

The focus on linguistics provided in Competency 001 underscores the interrelatedness of reading, writing, speaking, and listening in EL students' journey toward English proficiency. Interrelatedness means that these apparently distinct language proficiencies actually exist in the learner's linguistic repertoire as cohesive comprehension of L2 input. What does interrelatedness look like in a class? Let's consider a science lesson on arachnids in an elementary classroom where most of the students are EL intermediate level learners. This example, as helpful as it is for ESL instruction, does not segregate EL students; instead, it offers equitable participation opportunities for all learners.

Speaking: the teacher sets a large toy spider on the desk. Working in pairs, students construct a list of at least five adjectives to describe their affective response to spiders. Students share their responses orally, each pair explaining their choices, and the teacher responds distinctively to each pair as the response is written on the whiteboard.

Listening: the teacher presents a mini-lesson on basic arachnid anatomy, using visuals and stopping every few minutes to do quick assessments of students' understanding of the scientific terms.

Reading: students read a few pages from E.B. White's early draft of the first chapter of *Charlotte's Web* where he describes the spider in scientific terms. White rejected this opening and eventually constructed the one where Fern, the main character, is in the kitchen when her father walks out with the ax (Elledge, 1984, pp. 278–296). Then, the teacher reads the actual published version of the novel, asking students to contrast the scientific draft and the final story.

Writing: students do a quick write describing their reaction to spiders. The teacher offers three starter sentences for students to choose from: (1) I don't like spiders because . . . ; (2) I don't understand why so many people don't like spiders . . . ; (3) What would happen if we didn't have spiders?

As we consider what "interrelatedness of listening, speaking, reading, and writing means," we should keep in mind that EL students are not only acquiring a second language but are also learning the language and discourses of many different disciplines. Each content-area teacher, thus, should be a mentor, guide, and coach in helping EL students use their growing linguistic skills to join the conversation and productivity of each discipline. Knowing the basics of linguistics and having a full understanding of ELPS will enable you to *see* the progress that EL students are making. You will be able to see that "errors" actually point to attempts, to progress, and to growing competence.

Summary, Action Plan, and Chapter 1 Wrap-Up

You should use the descriptive statements in Competency 001 to consider hypothetical classroom scenarios that reflect the teaching knowledge and skills presented from descriptions A–D. Notice the verbs at the beginning of the descriptors: *understands, knows*. These are quite broad and don't delve into what might happen in the classroom; instead, they offer guidelines to steer a beginning teacher toward good decisions, student-centered pedagogy, and best practices in the context of fundamental concepts and the structure and conventions of the English language. The test items will very likely pose classroom scenarios that suggest activities that demonstrate teacher knowledge of linguistics. You should also anticipate items that directly ask about linguistic concepts and terms.

Self-Check

1. What is phonology?

2. What is morphology?

3. What is syntax?

4. What is semantics?

5. How does pragmatics reflect overall linguistic knowledge?

6. What is a register?

7. Why do content-area teachers need to have knowledge of linguistics?

8. Can you construct a teaching scenario in your discipline that creatively and effectively integrates speaking, listening, reading, and writing in a way that would support EL students' learning needs?

9. What does "interrelatedness" of listening, speaking, writing, and reading "look like" in a real ESL teaching situation?

Study Plan

➤ If you have had no courses in linguistics, it would be a smart study strategy to consult some texts such as the following:

Linguistics for Non-Linguists by Frank Parker and Kathryn Louise Riley (2010) offers just enough technicalities about each language system to enable non-linguists, like ESL content-area teachers, to gain confidence about helping EL students in understanding the structure and conventions of English.

Principles of Language Learning and Teaching by H. Douglas Brown (2014) provides a thorough background on first language and second language acquisition as well as topics addressed in the other nine competencies.

You should also add Literacy Glossary (ILA, 2019), a webpage from the International Literacy Association, to your bookmarks and consult this resource as you work through our Competency 001 chapter. Many of the linguistics terms relevant to Competency 001 are succinctly defined in the ILA Literacy Glossary.

Grammar to Get Things Done: A Practical Guide for Teachers Anchored in Real-World Usage by Darren Crovitz and Michelle D. Devereaux (2017) offers a clear, highly readable explanation of the grammar of English, focused on syntax. This is a good book for ESL teachers who may feel insecure about their knowledge of sentence structure. Crovitz and Devereaux have a follow-up book, *More Grammar to Get Things Done* (2019), that includes lessons to help students understand the "rules" of English. These two books are not workbooks; they are books that *explain* grammar so that teachers can help students make sense of and apply the rules that shape our use of English.

➤ Keep a copy of the ELPS at hand and annotate areas that reflect the descriptive statements of Competency 001. Note this excerpt from §74.4(a)(4) which we can connect to Competency 001.D and which clearly indicates that ESL teachers need foundational knowledge of linguistics to fulfill the district's ESL responsibilities:

[ELs in Grade 3 or higher who are at the beginning or intermediate level of English language proficiency in listening, speaking, reading, and/or writing] require focused, targeted, and systematic second language acquisition instruction to provide them with the foundation of English language vocabulary, grammar, syntax, and English mechanics necessary to support content-based instruction and accelerated learning in English. (TAC, 2007)

➤ Look carefully at TEKS in your subject area and teaching level to consider how content-area information, knowledge, and applications can be presented in ESL teaching environments.

Practice Items for Competency 001

1. A grade 4 beginning-level EL student includes the following sentence in a short report on rivers in Texas for his science class:

    The little rain make the rivers to be empty.

    The teacher has a short conference with the student as part of the whole-class formative assessment follow up on the report. Which of the following teacher comments to the learner most effectively shows that the teacher is using knowledge of structure and conventions of English to promote the student's content-area learning?

    A. The teacher says to the student, "This looks great. You are right about how not enough rain keeps river levels low."

B.   The teacher has the student orally read passages from the chapter where the words *drought* and *lower river levels* are used and guides the student to revise the sentence using the content vocabulary.

C.   The teacher says to the student, "You should reread the chapter, look up the key words on the first page, and write the definitions in your science spiral."

D.   The teacher marks the sentence as follows: "*Makes* should be *causes, to be empty* should be *to show reduced water levels*." The teacher also tells the student to rewrite the sentence correctly and resubmit the report.

Response B is correct. This item focuses on content-area vocabulary and concepts. The student's sentence suggests he understands the concepts but is not using the appropriate content-area vocabulary. The teacher's response guides the learner toward recognizing the specificity of content-area terminology and using the terminology to demonstrate his learning. Response A is incorrect because the teacher does not help the student move toward a higher level of proficiency in academic content. Response C does not show the student what the problem is or how to recognize key content-area vocabulary. Response D does not guide the learner toward recognizing content-area vocabulary and does not guide the learner toward developing awareness of his own learning processes.

2.   A middle school math teacher has a class in which about half the students are intermediate to advanced level EL students. The students are having trouble recognizing the structure of word problems. Which of the following initial strategies would promote EL students' linguistic knowledge in working out word problems?

A.   The teacher creates a paradigm for word problems, showing how the first sentence introduces the scenario with a statement, the next sentence poses a math operation, the next sentence clarifies the extent of the operation, and the last sentence sets up an instruction or directive.

B.   The teacher distributes manipulatives (pencils, crayons, marbles, and straws) and has students work in groups to create word problems using the objects as triggers for the problems.

C.   The teacher has students work in groups in a class contest to solve a set of word problems. The group that solves the most word problems in five minutes earns a bonus 10 points on the week's grade.

D.   The teacher writes a word problem on the board which includes confusing and extraneous information. The teacher leads a whole-class discussion in which learners rewrite the sentences to create a solvable problem.

Response A is correct. This response shows the teacher using knowledge of syntax (sentence functions) and the discourse of word problems to help students understand how math problems are constructed. Response B would be an effective next step in this lesson, once the students understand the discourse parameters of the word problem. Creating their own problems would show a higher level of problem-solving proficiency, but Response B would not be the best initial strategy in the item scenario. Response C would also work as an effective classroom strategy later in a lesson on understanding word problem construction. The collaboration and the competitiveness of a contest would boost learners' engagement in the activity, but this would not be the best initial activity for helping learners recognize the structure of word problems. Response D presents an interactive opportunity for learners to demonstrate their understanding of the discourse of word problems. However, this would be a higher-level activity that would work as a follow-up to the more fundamental discourse-centered strategy of Response A. Response D assumes that learners already know the way sentences function to create the discourse of word problems, which, as presented in the item stem, is the problem that the teacher is trying to address.

Competency 002

Competency 002: L1 and L2 Acquisition

The ESL teacher understands the processes of first-language (L1) and second-language (L2) acquisition and the interrelatedness of L1 and L2 development (Pearson, 2019a).

Competency 002 addresses the broad topic of **language acquisition** and is explained through five descriptive statements (A–E), which cover the following general areas:

- Theories, research, and concepts in L1 and L2 acquisition

- Connections between L1 and L2 acquisition research and ESL instruction to construct best teaching practices

- Cognitive processes that support L2 acquisition

- Linguistic scaffolding from L1 to L2

- Crossovers, "difficulties," and translingualism

■ Competency 002 Core Content

The following terms are integral to fully understanding the scope of Competency 002 and Standards I and III, which are aligned with Domain I.

Table 2.1.
Competency 002 Core Content

language acquisition	first language/L1	second language/L2	conversational support
cognitive processes	language rules	language development	communication
interlanguages	immersion	dual language	transfer
translingualism	interference	error	feedback
input	output	acquisition and learning	difficulties

Teaching ESL

ESL teachers have the special task of guiding EL students in the intricacies and possibilities of acquiring a second language (L2). Although the term L2 is used universally in discussion of second language acquisition, the reality is that many EL students have several languages other than English in their backgrounds, so that they are *multilingual* not just *bilingual*. A student, for example, could speak Korean, Spanish, *and* English. Students in our classes may have attended school in other countries where they learned English as a Foreign Language (EFL). Additionally, an increasing number of scholars talk not about bilingualism but instead about *translingualism*. **Translingualism** means that learners of multiple languages do not move smoothly and absolutely between L1 and L2; instead, individuals who have multiple linguistic systems in multiple languages reconstruct their output in L2 from both systems, creating innovative structures that are correct but that show distinct, creatively applied features of both languages (Newman & Garcia, 2019). Whether or not they have formal schooling in English, EL students bring to classrooms linguistic, cultural, social, and rhetorical diversity that can turn classroom spaces into sites for sociocultural, transgeographic engagement. ESL teachers are not starting from scratch in teaching English to EL students; instead, they guide students in identifying what they already know about other languages and appropriating that knowledge to promote growth in English.

L1 Acquisition

A starting point in establishing your framework for ESL teaching is that acquisition of a first language (L1) is markedly different from acquisition of a second language (L2). First languages are acquired *intuitively* with substantive support from caregivers and other individuals involved in the child's psychosocial growth. Children learn the complex linguistic systems of their L1 by "extracting" the rules of language from listening to and interacting with mature, experienced language speakers in authentic, meaningful contexts. The speed of acquisition without direct instruction has led to what is commonly called the "innateness hypothesis," which suggests that human beings are born with an innate "predisposition" for language learning (Yule, 2017; Fromkin, Rodman, & Hyams, 2017; Chomsky, 1959, rpt. 2004). Linguists discuss L1 acquisition in children in terms of stages and milestones: babbling stage, holophrastic stage, overextension, overgeneralization, telegraphic stage, and numerous other developmental phases (Fromkin, Rodman, & Hyams, 2017, pp. 383–407). Clearly, these initial stages do not occur in L2 acquisition, but some theorists suggest that there are comparable stages in SLA: non-verbal, single word, multiple words, phrases, the silent period, sentence-level utterances (Krashen & Terrell, 1983, p. 20).

Discussions of first language acquisition suggest that L1 acquisition is incremental and generative, with gradual understanding of language manifested in hierarchical stages which seem to culminate in learning to read and write, usually in formal, educational settings. Led by Noam Chomsky's classic discussions of language learning, language acquisition specialists agree that initial acquisition happens intuitively, that learners shape hypotheses about language "rules" to construct the grammar that supports an infinite variety of utterances, and that language users (even very young ones) can distinguish between grammatical and ungrammatical structures (Chomsky, 1959, rpt. 2004, pp. 45–47).

SLA and Learning Theories

Second language acquisition (SLA) necessarily integrates factors that apply to learning in general, such as Piaget's stages of cognitive development. Piaget's classic stages establish a learning hierarchy based on age and commensurate cognitive capabilities (Brown, 2014, pp. 60–61; Newman, 2019, pp. 12–13):

- Sensorimotor stage (birth through age 2)—physical, "body"-centric learning

- Preoperational state (ages 2 to 7)—acquisition of language and representational thought

- Concrete operational stage (ages 7 to 11)—learning to categorize, generalization, function in social settings

- Formal operational stage (ages 11 to 16)—abstract thinking

These stages are relevant to SLA because learning a second language inserts a learner into an expansive new universe of learning in which the learner may be required to "backtrack" to an earlier learning stage. Complicating the SLA circumstance is the natural learning of L1 simultaneously as the learner is moving through the cognitive stages. Piaget's cognitive hierarchy and Chomsky's innate learning constructs both place initial language learning at early ages where learning happens unconsciously via implicit learning. SLA forces learners to become conscious of their learning of the new language through explicit learning in school-based instruction. There are also the factors of the natural, untutored acquisition of first language and the schooled, tutored, sometimes externally driven SLA. SLA changes the context of learning: a young child learns language meaningfully, in traditional, "natural" stages; an older, second-language learner or a young L2 learner removed from the normalcy of the L1 acquisition environment has to construct new learning strategies in SLA (Brown, 2014, p. 61–63).

SLA operationalizes the impact of modeling, mentoring, and guidance in potential development in language. The zone of proximal development (ZPD), attributed to Lev Vygotsky, establishes that new learning is facilitated through the guidance of a mentor (a more capable guide or expert) who can support the learner in moving to a new learning that the learner would not have been able to achieve on his/her own (Gonzalez, Yawkey, & Minaya-Rowe, 2006, p. 158; Brown, 2014, p. 42).

The ESL Supplemental exam focuses on acquisition and development in L2, which is markedly different from acquisition and development in L1. The acquisition of L2 in classroom settings involves substantive direct instruction which cannot replicate L1 acquisition because learning a second language involves different cognitive and social competencies. Additionally, the variables that influence first language acquisition, such as relationships with caregivers, quality of the input, degree of reinforcement, and intuitive learning, significantly differ in formal classroom environments. Acquiring a language beyond the primary language is impacted by motivation, the learner's age, the quality and extent of instruction, the theoretical approach to instruction, meaningful use of L2, and the extra-curricular support and reinforcement for L2 learning. Whatever pedagogical approach is used in ESL instruction, there are psycholinguistic, sociolinguistic, and formal linguistic considerations that impact the EL student's progress toward proficiency (Gass, 2009).

Teaching ESL: Theories, Concepts, and Research

Descriptive statement 002.A invites us to consider the big question, "How are second languages learned?" Later competencies suggest operational, instructional choices for *teaching* L2 in ESL environments, but Competency 002 focuses on questions about theories and philosophies underlying L2 acquisition. SLA involves diverse and complex cognitive and social processes with intersections in psycholinguistics, linguistics, cognition, sociolinguistics, and general learning theory (Gass, 2013). Knowing classic theories of L2 acquisition *and* basic theories of cognitive development allows ESL teachers to construct a pluralistic, informed approach to guiding EL students toward proficiency. The school-based approaches to ESL have not always been in place. Many classic theories of L2 learning and acquisition were based on "distributed" learning—that is, learning that happened outside a school environment, motivated by the learner's pragmatic (economic, social, geographic, or personal) desire to learn L2. As a result of the **1965 Elementary and Secondary Education Act (ESEA)** and subsequent reauthorizations, most recently the 2015 **Every Student Succeeds Act (ESSA)**, ESL teaching has become a core responsibility of American public schools (U.S. Department of Education, 2017). Actual practices for teaching ESL can reflect the underlying classic principles of language learning.

Grammar-Based Approaches

Grammar-based approaches are based on learning *about* L2 through translation, drills, repetition, memorization, uncontextualized practice, rule learning, listening, and correctness. Instructional focus is not on meaningful use of the language for authentic communicative purposes but on objectified knowledge of L2 structures (Gonzalez, Yawkey, & Minaya-Rowe, 2006, pp. 162–165). Some grammar-based approaches rely on Chomsky's innateness hypothesis, suggesting that observation, exposure, and practice in L2 activates the language learning mechanisms that enable first language acquisition, such as the "universal grammar" that facilitated learning in L1. Grammar-based approaches include a lot of rote and drill activities, such as learning and repeating grammatical forms, learning common utterances out of context, and practicing scenarios.

For decades, before cognitive and affective factors were integrated into language teaching, grammar-based approaches were the prime methods for teaching a second language. These are some of the most well-known grammar methods:

- The grammar translation method—taught mostly in the learner's L1 with rules, words, grammar structures in L2. Generally did not focus on learner readiness, communicative viability, or growing proficiency (Gonzalez, Yawkey, & Minaya-Rowe, 2006, pp. 162–163).

- The audiolingual method—affiliated with military language training in World War II for military personnel to enable communication with indigenous groups in southeast Asia and the Pacific. Training involved dialogues and drills and practice with a native speaker and privileged oral skills over reading and writing. The method was considered successful and became a prime SLA method in instructional language programs (Krashen & Terrell, 1983, pp. 13–14).

- The direct method—also known as the Berlitz approach. Involved immersion in the target language. Focused rules, isolated utterances, and fixed grammatical structures in L2 (Gonzalez, Yawkey, & Minaya-Rowe, 2006, p. 165; Krashen & Terrell, 1983, p. 11).

All of the materials provided by TEA relevant to teaching ESL point to a far more holistic language approach than grammar-based approaches.

Communicative Approaches: Focus on Krashen

Communicative approaches to L2 instruction and learning serve as a contrast to grammar-based approaches by helping learners recognize the communicative efficacy of the new language. In communicative approaches, L2 is not just content to be acquired but is instead a vehicle for meaningful interaction in the world (Gonzalez, Yawkey, & Minaya-Rowe, 2006, p.165). Stephen D. Krashen is arguably the theorist most closely and enduringly affiliated with the communicative approach. Terms and concepts such as the input hypothesis, comprehensible input, competence precedes performance, the natural approach, and the monitor hypothesis are some of Krashen's signature contributions to L2 theory and practice.

Simply stated, Krashen's input hypothesis posits that L2 acquisition is supported not so much by knowledge of language—the grammar and systems—but by ***comprehensible input.*** In Krashen's own words, the **input hypothesis** is central to his overall theory of second language acquisition and is grounded in five hypotheses (Krashen, 1985, pp. vii–4):

1. The Acquisition-Learning Hypothesis: Krashen differentiates between *acquisition*, which is unconscious and reflects the construct of Chomsky's innateness hypothesis, and *learning*, which is deliberate and "results in 'knowing about' language" (1985, p. 1).

2. The Natural Order Hypothesis: Krashen suggests that L2 acquisition happens in a *predictable* "natural order" that reflects learners' readiness and receptiveness to gradations of structures in L2. Krashen suggests that forcing students to try to produce structures that they have not yet "naturally" acquired results in L2 errors (Krashen & Terrell, 1983, p. 59; Krashen, 1985, p. 9).

3. The Monitor Hypothesis: Krashen posits a "monitor" that functions as an "editor" in L2 output. The monitor enables the L2 user to self-correct *before* output, but this monitoring can occur only if the L2 performer is "concerned about correctness" and also knows relevant L2 rules and structures applicable to the output involved. Krashen suggests that the monitor is most likely to be in effect in writing output or situations where correctness matters, pointing out that in casual, out-of-class environments the monitor might not be activated (Krashen, 1985, p. 1–2; Krashen & Terrell, 1983, p. 59).

4. The Input Hypothesis: Krashen's signature input hypothesis construct suggests that the learner is mindful of forward movement in learning which can be supported with "extralinguistic information" such as mentoring, knowledge of context, and previous linguistic competence. (Krashen & Terrell, 1983, p. 2). Krashen's *i* (input) + 1 "formula" is frequently linked to Lev Vygotsky's **zone of proximal development (ZPD)** model of learning because both constructs connect new learning to a mentor or contiguous learning context that guides the learner toward higher levels of cognition and proficiency (Gonzalez, Yawkey, & Minaya-Rowe, 2006, p.158, 160).

5. The Affective Filter: Krashen suggests that L2 learning is dependent on a readiness to learn manifested as a "filter" that can be lowered or raised depending on the level of readiness. Conscious awareness that new information, new knowledge, and new competencies are contributing to L2 proficiency results in a lowered filter and by extension, new learning in L2. In contrast, input with limited connection in the learner's current L2 experience would trigger a raised filter and pose a barrier to new learning (Krashen & Terrell, 1983, pp. 37–38).

Although Krashen's hypotheses have been criticized as being limited or unsupported by full evidence but never debunked (Liu, 2015), his terms and constructs have persisted for decades as robust descriptors for what happens in L2 acquisition and how and why it happens (or doesn't happen).

Krashen also proposed the Natural Approach as a logical, learner-centered method for second language teaching. The method rests on the central hypothesis "that language acquisition occurs in only one way: by understanding messages. We acquire language when we obtain comprehensible input" (1983, p. 1). Another pivotal tenet of Krashen's natural approach method is that comprehension precedes production (p. 20), which simply means that the learner knows a lot more than what his/her output demonstrates.

Krashen's natural approach also posited stages (reflective of L1 acquisition):

- A silent period or pre-productive stage in which the learner seems reluctant to speak but is instead "building up competence by listening, via comprehensible input" (Krashen, 1985, p. 9)

- An early production period marked by single word responses

- Emergent speech period marked by combinations of several words

- A phrase-production period

- A sentence-production period

- Complex discourse production (1985, p. 20)

In Krashen's natural approach, learners should not be pressured to speak before they are ready because this causes anxiety and leads to "fall-back" reliance on L1 rules that may not apply to L2. Additionally, Krashen advocates that errors that do not interfere with communication should not be corrected (1983, p. 20; 1985, pp. 9–10).

In general, research and practice in SLA sees the EL student as an active, creative learner, utilizing a vast store of linguistic strategies in the journey from L1 to L2. Linguists suggest that as learners move from beginning to proficient levels, their growing competence can be described as "**interlanguage**," "a system that has a structurally intermediate status between the native and target languages" (Brown, 2014, p. 243). Interlanguages are idiosyncratic, learner-specific, and indicative of what the learner knows and can do at particular junctures in the trajectory from L1 to L2. SLA theories see that journey as a series of milestones that reflect how the learner is consciously, deliberately acquiring L2 proficiency. Interlanguages show how learners are processing data from L2 to formulate linguistic systems that show how learners are integrating knowledge from multiple linguistic systems to create meaningful output (Gass, 2013). For ESL teaching in the context of prepping for exam 154, this means that teachers need to be highly attuned to even apparently minor evidences of learner progress. The interlanguage construct does not include predetermined, expected performance levels but instead recognizes that progress toward L2 proficiency reflects learner readiness, motivation, effort, and sometimes serendipitous learning. Interlanguages are idiosyncratic, individual, fluid, and constantly evolving.

Immersion Approaches

Some SLA approaches *immerse* the learner in L2 environments, sometimes with L1 support, sometimes without. In non-school environments, there may be perceived expediency in learning L2 quickly but not primarily for meaningful communication (as when someone needs to move to another country and must learn a new language quickly). In such cases, immersion approaches offer the learner a quick, pragmatic understanding based on environment-specific but limited utterances that enable the learner to communicate and interact at a rudimentary level in L2 settings. In immersion approaches, with limited reference to L1, it is assumed that the learner may automatically, intuitively employ the same language learning strategies he/she used in learning L1 (Gass, 2013, pp. 117–118; Peregoy & Boyle, 2017, pp. 33–34). From a pedagogical standpoint, traditional immersion programs may seem draconian and not learner-centered because of the limited support from L1. However, many immersion programs, such as those used in Texas public schools, are actually *bilingual* programs where the target outcome is not just proficiency in L2 but *bilingualism* and *biliteracy*. We will discuss these programs more fully in Chapter 8, which includes a section on "Types of ESL Programs."

Fluency and Proficiency: BICS and CALP

Another foundation of ESL pedagogy, the distinction between **basic interpersonal communicative skills (BICS)** and **cognitive academic language proficiency (CALP)**, is connected to the research of Jim Cummins (1979). Cummins' work illuminates the reality that L2 proficiency operates on multiple platforms. In the context of ESL learning driven by in-school instruction, it is vital to distinguish between competence that supports phatic, social, pragmatic, and immediate **communication** in L2 and competence that enables effective performance in academic, disciplinary, and formal exchanges. Cummins points out that CALP is what schools endeavor to teach to all learners from the earliest grades. In the ESL environment, growth in CALP can be significantly complicated if no distinction is made among dimensions of proficiency (Cummins, 2000, p 59). Simply stated, the L2 language proficiency needed to just *communicate* is different from the L2 proficiency needed to participate meaningfully in academic discourse. Most ESL experts agree that BICS proficiency occurs much more easily and quickly than CALP, which can take years.

Cummins points out that CALP requires recognition of and facility in academic *registers* of schooling (Cummins, 2000, p. 67). Consider the cognitive load that this dual proficiency—BICS and CALP—imposes on EL students. Not only do they need to be working at acquiring L2 proficiency; they also need to be learning how to function in conversations and activities in all academic disciplines. TEKS materials relevant to EL instruction reflect this duality in proficiency (italics added):

In order for ELs to be successful, they must acquire both social and academic language proficiency in English. Social language proficiency in English consists of the English needed for daily social interactions. Academic language proficiency consists of the English needed to think critically, understand and learn new concepts, process complex academic material, and interact and communicate in English academic settings. (TAC, 2008)

Our discussion, explanations, and illustrations of Domain II, Competencies 003–007, Chapters 3–7, will show you how to operationalize this fundamental EL teaching responsibility to guide students to learn English while learning disciplinary content *in* English.

■ SLA Strategies

Competency 002 Descriptive Statements C, D, and E pull together some SLA processes that overlap and can be difficult to differentiate as distinct language acquisition processes. ESL teachers should expect students to rely substantively on L1, to use a variety of internalized learning and thinking strategies to process L2 learning, and to make errors that reveal the learner's growing competence.

Cognitive Strategies

Learning a second language requires significant self-consciousness about the learning process. Second language learners are generally almost hyperaware of how they are learning and what they are doing to promote their learning. The explicit information and knowledge that the learner is receiving in the formal classroom setting is fortified by the learner's implicit knowledge of how he/she is processing and internalizing the growing L2 knowledge. These awarenesses constitute the *cognitive processes* referenced in Competency 002.C.

Teachers of ESL should be aware of key cognitive strategies used by EL students as they move toward L2 proficiency (Gonzalez, Yawkey, & Minaya-Rowe, 2006, pp. 142–145; O'Malley, 1988; Bialystok, 1981, p. 25):

- Translation: reconstructing an L2 utterance in L1 in order to understand the meaning. Most EL students prefer not to translate because it is time consuming and because the learners recognize that translation impedes growth toward L2 proficiency. Additionally, correct translation requires full understanding of the L2 utterance. More common is the translation of specific words or segments of an utterance to aid the learner in understanding a difficult utterance. Translation is a cognitive not a performative activity; in other words, the learner uses translation privately not in public communicative transactions. In communicative transactions, EL students may say something like, "I don't know the word . . ." which in many cases prompts others in the communicative interaction to help the learner fill in the L2 word based on the context. This happens frequently in classroom interactions as learners in the classroom community support the language learning of their EL classmates.

- Repetition—saying or writing a structure repeatedly in order to internalize the form. Repetition is also a form of rehearsal for speaking or writing in L2.

- Generalization or categorization—contextualizing a new form by recognizing characteristics shared with known forms. For example, a new learner could start categorizing *–ed* or *–ing* forms as probable verb forms, *-s* and *–es* structures as probable plurals. Generalization, however, can lead to "errors," such as *childrens* as a plural for *child* or *thinked*. The learner is clearly showing knowledge of plural formation and past tense formation. An extreme form of generalization is *over-generalization*, which shows excessive and/or undifferentiated application of a newly internalized L2 rule.

- Metacognition—awareness of how specific thinking processes and/or study activities can support new learning in L2. Ideally, EL students should be aware of what internalized thinking strategies contribute to his/her growth as a language learner. For example, if actually asked about how he/she gets through a challenging L2 task, the learner might say, "I read it aloud, very slowly" or "I start over" or "I try to write a summary of what I just read."

- Cooperation/collaboration—participating in self-directed group activities that support L2 growth.

- Questioning—posing questions in class or seeking L2 clarification from other experts, including online sources.

- Practice—creating opportunities among peers, family, and/or experts for targeted practice in L2. Practice is modulated by the learner not by the ESL instructor and thus represents the learner's internal motivation to affect L2 acquisition.

- Code-switching—mixing structures from L1 and L2 in utterances that make linguistic sense within the context of the conflation. Code-switching could be considered a strategy when the learner is at a loss in a communicative transaction because the L2 word or structure cannot be accessed from the learner's current interlanguage repertoire and he/she substitutes a readily accessible structure from L1. Learners who code-switch generally do so when the register is appropriate, such as in communicative transactions with peers. With older learners who are more experienced in L1 to L2 transfer, in many cases, code-switching demonstrates deliberate rhetorical and sometimes political intent to integrate structures across linguistic platforms. Depending on the discourse and register parameters, code-switching could be considered an error or an obstacle to demonstrating English proficiency, but it could also be a deliberate assertion and demonstration of the importance of L1 in the speaker's linguistic universe.

While these cognitive strategies are the province of the learner, the teacher can encourage the use of strategies appropriate for specific learners through in-class guided practice. The cognitive strategies listed here can also form the core of responsive ESL teaching (which we will discuss in Chapters 3–7).

Transfer and Interrelatedness of L1 and L2

Of necessity, EL students will contrast and compare L1 and L2 structures and scaffold L2 learning on L1 competence. L1 offers a vast data bank of prior knowledge not just in linguistic forms but in the experiences that allow learners to create schemas that make learning meaningful. Most people who know more than one language point to the moment when they start thinking in L2 as a significant milestone in SLA. But, before that momentous learning point occurs, there is a lot of transfer from, a lot of reliance on, a lot of dependence on L1. Krashen creatively labels this interrelatedness the "din in the head," a phenomenon that reflects the L2 learner's growing desire to communicate meaningfully in L2: "words, sounds, intonations, phrases, all swimming about in the voices of the people [the L2 learner interacts with]" (1985, p. 37).

In ESL teaching, a significant variable that creates vast differentiation among learners is the level of L1 formal instruction which contributes to developing proficiency in L2. Consider the differences among four hypothetical EL students: (1) a very young newcomer with limited, interrupted, or no formal education, (2) an adolescent-age newcomer with limited, interrupted, or no formal education, (3) an immigrant child who has attended several years of school in his/her native country and thus can read, speak, listen, and write in the native language, and (4) an immigrant child with several years of formal education in his/her native country that included learning English as a Foreign Language. The scope of Exam 154 preparation cannot delve into the variations in teaching that these learner differences would involve but we can assert that SLA for learners (3) and (4) would allow for a much higher level of L1 and L2 interrelatedness or *transfer* than would be possible for learners (1) and (2). The issues of interrelatedness and transfer from L1 to L2 are both logical and idiosyncratic: linguistic knowledge and some literacy in L1 seems to support enhanced learning and performance in L2 but there are factors of motivation, family support, self-selected use of L2, and classroom environment that impact the learner's trajectory toward L2 proficiency (Bialystok, 2007).

Interrelatedness of L1 and L2 does not mean reliance on translation of new structures into the native language but it suggests the pedagogical power of *contrastive analysis*. Although classic discussions of contrastive analysis seem to focus on interference (and incorrect forms) generated by applying structures from L1 in producing L2 (Brown, 2014, pp. 254–256), comparisons of the native and target language forms has robust pedagogical possibilities. From the earliest experience in L2 acquisition, EL students should be guided in recognizing *similarities* in sounds, roots, syntax, semantics, conventions, and even more expansive structures such as genre expectations. ESL teachers should be aware that EL students may not see the interrelatedness, but recognizing, for example, that the Spanish word for *father* (*padre*) shares a Latin root with *paternal* and *patriarch* may help learners develop inquisitiveness about and receptiveness to possible connections among other L1 and L2 words. Phonemic similarities are especially important in developing speaking and writing proficiency, so EL students should have guidance in vocabulary growth through comparisons between similar L2 and L1 words when appropriate. In some situations, syntactic structures in L1 can also be used to demonstrate how syntax combines semantics, rhetoric, and intentionality which can be constructed using appropriate structures from L2.

In short, EL students rely on connections, similarities, differences, crossovers, and opportunities in the interrelatedness of L1 and L2. That is a natural part of SLA, and ESL teachers can use interrelatedness of native and target languages to bolster students' confidence in their growing proficiency in L2.

Error and Growth

When we talk about *error* in SLA acquisition, we need to start with the understanding that error is a sign of growth. Traditionally, error in SLA has been seen as evidence of interference from L1 in attempting to produce L2 structures. *Error analysis* is a branch of SLA studies that explores the provenance of errors in L2 production with a focus on the rationale of the mismatch between the expected, correct structure and the produced incorrect structure (Brown, 2014, pp. 250–251). If we go back to considering the differences between L1 and L2 acquisition, we can see a significant difference in attitude between language errors produced by young learners, acquiring language naturally and intuitively, and errors produced by older L2 learners. The errors produced by EL students should not be seen as careless mistakes that show inattentiveness to L2 structures but should instead be seen as "hypothesis testing" of new structures and new possibilities in L2 (Corder, 1974, p. 25). In the classic article, "The Study of Error" (1980), David Bartholomae offers an alternative, highly learner-centered view of error: he suggests that error does not show failure but instead shows what the learner knows and is trying to do; hence, error is evidence of growth:

> errors are seen as (1) necessary stages of individual development and (2) data that provide insight into the idiosyncratic strategies of a particular language user at a particular point in his [or her] acquisition of a target language. (p. 256)

Part of recognizing the "idiosyncratic strategies" evidenced by particular errors is knowing the typical errors that EL students make in attempting meaningful L2 communication. Let's consider some of the most common errors:

Interference errors—this is a broad term that encompasses errors that can be traced to incorrect application of L1 structures in the L2 framework. Interference errors can occur at all levels of the grammatical spectrum, from phonological errors to errors in pragmatics. Interference errors are logical and frequently represent approximations of structures from L1 into L2 environments.

Idiomatic structures—because idioms are language-specific and generally do not translate logically, they are the source of common errors. Idiomatic structures can be misunderstood or misinterpreted resulting in holistic failure to understand the greater context of the discourse in which the idiom occurs. An example of a Spanish idiom that does not logically translate into English is the colloquial *te aventaste*, an expression that means something like "you outdid yourself, you rocked!" *Aventar* means *throw*, so there is no literal semantic interrelatedness that could support saying "you threw yourself" as a viable, correct, logical translation. Because it is an idiom, a literal translation would destroy the meaning intended by the idiom; there would have to be a comparable idiom in L2 to express the same colloquial meaning. Idioms may have etymological or historical backstories to explain the origin of the expression, but for the most part, idioms are linguistically idiosyncratic and literally impossible to translate; thus, they are a source of L2 error.

False cognates—when learners assume that a word is a direct match in phonology, morphology, or semantics in L1 and L2 but is not, we have a false cognate. Consider the English word *assist*, which means *to help*. In Spanish, *asistir* means *to attend*, so an EL student who says, "I assisted classes all day" is demonstrating a false cognate error. Prefixes can also create false cognate errors as in the use of the word *intoxicate* in a discussion of environmental poisoning of a forest with chemical runoff: "the wild life in the forest was intoxicated by the chemicals." Or using the word *distressed* to mean "without stress" because of the conflation of prefixes *de-* and *dis-* and the literal appending of the word *stress* to these prefixes, ending up with a false cognate that actually means the opposite of the constructed structure: "running helped me be distressed."

Approximations—these are common errors that arise when an EL student tries to produce a sound or other structure in L2 using the closest, relevant structures from L1 and ends up substituting an incorrect structure. When L2 includes sounds that are not used in L1, the logical remedy is to substitute a sound from L1 that approximates the sound of L2.

The ELPS emphasis on the interrelatedness of the listening, speaking, reading, and writing is particularly relevant in helping teachers identify errors in one domain so that they do not carry over into others.

Direct translation—these errors can be triggered by false cognates or approximations. The EL student might recognize a linguistic similarity in L1 or L2 structures but the actual connection is tenuous, as when an EL students says, "We made a party to celebrate my *Abuelo's* 95 years," reflecting the direct translation of *hiciemos una fiesta.*

Invented spellings—we celebrate invented spelling in primary grades as evidence that young learners are operationalizing phonetic and orthographic knowledge. However, when invented spellings show up in the writing of EL students, they are seen as marks of deficiency. Invented spellings in the writing of EL students at all grade levels show attempts to employ phonetic knowledge to produce graphic communication. ESL teachers should recognize what the invented spelling says about the writer's current L2 competence and use that analysis to help the student progress to higher levels of proficiency, instead of simply marking the aberrant spelling as a mistake.

Code-switching—the conscious practice of inserting L1 structures in L2 output. We could argue that code switching is more a cognitive strategy or evidence of the interrelatedness of L1 and L2 than an error. Code-switching, however, reveals the learner's ability to smoothly transition within phonological, morphological, semantic, and syntactic systems of L1 and L2. Code-switching shows *correct* cross over; in other words, the code switcher would not likely insert an L1 noun in the syntactic slot for a verb. Some discussions of code-switching focus on the way that code-switching can be used deliberately to emphasize the second language speaker's affiliation with the culture, politics, and history of L1. When code-switching shows failure to recognize the parameters of discourses or registers, it could be considered an error.

Being attuned to the errors involves knowing how to use full linguistic knowledge to explain the error to the learner and to guide the learner in correcting the error. In looking at errors, an ESL teacher should compare prescriptive expectations for what is "right" or "acceptable" in L2 to descriptive analysis of what the learner is doing. In other words, seeing error as failing to meet a prescriptive standard creates a deficit view of linguistic experimentation (Crovitz & Devereaux, 2017, p. 6). A thorough knowledge of all aspects of linguistics, the topic of Competency 001, gives ESL teachers expertise in recognizing errors as contextualized applications of developing L2 proficiency. ESL teachers are in the position of being Krashen's +1 in his *i* (input) + 1 (extra linguistic information) formula, which channels Vygotsky's ZPD construct. With the linguistic, contextual, and rhetorical explanation provided by the ESL teacher, an EL student can use error to move from the current *i* (input) level to a higher level of proficiency.

Best Practices for ESL Teaching

Domain II will fully address what ESL teachers can do through classroom activities and teaching practices to promote EL students' proficiency. Here we offer a few general principles that will be illuminated in Chapters 3–7 but that address Competency 002.B which includes the responsibility "to select effective, appropriate methods and strategies for promoting students' English-language development at various stages":

- Manageable, comprehensible input—lessons should be presented in segments that allow learners to process new knowledge in terms and activities that reflect learner readiness and break down large bodies of content into discrete, manageable portions.

- Anticipation, prediction, expectation—learners can be primed for new learning with lists of content-specific vocabulary, activities that activate prior knowledge, and learning agendas that show what will happen in a specified learning period.

- Reinforcement—teachers can repeat information, can present it orally and visually, can ask targeted, meaningful questions.

- Redundancy—information can be presented in a variety of ways and in multiple learning platforms.

- Collaborative opportunities—while native L2 speakers should not be designated as coaches or teacher aides, collaborative work, such as think-pair-share activities, allow EL students to experiment in low-risk situations.

- L1 support—when appropriate, supporting materials in L1 should be provided for EL students.

- Recognition of L2 learning stages—EL students should not be rushed into performance levels for which they are not ready. Teachers should be aware of learners' silent period when the predominant learning activity is non-verbal acquisition of L2 knowledge. Teachers should also recognize that EL students, especially at the beginning and intermediate levels, may offer evidence of learning in shorter, simpler utterances than L2 speakers.

- Integration of language skills—ESL teachers should consistently reinforce learning through integrated listening, speaking, reading, and writing activities.

- Specialized content-area support—content-area teachers should provide specialized scaffolding to support EL students' acquisition of disciplinary knowledge that also supports overall L2 proficiency.

- Differentiation—ESL teachers should recognize the individual distinctions among EL students' current proficiency. Learners may share generic qualities as second language learners, but individually, they require learner-specific pedagogical attention.

- Feedback—the teacher's response to the learner's output. In ESL instruction, feedback is a vital conduit for learner growth. Teachers should be alert for authentic assessment opportunities that allow just-in-time feedback as EL students interact with other class members and the teacher and as learners submit learning products. Feedback should always be shaped by identifying what the learner has done effectively and what the learner needs to do to improve. A more detailed discussion of feedback occurs in Chapter 4.

- Total Physical Response (TPR)—a classic second language teaching strategy that engages learners in physical activities to demonstrate comprehension of vocabulary and simple directions and commands. Learners may be asked to act out verbs like *run, jump* or to identify objects or images relevant to designated activities. Sometimes learners may be asked to follow simple instructions like "Show me which is your left hand" or "Pick up your math book." For older learners, TPR can be used to demonstrate understanding of content-relevant activities, such as performing tasks for science experiences or acting out literary or historical scenes. TPR can promote learners' sense of accomplishment, participation in the class community, and communicative competence (Herrell & Jordan, 2020, pp. 28–31; Peregoy & Boyle, 2017, pp. 270–271).

■ Summary, Action Plan, and Chapter 2 Wrap-Up

Competency 002 covers the expansive topic of L1 and L2 acquisition, calling Exam 154 candidates' attention to the differences in these two kinds of language acquisition. However, SLA is literally impossible without reliance on existing knowledge and experience from L1.

Self-Check

1. Explain your understanding of L1 acquisition.

2. Explain your understanding of L2 acquisition, focusing on *differences* between L1 and L2 acquisition.

3. Explain some of the cognitive processes EL students use to demonstrate their awareness of how they are learning L2.

4. Explain some of the connectivity between L1 and L2 that is relevant to L2 acquisition.

5. Consider how integration of listening, speaking, reading, and writing might be manifested in specific content areas. Try to imagine a short lesson on a designated topic and consider how you might teach a lesson that would address the needs of EL students.

Study Plan

1. Comprehensive discussions of SLA, such as H. Douglas Brown's *Principles of Language Learning and Teaching: A Course in Second Language Acquisition* (2014) and Frank Parker's and Kathryn Riley's *Linguistics for Non-Linguists: A Primer with Exercises* (2010) include chapters on first language acquisition. Reading at least one such section will be a great help in understanding Competency 002.

2. *English-as-a-Second-Language (ESL) Teaching and Learning: Pre-K–12 Classroom Applications for Students' Academic Achievement and Development* by Virginia Gonzalez, Thomas Yawkey, and Liliana Minaya-Rowe (2006) includes a strong chapter on instructional approaches for ESL students which provides an extended discussion of the approaches touched on in our Competency 002 chapter.

3. Theories of L2 acquisition are vast, linked to historical understandings of language teaching practices, and interrelated with overall learning theory. You should make some time to read some chapters from Brown and from Parker and Riley on classic approaches to second language teaching.

4. Anticipate test items for Competency 002 that pose teaching scenarios that reflect best practices in ESL.

5. Anticipate test items that ask you to recognize examples of specific terms or concepts.

Practice Items for Competency 002

1. A middle school science teacher is launching a group project on wildlife indigenous to South Texas. She has mounted six posters throughout the room with names and illustrations of the opossum, jackrabbit, coyote, raccoon, armadillo, and jaguarundi. She is doing a quick info talk on each animal and then going back to ask for volunteers for each creature. When she gets to the jaguarundi, Jaime waves his hand and says, "*Yo! Yo!* Miss, I want *el* jaguarundi for my report!" Jaime's utterance is an example of which of the following SLA strategies?

    A.   Transference

    B.   Interference

    C.   Code-switching

    D.   Approximation

    Response C is correct. The student's utterance is a classic example of code-switching. The student has inserted Spanish words in correct syntactic and semantic form to create an L2 utterance that relies on deliberately merging L1 structures into L2 utterances. Response A is incorrect because the student's utterance does not show that the student is appropriating an L1 structure as scaffolding for an L2 utterance. The full utterance shows that the student indeed knows pronoun and article forms in English as well as Spanish. Response B is incorrect because interference refers to an incorrectly constructed L2 form created when an EL speaker uses an L1 structure because the L2 form has not yet been learned. Response D is incorrect because approximation involves the use of an L2 form that is closely related to the intended output when the speaker has not yet acquired the correct form.

2. A fourth grade ESL teacher is preparing students for the state-mandated mathematics exam. The teacher presents a word problem on the document camera and asks for student volunteers to create step-by-step protocol on the whiteboard to consider response strategies for solving the problem. What aspect of ESL teaching does this strategy most closely represent?

    A.   Cognitive Academic Language Proficiency

    B.   Segmenting

    C.   Collaborative reinforcement

    D.   Content-area vocabulary emphasis

    Response A is correct. The teacher is trying to get students to activate cognitive strategies for tackling the word problem which would reinforce the students' proficiency in the academic content of math. The protocol would activate students' cognitive processing of their response to word problem discourse. Response B is incorrect. Segmenting, one of the strategies recommended in ELPS for linguistic accommodation, means breaking up a lesson into smaller, manageable units. The activity explained in the item stem could be an example of segmenting if we knew what the teacher did in the rest of the class. Response C is incorrect because although collaboration is clearly a major part of this activity, the teacher's focus is on content-area preparation not on a communicative interaction. The protocol strategy is a powerful indication that the teacher is focused on the math content. Response D is incorrect because while the protocol activity is likely to bring up relevant vocabulary, the activity is not tailored toward emphasis on vocabulary.

PART II: DOMAIN II

ESL Instruction and Assessment

ESL Instruction and Assessment

▪ Overview of Domain II

Domain II focuses on how knowledge and practices in general pedagogy can be adjusted for teaching ESL. If you are taking the ESL (154) exam, you have already succeeded on the PPR (160) exam, and thus know the fundamentals of pedagogy. Teaching ESL does not require *different* pedagogical practices, but it does require fine tuning and adjusting what we do in a classroom of native speakers in order to meet the needs of students who are both learning English and learning *in* English.

Domain II Competencies

Competency 003: The ESL teacher understands ESL teaching methods and uses this knowledge to plan and implement effective, developmentally appropriate instruction.

Competency 004: The ESL teacher understands how to promote students communicative language development in English.

Competency 005: The ESL teacher understands how to promote students' literacy development in English.

Competency 006: The ESL teacher understands how to promote students' content-area learning, academic-language development and achievement across the curriculum.

Competency 007: The ESL teacher understands formal and informal assessment procedures and instruments used in ESL programs and uses assessment results to plan and adapt instruction.

(Pearson, 2019a)

Core Content from Domain II Competencies

Table D2.1.
Core Content from ESL (154) Domain II

Competency # and General Topic	Core Ideas from Descriptive Statements
003 ESL teaching strategies and instruction (5 descriptive statements)	• Using TEKS and ELPS to modulate ESL instruction • Knowing methods, techniques, and resources to address EL students' diverse needs • Knowing content-specific strategies for promoting EL students' content-area competency • Using technology to enhance learning in ESL environments • Knowing how to implement effective classroom management in ESL environments
004 Communicative competence (7 descriptive statements)	• Knowing TEKS and ELPS for listening and speaking • Understanding how listening and speaking skills contribute to communicative competence • Knowing strategies for fostering growth in communicative competence • Recognizing individual differences in EL students and using targeted instruction to promote communicative competence in L2
005 Literacy development (7 descriptive statements)	• Knowing TEKS and ELPS for reading and writing • Knowing that linguistic foundations support literacy growth • Using L1 literacy to support growth in L2 literacy • Recognizing individual differences in EL students and using targeted instruction to promote literacy in L2
006 Content-area responsibilities (4 descriptive statements)	• Knowing how to create linguistically accommodated instruction to promote cognitive-academic language proficiency • Using a variety of delivery methods to enhance students' learning in content areas • Recognizing individual differences in EL students and using targeted instruction to promote growth in content-area understanding
007 Assessment (6 descriptive statements)	• Adapting comprehensive knowledge of assessment for the ESL teaching and learning environment • Being operationally familiar with ESL testing and assessment practices in Texas • Using ongoing formal and informal assessment to promote continual achievement in EL students

ELPS and Domain II Content

Knowledge of ELPS is included as a descriptive statement in three Domain II competencies. If you have not already looked carefully at ELPS, you should do so now, noting the multi-level organization that will enable you to negotiate sections of ELPS as you need to reference them for clarifying the Domain II expectations:

§74.4(c)(1)–(5)   Cross-curricular second-language acquisition essential knowledge and skills. Think of the term *cross-curricular* as generally equivalent to *content area* or *academic language*. This section is a valuable ESL Exam (154) study aid because it identifies targeted student performance expectations for listening, speaking, reading, and writing which can be used to infer appropriate teaching strategies. (TAC, 2007)

§74.4(c)   Proficiency level descriptors. This lengthy section breaks down the four proficiency levels—beginning, intermediate, advanced, and advanced high—by grade level (Kindergarten through Grade 12 or Kindergarten through Grade 1 and Grade 2 through Grade 12). There are detailed performance descriptors for each proficiency level in the areas of listening, speaking, reading, and writing. These bulleted lists of ELPS content offer a way to "translate" SLA pedagogies into specific teaching activities that elicit specific learner behavior or outcomes. Deep knowledge of these proficiency level descriptors matters to ESL Supplemental Exam (154) candidates because you are likely to have numerous test items that ask you to identify an EL student proficiency level based on student behavior described in the stem. (TAC, 2007)

§74.4(b)(3)   Linguistic accommodations. ELPS stipulates that essential knowledge and skills must be provided in a linguistically accommodated manner.

§74.4(c)(1)–(5) Linguistic accommodations. The student expectations sections in listening, speaking, reading, and writing define linguistic accommodation as instruction that is "communicated, sequenced, and scaffolded." (TAC, 2007)

According to the English as a Second Language Supplemental (154) Preparation Materials website, Domain II items compose 45 percent of the 80 test items (Pearson, 2019a).

CHAPTER 3

Competency 003

Competency 003: ESL Teaching Methods

The ESL teacher understands ESL teaching methods and uses this knowledge to plan and implement effective, developmentally appropriate instruction (Pearson, 2019a).

Teaching in an ESL environment is the broad area addressed by Competency 003. Five descriptive statements (A–E) in this competency cover the following general topics:

- Operational familiarity with TEKS and ELPS

- Best practices for ESL instruction

- Integration of technology to enhance ESL instruction

- Creation of a hospitable classroom environment for ESL learning

Competency 003 Core Content

Competency 003 focuses on pedagogical skills and strategies that enhance teaching and learning in ESL environments. Competency 003 does not suggest that different teaching strategies are required for teaching ESL; instead, it addresses the need to shape what works in all pedagogy for the special circumstances of ESL teaching. Table 3.1 presents important terms from Competency 003 and the aligned educator standards—Standard I and Standards III–VI.

Table 3.1.
Competency 003 Core Content

Texas Essential Knowledge and Skills (TEKS)	ELPS	instructional goals	teaching methods
content area teaching	diversity	technology	classroom management

TEA Materials: TEKS and ELPS

All TEA materials offer an abundance of insights into expectations for the ESL Supplemental (154) exam. As you work through Chapter 3, you should have a copy of the TEKS relevant to your target content area and grade level as well as the ELPS. Competency 003 focuses on teaching methods; while TEKS does not specify teaching methods, the content-area specifications in grade level TEKS enable you to envision classroom activities in ESL context for the specific curricular expectations, articulated in Competency 003.A as "knows how to *design and implement* appropriate instruction" [italics added]. Competency 003.A ends with a focus on the interrelatedness of listening, speaking, writing, and reading skills, a pedagogical foundation that runs through all sections of ELPS. Competency 003.C reiterates the ESL teacher's responsibility to foster communicative skills as well as deep understanding of discipline-related content (Pearson, 2019a). A close look at ELPS reveals some key pedagogical practices designed to support these responsibilities.

What ELPS Says About Teaching ESL in Content Areas

ELPS §74.4(c)(1)(A–H), presented as student expectations, suggest specified strategies for addressing the pedagogical responsibilities in Competency 003:

- Activating prior knowledge

- Promoting self-correction

- Devising strategies for learning relevant vocabulary, such as concept mapping, drawing, memorizing, comparing, contrasting, and reviewing

- Reinforcing content-area knowledge through targeted speaking and writing activities

- Promoting new learning of academic content through accessible input

- Helping the learner understand the difference between formal and informal L2 (which reflects Competency 001 points about registers and discourse)

- Supporting cognitive development of inductive/deductive thinking, patterns recognition, and holistic semantic development. (TAC, 2007)

The ELPS items in content-area student expectations in listening, speaking, reading, and writing presented in §74.4(c) (2)–(5) offer remarkably specific details on how content-area teachers might present disciplinary information to EL students. For test candidates, the extremely specific strategies, techniques, concepts, and approaches integrated into descriptions of content area ELPS expectations offer a window into what might be on the ESL Supplemental (154) exam. This chart of selected items actually integrated into ELPS gives you a good overview of the specificity of terms and concepts included in ELPS for cross-curricular ESL teaching:

Table 3.2.
Selected Terms and Concepts Relevant to
Cross-Curricular Instruction from ELPS §74.4 (C)

prior knowledge	self-correction	concept mapping	drawing	memorizing	comparing/ contrasting
reviewing	non-verbal clues	requesting assistance	synonyms	circumlocution	meaningful use of academic language
formal/informal usage	reasoning strategies	patterns	analysis of sayings and expressions	intonations	phonological knowledge
visual support	media support	summarizing	collaboration	syntactic performance	opinion formation in the context of academic content
prereading strategies for academic texts	linguistic accommodation	inferential skills	critical analysis	editing	conventions of writing
grammatical correctness	syntactic variety	writing in a variety of genres to reflect content knowledge	alphabetic knowledge	silent reading	comprehension of content-area material

If you have not seriously looked at the content-area ELPS, you should take some time right now to explore the detailed presentations of EL student performance bulleted in the ELPS §74.4(c) (1)–(5) (TAC, 2007). The terms presented in Table 3.2 offer a powerful indication of the depth and breadth of ESL teaching knowledge and skills required to succeed on the ESL Supplemental (154) exam.

Listening, Speaking, Reading, and Writing Expectations Presented in ELPS

The overriding feature of ELPS for listening, speaking, reading, and writing is the articulation of proficiency level descriptors for Kindergarten through Grade 1 and Grades 2–12 in §74.4(d) (TAC, 2007). The proficiency level descriptors for listening, speaking, reading, and writing represent holistic competencies that apply to all subject areas and that show the EL student's growing capabilities in L2 competence and performance. Table 3.3 shows selected comparison of similar expected performances across proficiency levels for *listening*. Note the generic adjectival descriptors for each proficiency level (TAC, 2007, pp. 8–9).

Table 3.3.
Comparable Performance Descriptors for Listening

Beginning	Intermediate	Advanced	Advanced High
§74.4(d)(1)(A)(ii) struggle to identify and distinguish individual words and phrases during social and instructional interactions that have not been intentionally modified for ELs	§74.4(d)(1)(B)(ii) often identify and distinguish individual words and phrases necessary to understand the general meaning during social and instructional interactions that have not been intentionally modified for ELs	§74.4(d)(1)(C)(ii) understand most main points, most important details, and some implicit information during social and basic instructional interactions that have not been intentionally modified for ELs	§74.4(d)(1)(D)(ii) understand main points, important details, and implicit information at a level nearly comparable to native English-speaking peers during social and instructional interactions

The consistent, defining point of the Advanced High proficiency level is the "level nearly comparable to native English-speaking peers" as the marker for reaching this top ESL proficiency level. The goal for ESL instructors is to support EL students' achievement of Advanced High performance by adapting teaching practices to meet their communicative and academic language needs.

Adapting Best Teaching Practices for ESL Environments

Effective ESL instruction starts with a firm foundation in best practices for reaching *all* learners. ESL instruction does not draw on different practices but instead focuses on what helps engage learners in the challenging task of achieving L2 proficiency. Most ESL experts designate specific instructional strategies as particularly effective for teaching EL students:

- Collaborative learning. Learners are grouped randomly or selectively to provide opportunities for learning new knowledge, for reporting in-progress activities, for learning from each other, and for supporting peers in moving toward new achievements. **Collaborative learning** can occur in pairs or in groups of varying sizes, maximizing communicative opportunities among learners. Teachers can assign all levels of activities as group tasks, such as simple identification of core information for a class lesson, analysis of pivotal, lesson-relevant topics, creation of learning products, and formal or informal presentations. For groups to function effectively, learners need to use basic communicative skills to do the interactive work of the group and apply content-area language and knowledge to complete targeted tasks. Thus, for EL students, collaborative learning in small groups vs. whole-class settings can promote development of BICS and CALP. Additionally, collaborative learning in small groups can provide opportunities for EL students to demonstrate their competence and capabilities more readily than the anxiety-producing, "performance type" participation of whole-group discussions. (Peregoy & Boyle, 2017, p. 115)

- Thematic units. When content-area units are constructed coherently on a theme, the singular focus of unit activities supports increasingly higher levels of learning as learners scaffold new knowledge on the thematic platform. **Thematic units** allow teachers to create a variety of instructional activities that activate a variety of learning strategies at different cognitive levels, thereby reinforcing holistic, incremental achievement across the domains of listening, speaking, reading, and writing. Thematic units enhance EL students' comprehensible input through cross-curricular connections, integration of language skills, opportunities to draw on prior knowledge, and increased participation and motivation. (Peregoy & Boyle, 2017, pp. 109–114)

- Scaffolding. Sequential lessons and activities contribute to learners' growing competence as they approach new information in incremental segments matched to their learning readiness. **Scaffolding** allows teachers to operate within the student's zone of proximal development, providing necessary instructional support to move to higher levels of learning that they can achieve through that support (Peregoy & Boyle, 2017, p. 116). ESL teachers should rely on **Bloom's Taxonomy** to construct activities that reflect learner readiness for successively higher cognitive engagement (applying, analyzing, evaluating, and creating) instead of centering instruction on the basic levels (remembering and understanding) (Burden & Byrd, 2013, pp. 99–102; Anderson & Krathwohl, 2001). The learning categories of Bloom's Taxonomy enable EL teachers to provide appropriate accommodations, predict learner outcomes, and observe behavioral changes that can be matched to ELPS student expectations and proficiencies.

- Modeling. Instructors should show learners how learning activities can be approached. **Modeling** can involve teacher or student demonstrations, internet videos showing the activity in action, or group presentations that demonstrate diverse approaches to a task.

- Recursiveness. Learners need to see that learning happens by moving forward, sometimes backtracking, and then finding new paths forward. In ESL instructional settings, **recursiveness** should be recognized as evidence of the productivity of error.

- High expectations. Teachers should convey a success attitude that encourages learners to keep trying even when they may falter in their journey toward achievement. Teachers can foster a culture of **high expectations** by creating low-stakes assessment opportunities that motivate learners by showing immediate, manageable accomplishments. Teachers should keep in mind that even apparently small increments of achievement should be recognized to show learners that their accomplishments are being noticed.

- Interrelation of listening, speaking, reading, and writing. These routes to understanding must be continually integrated to create redundancy and to recognize different learning styles.

- Celebration of difference. EL students' linguistic and cultural distinctiveness should never be seen as a deficit, but instead should be seen as a contribution to the **diversity** of the classroom space.

Special Circumstances of Content-Area Instruction

Content-area ESL instruction will be discussed in more detail in Chapter 6, which addresses Competency 006, but we can start here with basic responsibilities that ESL teachers have for helping EL students enter the conversations of academic disciplines.

- ESL teachers should demonstrate an authentic affinity for the discipline they teach by sharing with students' stories of their own experience in the discipline and explaining how the discipline matters globally and locally.

- ESL teachers should show, explain, and model the discipline-specific ways of thinking distinct to content areas.

- ESL teachers should strive to involve students in authentic activities that reflect content-area expertise, mindsets, and behaviors.

- ESL teachers should guide students in learning the basics of the content area, such as vocabulary, problem solving approaches, historical context, and current relevance.

- ESL teachers should have artifacts, realia, representations, books, and models in the classroom to show learners the context of the content area.

- ESL teachers should strive to integrate **culturally relevant** materials to support EL students' understanding of content-area information.

Linguistic Accommodations

An "accommodation" is an adjustment made in instruction or materials to make content more accessible for learners. In the context of ESL instruction, linguistic accommodations refer to teacher practices that enhance the quality of the input for the EL student, thereby promoting learning. Accommodation does not mean changing the instructional content but instead refers to creative, specific, learner-centered strategies that make academic content input more comprehensible for learners. Here are some instructional adjustments that ESL teachers can make:

- Delivery. Teachers can slow down the pace of lecture-type presentations by modulating their speed, voice, and even their circulation throughout the classroom space. Teachers can put key information on the whiteboard or document camera in bulleted lists to reinforce lecture content.

- Segmenting. Instead of presenting new information in a large, undifferentiated chunk, teachers can use **segmenting** to break up lessons into mini-lessons targeting specific objectives. Each mini-lesson can include self-checks that allow learners either to work collaboratively to check their understanding or independently to perform a short task that the teacher can check easily and quickly.

- Content-area accessibility. Textbooks are written by experts who do not always write at a level that can be understood by student readers. Teachers can create linguistic accessibility of challenging course content by restating key content material in simpler terms and simpler sentence structures.

- Learning styles. Teachers should vary the way information is presented to reflect awareness of varied **learning styles**. There should be a variety of delivery systems used besides traditional lecture. Teachers can use visuals, clips of films or other media, interactive computer work, guided practice, demonstrations, modeling, guest speakers, and kinesthetic activities. Sometimes, even something as simple as changing the configuration of the desks can create a new way of learning for students.

- Disciplinary content. Each subject area has distinct vocabulary, ways of thinking, ways of presenting results, distinct writing styles, and expected prior knowledge. Content-area vocabulary should be displayed around the room. Posters and other visuals should reinforce student knowledge of important individuals, dates, genres, problem-solving strategies, and any other elements deeply connected to the content area.

- Instructions. Instructions should be delivered in multiple ways to create redundancy and enrich the comprehensible input. For example, students can be asked to copy instructions presented on a screen and then, the teacher can highlight key words in the instructions or create a bullet list on the whiteboard to reinforce what is expected. For major task instructions, teachers can call on students to repeat the sequence of steps.

- Nonverbals. Teachers can use body language, gestures, and movement to reinforce delivery.

- Lesson set-up. Teachers should plan an "entering the learning space" activity for each class meeting in schools where students are moving from class to class. This entry activity can be something content-related such as presenting an entrance ticket or more communicative such as writing something on the class bulletin board. Starting each lesson with a simple class agenda and/or lesson outcomes creates a context for the lesson. For example, a simple enumerated list of what the class will do that day allows learners to understand what's going on at different points in the class. Creating a list of important vocabulary will alert learners to pay closer attention as those terms are mentioned in the lecture. Having a class wrap-up will reinforce what should be the major takeaways. Leaving time for targeted questions allows the teacher to sense what might have been misunderstood. Questions should not be an open-ended "does anyone have questions" but perhaps, "Can I get two volunteers to draw a plant on the board and label the parts?" Teachers should leave a few minutes of "cool down" time at the end of the period instead of running the lesson up until the bell rings.

- Wait time. The time between a teacher question and student response can sometimes seem interminable. **Wait time** is the interval between the point when the teacher asks a question and students respond. Wait time can be truncated when teachers jump in, for whatever reason, to push students to respond before they are ready. Students, especially EL students who are processing not just the content of the question but also the linguistic framework of the question, need time to process the question. Teachers should repeat the question if necessary. Questions can also reflect Bloom's Taxonomy: some questions may be intended to elicit evidence that students did an assigned reading and might focus on remembering; other questions could ask students to form an opinion or evaluate. The wait time should reflect the rigor of the question and the level of the cognitive activities required to construct a response.

Technology in the ESL Classroom

Technology enables ESL teachers to both expand and differentiate learning for EL students. However, the vast range of general learning readiness significantly impacts the benefits of technology integration. Nonetheless, ESL teachers can prolifically integrate technology in all areas of learning to promote L2 proficiency because of the foundational premises of technology applications:

- ESL teachers should use technology not as an addition to instruction but as a tool for constructing versatile approaches to learning.

- ESL teachers should view technology as a means of interrelating listening, speaking, reading, and writing.

- ESL teachers should recognize that newcomers and learners at the beginning and intermediate levels will need substantive instructional support in entering technology-based learning environments.

- ESL teachers should create technology-based learning opportunities that maintain equity and access for all learners, recognizing that some students may not have access to technology outside of the school environment.

- ESL teachers should adeptly integrate content-area learning with appropriate technology platforms to enhance EL students' academic language proficiency.

- ESL teachers should match technology resources to the parameters and expectations of the specific content area.

- ESL teachers should be prepared to guide students in learning technology applications relevant to the content area.

Technology can provide multiple ways to enhance EL students' learning experiences. A short video, "Differentiated with Technology for ELs" (ASCD, 2010), identifies real strategies for enhanced learning made possible through technology:

- Videos and live demonstrations online can build learners' background knowledge.

- Students can work on their pronunciation by recording and listening to themselves in L2.

- Students can listen to a book being read in L2.

- Tablets, computers, even cell phones, and interactive software can help learners work through challenging content by allowing a different venue for problem-solving and by allowing indefinite repetition of lessons or examples.

- Technology can empower learners to take ownership of their own learning.

Technology and Content-Area Learning

Technology can enhance the best practices and delivery of content-area instruction as well as communicative skills:

- Electronic discussion boards or blogs offer venues for learner interaction that support BICS and can promote CALP when instructors create targeted discussion items. For example, learners could be asked to create a discussion board post that identifies a "golden line" from assigned reading and explains why the line stands out.

- Social media can be used to allow students to record and share videos of themselves as they complete specific class activities. For example, for a science class project in which students have to collect leaves and describe them on the basis of botanical features, students could make a video that includes images of the leaves and a think aloud as they identify the leaf features. This think aloud activity could also work effectively with a math problem, especially if students have to do back tracking, revision of strategies, and starting over.

- Multi-modal projects. Projects that include visuals, text, research, audio, and animation on presentation software can powerfully enhance learner engagement. Completing such projects as group projects adds the benefits of collaborative and cooperative learning.

- Writing processes. All aspects of the writing process, from initial brainstorming or research through drafting and final presentation, can be enacted in technology-supported platforms. Generating a writing product at a computer allows learners to do just-in-time searches and follow breadcrumbs as they construct the project. Students can look for translations of words from L1 that they want to integrate into their L2 writing. There can be instant messaging with the teacher or classmates during the project. And parts of the writing can be repositioned or deleted easily during revision. Word-processing tools can be used to explore verb forms, syntactic structure, academic vocabulary, grade-appropriate expression, and formatting.

- Translation. Technology can be used to provide some linguistic accommodation via translation. Students who have learned English as a second language sometimes admit that they started out by writing things out in L1 and then translating, but they almost always say that once they start thinking in L2, that is not necessary. Nonetheless, translation possibilities allow learners to discover L2 meanings independently and right at the moment of learning.

Teaching ESL online

Full online teaching far extends the realm of integrating technology into teaching. In online teaching, technology is the medium by which instruction and learning happens. In online teaching, the special needs of EL students are intensified as the crucial elements of affective, individualized instruction must be reconfigured for the cyber teaching world.

True online teaching reconstructs face-to-face teaching by applying strategies that enable learners to recreate their learning spaces in an online space. Basic things to do in these circumstances include the following (Loomis, 2020; Snelling & Fingal, 2020; Yang, 2020):

- Focusing on clear, target objectives for each lesson

- Crafting lessons that are manageable, clear, and simple (not simplistic) for learners to complete on their own

- Creating a teacher presence that reminds students of the in-person teacher in the face-to-face classroom

- Operationalizing the less-is-more principle by creating shorter, tightly targeted lessons

- Integrating opportunities to practice new learning before assessment occurs

- Providing feedback and redos to increase learners' opportunities to succeed

- Being available at designated times for online connections with students

- Learning your campus Learning Management System

- Learning to make short, teacher-created instructional videos

- Using instruction-creating tools such as SoftChalk, Flipgrid, VoiceThread, and screen-capture software to promote and present instructional activities

Online teaching experts concede that moving to online instruction begets a steep learning curve. We know how to engage learners when we are looking at them face-to-face in our classrooms, but what about the asynchronous way that much of online learning happens? Furthermore, the socioeconomic status of many of our EL students creates a roadblock to successful online learning if they do not have home access to internet connections, hardware, or software. Clearly, the ESL teacher cannot solve the access issue; that is the province of school districts or individual campuses. However, individual teachers *can* be proactive in learning how to take their best teaching selves into the space of online teaching.

ESL teachers should develop a paradigm for their lessons:

- targeted, concise, manageable lesson objectives

- a short lesson delivered as a short, written lesson or a video (videos no more than 5 minutes long)

- opportunity to practice and experiment with new knowledge

- low-stakes assignments to demonstrate understanding of new knowledge

- feedback with clear explanations of how to improve

- resubmission options to maintain high expectations. (Loomis, 2020)

Online learning creates both opportunities for learners as well as obstacles: some learners will thrive in a self-directed learning environment; others will feel rudderless without their teachers (Caruso, 2008). Teaching online requires that we anticipate these differences and modulate our online instruction to fully accommodate the continued needs of EL students.

Some online teaching advice for ESL teachers:

- If you are a complete novice to online learning, take time to read some basic materials on online and blended teaching such as Jon Bergmann's and Aaron Sam's great book *Flip Your Classroom* (2012), where the authors trace their entry into learning that shifted student involvement in learning to times and spaces that the students controlled vs. the teacher-modulated space of the classroom.

- Participate in teaching organizations such as ASCD.org and the International Society for Technology in Education (ISTE) to keep up with the latest articles and books on innovative online teaching.

- Online teachers believe that students need twice as much processing and producing time when they are learning online (Loomis, 2020; Yang, 2020). Add to that the additional needs of EL students whose learning time is magnified as they learn English while they are learning academic content *in* English. The accommodations that work in classrooms—communication, sequencing, modeling, scaffolding, multiple ways of presenting content—also work in online teaching. ESL teachers need to be proactive in devising learner-centered online instruction that keeps EL students' needs in mind.

- Realize that you cannot make access happen for students who do not have technology access. However, if the campus or district has done everything possible to create equitable access to technology, ESL teachers *can* create focused, clear, targeted lessons that allow EL students to learn independently, at their own pace, but with the virtual presence of the teacher to guide and support their learning.

Managing the ESL Classroom

The classroom is a space that can be modulated as much by environmental configuration as by attitudinal factors. ESL teachers should consider what an "ideal" classroom space could look like and identify negotiable factors that can be operationalized into creating that space. For EL students, the configuration of the classroom can promote or inhibit social interaction, and social interaction is vital to creating meaningful, authentic contexts for L2 learning (Freeman, Freeman, Soto, & Ebe, 2016, pp. 182–183). Let's consider what ESL teachers can do to shape a learning space that effectively and efficiently supports learners' diverse needs:

- Teachers should organize the classroom space to maximize social interaction among learners. If possible, desks should be grouped so that learners sit together instead of in rows, students should be allowed some freedom in moving about the room, and students should have "ownership" of the space by sharing responsibility for maintaining orderly storage and distribution of materials (Freeman, Freeman, Soto, & Ebe, 2016, pp. 182).

- Teachers should implement routines that allow learners to feel comfortable in the classroom space. Learners should know expectations for entering and leaving the room, for accessing supplies, for working independently or in groups, for stowing materials. Routines can be reinforced with signs throughout the classroom.

- Teachers should create opportunities for native speakers to mentor L2 learners in learning culturally-specific behavioral expectations for classroom space, such as ways to respond to questions during whole class discussions. Instead of directly calling on native speakers, the teacher can model behaviors using fishbowl activities. Fishbowl sessions create kinesthetic and cognitive involvement as students position themselves as observers, ideally in a circle, while one or more students sit in the center (in the "fishbowl") and demonstrate a task. Fishbowls can yield a high level of participation especially if students can question the "fish" in the bowl or comment if the fish seem to be headed in a wrong direction with the activity. Fishbowl sessions usually result in a lot of laughter, especially if students feel comfortable enough to good-naturedly criticize each other, but these interactive sessions can also serve to demonstrate important content to EL students.

- Teachers should vary learning approaches to allow EL students to continually practice listening, speaking, reading, and writing skills and to keep all learners engaged. Teachers should create opportunities for learners to interact with each other, to move around the classroom in doing targeted tasks, to demonstrate understanding of new content not just through quizzes but perhaps through interactive, immediate feedback computer applications.

- Teachers should be aware that EL students' cultural background may inhibit ready or full participation in some classroom activities and should be ready to implement accommodations for full, equitable participation. For example, in some cultures, affective demonstrations are considered inappropriate. Teachers should be pro-active in recognizing that what appears to be non-participation may reflect the EL student's cultural norms.

- Teachers should create an environment of inclusivity, acceptance, and equity to encourage all learners to feel that they are a part of the classroom community.

- Teachers should promote a culture of high expectations. Motivational posters that reflect the teacher's approach to achievement serve as continual reminders that success is possible for all learners and they add light, color, and visuals to the classroom.

- Teachers should create a space that sends out good "vibes." There should be artifacts in the class that reflect the teacher's special interests, whether whimsical, personal, professional, or academic. Posters or photographs should highlight places, objects, scenes, or people relevant to the subject area. There should be bookcases with books that students can read during Drop Everything and Read sessions. The teacher should have a stack on the desk of books he/she is currently reading, ideally relevant to the subject area. Supplies should be stored in accessible, colorful, attractive storage containers. Placement of the teacher's desk should offer a clear signal about the teacher's attitude toward interactions with learners.

Summary, Action Plan, and Chapter 3 Wrap-Up

Chapter 3 should help you remember pedagogical strategies you channeled in passing the PPR exam. Chapter 3 does not present teaching strategies unique to ESL teaching; instead, Competency 003 adds the special circumstances of ESL teaching to the best teaching strategies that should be utilized in all classrooms.

Self-Check

1. Have you reviewed ELPS to locate the terms presented in Table 3.2?

2. Can you explain some good teaching practices to promote learning in EL students?

3. What are linguistic accommodations?

4. How can technology contribute to EL students' growing proficiency in English?

Study Plan

1. If you have not already read through ELPS with pen and highlighter in hand, you should do so now. We cannot over emphasize the centrality of ELPS in ensuring that your study is targeted at what will be on the ESL Supplemental (154) Exam.

2. If you have had no college courses in ESL or bilingual education, you should look at some of the best books on ESL teaching: *ESL Teaching: Principles for Success* (Freeman, Freeman, Soto, & Ebe, 2016) and *Reading, Writing, and Learning in ESL: A Resource Book for Teaching K–12 English Learners* (Peregoy & Boyle, 2017). These two books contextualize sample class activities within the theories that drive learner-centered instructional choices.

3. Look up any terms from the chapter that you don't understand. Our glossary is a good start, but you might want to consult another resource: *English-as-a-Second-Language (ESL) Teaching and Learning: Pre-K–12 Classroom Applications for Students' Academic Achievement and Development* (Gonzalez, Yawkey, & Minaya-Rowe, 2006). This book includes substantive discussion of ESL background and theory and suggested teaching strategies, with a glossary at the end of each chapter.

4. Explore the website of the International Society for Technology in Education (ISTE). This website presents standards for integrating technology but also includes resources that can help teachers understand the role that technology can play in supporting student learning. ISTE does not specifically address ESL applications of technology but the materials on the website illuminate possibilities for enhancing learning through well-chosen technology platforms and applications.

Practice Items for Competency 003

1. Which of the following explanations best presents the intention of linguistic accommodations for EL students?

    A. Linguistic accommodations call for campuses to provide individual peer tutors for all EL students.

    B. Linguistic accommodations are pedagogical adjustments that ESL teachers make to increase accessibility of content for EL students.

    C. Linguistic accommodations are designated by the Language Proficiency Assessment Committee (LPAC) on the basis of EL students' annual test scores.

D.   Linguistic accommodations are not necessary if ESL teachers have an assigned paraprofessional in the classroom.

Response B is correct. Linguistic accommodations are clearly identified in ELPS as specific teaching adjustments that enable teachers to make content accessible for EL students. Specific accommodations mentioned in ELPS are communication, sequencing, and scaffolding, all of which can be operationalized in creative, robust ways in classroom instruction. Response A is incorrect because peer tutors are not mandated in any aspect of the state's requirements for ESL instruction. Response C is incorrect because the classroom teacher, not the LPAC, has full responsibility for implementing necessary accommodations for EL students. Response D is incorrect because paraprofessionals can help teachers carry out classroom activities, but their presence in an ESL classroom does not constitute evidence of accommodations.

2.   Which TWO of the following applications best illustrate how teachers can integrate technology to enhance EL students' learning?

A.   Technology enables teachers to direct learners to simplified, online presentations of class content.

B.   Technology enables EL students to reinforce class content by watching supplementary instructional videos.

C.   Technology enables EL students to create learning connections with other learners in local and more distant learning spaces.

D.   Technology enables EL students to seek tutoring for content that was not adequately presented in class.

E.   Technology enables teachers to identify test-preparation tutorials to boost EL students' chances to pass mandated state exams.

Responses B and C best illustrate possibilities for enhancing EL students' learning through technology. Response B reflects common student comments about how having a designated learning video enables them to rewatch lessons that are challenging. Response C reflects the community-shaping possibilities of platforms like blogs and discussion boards that enable EL students to learn content-relevant strategies from other learners. Response A incorrectly suggests that technology simplifies lessons. Response D is incorrect because technology is not intended as a substitute or replacement for inadequate teaching. Response E is incorrect because test-preparation, according to the ESL 154 competencies, should be integrated into classroom teaching with the teacher connecting test standards to specific curricular content.

Competency 004

4

Competency 004: Communicative Language Development

The ESL teacher knows how to promote students' communicative language development in English (Pearson, 2019a).

Competency 004 focuses on listening and speaking proficiencies, collectively labeled communicative language development. Seven descriptive statements (A–G) address the following ESL teaching topics:

- Knowing TEKS and ELPS relevant to listening and speaking

- Recognizing conversational competence as an important part of English proficiency

- Applying appropriate teaching techniques to promote communicative competence

- Recognizing the interrelatedness of listening, speaking, reading, and writing skills

- Understanding how the student's native language competence can support listening and speaking proficiency in English

- Devising instruction that recognizes individual differences

- Offering feedback that promotes EL students' communicative competence

Competency 004 Core Content

Table 4.1 identifies key terms from Competency 004 and Standards I and III-VI that you should be able to define and apply in envisioning ESL teaching scenarios.

Table 4.1.
Competency 004 Core Content

ELPS for listening	ELPS for speaking	linguistic environment	conversational support	comprehensible language environment
teaching techniques	interrelatedness of language domains	transfer from L1 to L2	individual differences	appropriate feedback
communicative competence	BICS	CALP	linguistic accommodation	assessment
registers	conversational support	developmental characteristics and individual needs	student variation	classroom management

Listening and Speaking ELPS

Fully understanding the scope of Competency 004 involves close attention to two relevant areas of ELPS (TAC, 2007):

§74.4(c)(2)–(3)   describe student expectations in listening and speaking in **cross-curricular** areas.

§74.4(d)(1)–(2)   present descriptors of student performance in listening and speaking in the four **proficiency levels**.

ELPS describes EL students' observable behaviors using specific, distinct terminology. Thus, we can hypothesize about teacher behaviors and instructional techniques that enable learners to move to the advanced high level. Consider, for example, how an ESL teacher might support developing communicative proficiency in learners who "struggle to identify and distinguish individual words and phrases during social and instructional interactions that have not been intentionally modified for ELs," a performance descriptor for beginning ELs' listening proficiency in §74.4(d) (1)(A)(ii), (TAC, 2007). The very specific ELPS descriptors in listening and speaking student performance point to the teacher's responsibility to apply knowledge from phonology, pragmatics, discourse, registers, and general learning theory. The ESL teacher's responsibility, as presented in Competency 004, is to use knowledge, skills, resources, and classroom activities to move EL students toward the optimal proficiency level in listening and speaking.

Communicative Competence

The focus on communicative language development in Competency 004 channels the theory of **communicative competence**, which endorses the development of social skills, authentic communicative opportunities, and confidence shaped by meaningful input and output. Unlike with academic or cognitive competencies which researchers believe transfer from L1 into L2, communicative competence is supported through social contexts that allow learners to experiment with language and develop enhanced motivation for communicating in L2 (Gonzalez, Yawkey, & Minaya-Rowe, 2006, pp. 136–137; Cummins, 1979). ESL teachers can support EL students' communicative language development in several broad categories (Gonzalez, Yawkey, & Minaya-Rowe, 2006, p. 137; Gee, 2001, p. 719):

- Sociolinguistics: Cultural and performative "rules" in L2 that impact communicative effectiveness;

- Grammar: Foundational linguistic knowledge in phonology, syntax, semantics, and pragmatics (which we covered in Chapter 1);

- Nonverbals: Effective listening and speaking includes knowing how to interpret and use gestures, body language, spatial boundaries, and embodiment of space as part of communication;

- Discourse knowledge: Effective communication requires recognizing linguistic and behavioral expectations that "mark" expectations for groups in which an individual may want to participate.

In the context of overall L2 proficiency, communicative skills are usually addressed as BICS, Basic Interpersonal Communicative Skills that are intertwined with the EL student's developing competence in academic areas because increased BICS usually results in increased motivation and positive affect regarding L2 learning. Communicative skills include areas such as pronunciation, oral fluency, listening comprehension, meaningful interaction with L2 speakers, and social skills (Freeman, Freeman, Soto, & Ebe, 2016, pp. 179–182; Cummins, 1979).

In the real world, communicative competence reflects the L2 speaker's pragmatic, immediate, and possibly economic exigencies. In a classic article, Krashen recounts the story of Armando, an immigrant from Mexico who "speaks English quite well but . . . speaks Hebrew better." He learned Hebrew on his own in the environment of his job in an Israeli restaurant where everyone, the bosses, the staff, and the customers, spoke Hebrew. The major point in Krashen's article is that Armando achieved communicative competence in Hebrew, to the extent that even native speakers assessed his output as meaningful and almost equivalent to native speakers. Armando's motivation was his job: to interact with his Hebrew co-workers and customers, he had to demonstrate communicative competence which he achieved through immersion in the linguistic environment in which he wanted to participate (Krashen, 2000)

In the context of TExES ESL (154), we are focusing on communicative competence as promoted and supported in the school space by well-constructed instructional strategies and learner-centered teacher affect. Shortly after the term *communicative competence* gained traction as a "type" of L2 competence, Mary McGroarty offered this somewhat daunting explanation of how SLA happens in schools:

> In schools, students must learn to follow schedules; use textbooks; solve math problems; learn to print; learn to write in script; learn to read stories, textbooks, schedules, and notices; spell words; make friends; get rewards-both social and academic-from teachers and peers; pass tests; fill in blanks; do grammar exercises; define vocabulary words, draw pictures, play dodge-ball, basketball, or volleyball; write (at least) correct sentences, perhaps even coherent themes and letters; absorb information on the evils of drugs, the responsibilities of parenthood, and the turning points in history. The list is long. Fortunately, students need not master all of these skills at once, but even so, the diversity and variety are almost overwhelming if considered in total. (1984, p. 264)

Remarkably, we can detect direct reflection of McGroarty's explanation in ELPS, ESL Educator Standards, and the exam 154 competencies. This chapter is aimed at helping you "see" how ELPS, Competency 004, and relevant TEKS can be operationalized as teaching strategies in order to help EL students achieve the listening and speaking skills required to participate meaningfully in the environment so aptly described by McGroarty.

Instructional Strategies for Listening and Speaking

To create a learning environment that offers linguistic and conversational support, connects the four language domains, and recognizes learner diversity, ESL teachers can implement targeted approaches, techniques, and strategies in the classroom. Whatever strategies are used, teachers should do a "check" on whether the planned strategies offer equitable participation for all levels of learners, meet students' current ESL developmental levels, meaningfully promote listening and/or speaking skills, and coherently fit into overall integration of the four language domains.

Most listening and speaking skills techniques can be categorized in several core areas.

- Teacher talk. The teacher orchestrates the discourse of the classroom, to a great extent through **teacher talk**. When there are EL learners in a class, teachers need to be especially conscious of how teacher talk is modulated. Teachers should always speak loud enough to be heard throughout the room, perhaps even asking the students who are furthest from the teacher whether they can hear. Teachers should take care not to ramble or mumble. They should use transitional markers like *first, second, most important, last point* to help learners be active listeners. Teacher talk should also be punctuated with appropriate facial gestures, body language, and kinesthetic support. Teachers should not speak for long periods without giving students time to process information. Teachers should be aware of the reality that students' attention drifts easily; thus, teacher talk should be integrated with opportunities for students to process information, ask questions, and apply new knowledge. Although most of us use idioms and expressions that seem to reflect collective, linguistic knowledge, teachers need to be conscious that even something as simple as "are we all on track?" might linguistically muddle an EL student. Routine things like getting learners to listen to class procedure instructions (like information about entering and exiting the room, classroom period changes, work station procedures, safety procedures) may be a challenge for EL students if the instructions are delivered too quickly or sketchily. To ensure EL students are given an opportunity to derive instructional benefit from teacher talk, teachers need to use redundancies such as bulleting items on the white board or summing up high points. In short, teacher talk needs to be delivered with the aim of reaching all learners.

- Class discussions. For EL students, whole class discussions can be daunting, especially for students still in the **silent period**. Effective class discussions should reflect pre-set "rules" about participation so that learners participate equitably and meaningfully. Teachers should consider that whole class discussions can include a lot of phatic communication. EL students may not be able to follow along with everything that is happening in a noisy, active discussion that may have begun coherently but then absorbs a lot of input from class members. Questioning should reflect learner readiness, instructional objectives, and authentic assessment opportunities. **Wait time** should be tailored to learner readiness, diversity, and the cognitive rigor of the questions. Calling on students should be done with care, especially if EL students are obviously in the silent period. Teachers should work consciously to make whole class discussions an event that everyone can join into, either as participants or engaged, silent observers.

- Meaningful Practice. ESL classrooms should include abundant practice in meaningful, real-world uses of listening and speaking skills. Role-playing, scenarios, reader's theater, and simulations (real world and academic) can be used across disciplinary and grade level classrooms. In history classrooms, for example, simulations can be used to enact historical events. Role-playing can be used to recreate scenes from literary works or to anticipate real-world scenarios relevant to the academic subject or a unit the class is currently engaged in. Reader's theater is traditionally an English language arts activity, but teachers in all subject areas can adapt this prolific activity to support learners' listening and speaking skills. A common listening and speaking activity, such as asking or giving instructions, can help EL students learn rules of discourse, pragmatics, and non-verbal communication.

- Group activities. **Collaborative activities** are among the most versatile teaching techniques that teachers can use to support listening and speaking skills. A hallmark of well-constructed group activities is the buzz that we hear when students work in groups to tackle learning tasks collaboratively. Group activities allow learners to shift their focus from the teacher as authority to class members as learning and teaching peers. For EL students who may be uncomfortable participating in whole class discussions, small group activities allow more relaxed, social exchanges that support learning with peers. Group activities can be highly organized with designated tasks for each group member or more relaxed with learners just collaborating on responding to an assigned task. Jigsaw activities allow teachers to subdivide a challenging task to enable all learners to contribute to the whole class understanding. Adaptations of games, such as round robins, are productive, yet fun. Teachers should celebrate the opportunity for social interaction afforded by group work: when students are grouped and given learning tasks, it's not long before they are talking freely about things that may be only tangentially related to the task. In short, collaborative activities foster comprehensible input that promotes listening and speaking proficiency for EL students.

- Academic listening and speaking skills. Teachers should strive to integrate speaking activities such as interviews and formal and informal oral presentations as a means of integrating CALP and BICS. Additionally, teachers should be aware that students need direct instruction in conducting interviews so that appropriate questions are created and appropriate speaking skills are used. Mock interviews can be used across most academic areas. Oral presentations are among the most anxiety-producing academic ventures in classroom settings. Students need to be taught how to do oral presentations, including coaching and instructions in eye contact, movement, gestures, volume, stance, pace of speaking, as well as how to "transform" material into appropriate oral delivery.

- Instructions for major assignments. When instructions for major assignments are delivered orally, teachers should take abundant care to reinforce the presentation with visuals, bullets or key points on the board, plentiful pauses to let learners process the information and possibly construct questions.

Talking and listening occur in the classroom from the moment learners enter the classroom space until the moment they leave. There are continual opportunities for ESL teachers to promote EL students' communicative competence by discovering ways to enhance active listening and meaningful speaking while fully integrating these skills into the spectrum of academic language and general literacy skills.

What Listening and Speaking Strategies Look like in Classrooms

Listening and speaking are the media through which a lot of teaching and learning happens in classrooms. In ESL teaching, listening and speaking are far more than instruments for classroom transactions; these modes of delivery are also instructional opportunities for teachers to develop EL students' English proficiency. ESL teachers also need to be aware of how distinct communicative interactions support EL students' basic communicative skills (BICS) and how listening and speaking can be integrated to enhance understanding of course content. Let's look at some possibilities for listening and speaking activities in ESL environments.

Table 4.2.
Listening and Speaking Strategies for
Promoting Communicative Language Development

Activity	Description	Support for Communicative Language Development	BICS/CALP
Entering the class greeting	Teacher can stand at the door and offer an individual greeting to students by name, offering student-specific comments to encourage responses.	Teacher models common greetings, shows students how to engage personally in a typical greeting, gives students an opportunity to practice speaking skills in responding to the teacher's comments.	BICS
Status-of-the-class session	A state of the class session allows learners to quickly "report," in a round robin type of format, how they are progressing on an assignment (Atwell, 1998, p. 141).	Classroom learning community is bolstered as class members listen to each other's comments on their progress. Students practice speaking in a specific context. In classes where students may be at beginning or intermediate ELPS speaking levels, the teacher may model the responses by writing some response options on the board for students to complete: My progress is going great/not so good because I got stuck on ____, because I didn't have time to do the assignment ____, because I need help with ____. The teacher records the student responses on a status-of-the-class ledger which can be a reference point later in the class.	CALP
Activity instructions	Teacher provides instructions at the beginning of the class on how the lesson will be segmented and what is expected from class members.	Teacher ensures that instructions are communicated in clear language accessible to all learners. The instructions should be reinforced with bullet items on the whiteboard or document camera. Students should be required to jot down the instructions to integrate listening and writing skills.	CALP
Lesson presentation	Teacher uses lecture, demonstration, examples, mini-lessons to present new information to students primarily through speaking.	Teacher alerts students that active listening will be required, calling their attention to objectives and key vocabulary. During the presentation, the teacher modulates his/her voice to reflect lesson components. Teacher uses appropriate body language and gestures for emphasis. Teacher stops at appropriate junctures to allow students time to process what the teacher is saying.	CALP and BICS

Activity	Description	Support for Communicative Language Development	BICS/ CALP
Guided practice	Teacher works in time after major lesson segments for students to practice mastery of new information in short collaborative activities like think-pair-share or kinesthetic activities like recording responses on the whiteboard.	Knowing that there will be a just-in-time practice at the end of lesson segments encourages learners to listen actively. Collaborative application activities allow learners to engage in social interaction prior to addressing the targeted application task.	CALP and BICS
Class discussion	Teacher asks questions ranging from basic recall to critical thinking about the topic. Discussion can be conducted with the whole class or in groups, depending on student readiness to respond.	Teacher needs to be attuned to the class readiness for whole-class discussion. Often, small group discussions are far more productive because learners feel less put on-the-spot when they are interacting with peers. Teacher should model how students respond orally. For example, the teacher could invite students to use lead ins like "I agree, I think, I'm confused, I wonder, I thought, I think ___ is wrong." Teachers should steer clear of open-ended questions like "Who has a question?" or "What do you think about ___?"	CALP and BICS

Diversity

Because of the idiosyncratic, learner-specific trajectory of L2 acquisition and learning, diversity and heterogeneity are pillars of classroom dynamics in ESL teaching. ESL teachers should anticipate having EL students on a wide spectrum of cognitive and communicative proficiencies, which means that instruction needs to be **differentiated**. Teachers need to have a set of guiding principles to ensure that their classrooms celebrate diversity, promote access and equity for all learners, and create an environment where EL students feel affectively supported.

Let's start by examining the realm of diversity among EL students (Short & Echevarria, 2004/2005; Guild, 1994):

- The concept of **interlanguage** poses a challenge for ESL teachers because if the individual learner is reconstructing the interlanguage constantly as his/her trajectory toward L2 proficiency improves (Brown, 2014, p. 243), instruction must constantly change to keep up with the learner's progress. In a classroom with 20 EL students, a teacher can expect a diversity of performance levels even if all the learners in the class meet performance levels for the same ELPS level. The interlanguage construct hypothesizes constant reconstructions of current L2 competence as the learner approximates structures in the target language. A teacher needs to be attuned to individual differences in competence and ready with differentiated instruction to support EL students' continued growth.

- EL students' socio-economic status directly impacts levels of access to materials outside the classroom and degree of parental support for L2 learning.

- Educational history will vary among learners. Recent immigrants, for example, may have strong academic backgrounds due to formal schooling in their country of origin; others may have limited, interrupted, or no formal schooling. Cognitive development will vary substantively among learners for reasons ranging from the degree of formal schooling to negative classroom experiences that result in reduced motivation to learn in school settings.

- The linguistic system of the EL student's L1 may be so different from English that L2 acquisition is more challenging as the learner is faced with acquiring a new alphabet and has limited language transfer possibilities.

- Cultural differences between the native culture and the L2 culture may be extreme and difficult for the learner to negotiate.

- Students' cultural background impacts learning style preferences. Factors such as interpersonal connectivity, reliance on oral communication, independent thinking, visually-based learning, and social norms established by the culture all impact EL students' learning and create the exigency of teacher readiness to meet each learner's needs.

In light of this range of diversity among EL students, the question, then, is how can an ESL teacher create a classroom that celebrates learner diversity, promotes listening and speaking skills, and pulls all learners into the class community? Here are some suggested instructional strategies that address diversity:

- Teachers should strive to create a community of learners by creating opportunities for learners to learn about each other. Activities that allow class members to share stories about their culture should be started very early in the semester and continued so that the entire class is constantly learning new things about each other. Community activities can be oral, visual, or written. Teachers can contribute to the community by sharing informational items about the cultures represented in the classroom and by reading texts from different cultures.

- Teachers should use a variety of delivery methods in every class session to ensure that all learners—native speakers and EL students—are receiving comprehensible input in a variety of ways, such as through traditional lecture, visual materials, kinesthetic activities, and independent activities.

- Group activities should be a mainstay of every ESL teacher's pedagogical repertoire. Group activities can be a just-in-time application through think-pair-share or a formal collaborative project that spans several class periods. Group activities allow EL students to experiment with what works in social interaction and promote understandings about interpersonal dynamics, a vital part of affective learning in L2.

Feedback

Feedback is a component of assessment which we will discuss in detail in Chapter 7 on Competency 007. Feedback can be defined as a response to student performance designed to identify accomplishment and provide guidance toward improvement. As we'll explain in more detail in Chapter 7, feedback can be formative, which means it is offered in-progress as the learner is working on a learning task. Or it can be summative, which means that it provides a culminating assessment when the learner completes a learning task. In the context of promoting communicative competence, feedback can be provided immediately and frequently as learners interact in daily classroom routines and activities or it can be provided in more formal assessment settings, such as during read alouds or presentations.

There are some target behaviors that teachers should aim for in offering feedback to students, as well as some behaviors to avoid.

- Feedback should be clear and specific and connected to observable learner behavior. The learner should understand exactly what the teacher is commenting on. Comments like "good job," "great," or "you need to work on that" do not help the learner. But a comment like "Norrie, I hear your question intonation. That really sounded like a question because your voice went up a little at the end of the sentence" will help a learner who is having trouble with English pragmatics.

- Feedback should focus on the behavior or output, not on the learner. Consider a teacher who is trying to improve EL learner's active listening skills. The teacher has just gone over instructions for an in-class science reading activity and as she is walking through the class to see if anyone has questions, she notices that Norrie, an EL student, jotted down several instructional notes in his notebook. The teacher can reinforce the behavior by saying, "Norrie, the notes you jotted down show that you were really listening carefully. That will help you do the reading tasks in order when we start our reading project." An example of a behavior to avoid in a similar situation would be to tell a student who seems not to be listening, "Norrie, would you like to tell the class what you're thinking about?"

- Feedback, especially formative feedback, should be aimed at improvement. Teachers should target what the learner has done and suggest a modification that can be made next time or as the task is being completed. For example, in watching students practice an upcoming oral presentation, a teacher can sit in during their group practice, with a pre-distributed checklist, and say something like, "Norrie, I see that you are standing very still while you do your part of the presentation. Next time, walk toward the poster when you mention the chart and look at your audience to see if they are looking at the graph your group is sharing."

- Feedback should never be insulting, critical, or punitive. Feedback impacts learner affect and motivation. Teachers need to remember that feedback is a valuable tool for helping learners feel good about the classroom space and about their involvement in the learning community. Feedback that embarrasses a learner, either deliberately or unintentionally, marginalizes the learner. Additionally, ESL teachers need to remember that meaning is holistic; thus, even a learning product or utterance that appears to show a lot of errors can convey substantive holistic meaning, and that should be noted in feedback.

- Feedback should be immediate and frequent. With listening and speaking skills, ESL teachers can offer on-the-spot feedback, perhaps focused on affirmation of production of a new form. Written work should also be evaluated in quick turnaround to allow learners to connect effort to outcomes and to strive toward improvement. In Chapter 7, we will address types of feedback to enhance learner motivation.

When ESL teachers work from the mindset of authentic assessment, feedback relevant to listening and speaking skills can be almost on-going throughout the lesson. Teachers can recognize opportunities to praise learners even for apparently small gains, such as when a student who has never offered a comment in class finally volunteers a response during a whole class session, the teacher can praise the student's participation by saying, "Norrie, I am glad you are sharing how the second sentence in the problem is confusing.

Your comment will help all of us pay special attention to that sentence when we work on the problem." During oral reading sessions, feedback can be used to improve pronunciations, intonation, pacing, segmenting, and overall fluency. Finally, feedback should be learner-centered, focused on helping the learner take ownership of his/her listening and speaking. Thus, correction should be reworked as explanation of how the listening or speaking output can be improved, not on what was done wrong.

Summary, Action Plan, and Chapter 4 Wrap-Up

Competency 004 focuses on the ESL teacher's responsibilities in helping EL students achieve higher levels of communicative competence. To demonstrate proficiency in L2, EL students must be provided varied opportunities to receive comprehensible input and produce meaningful output. In ESL environments, communicative competence is promoted through social interaction in the classroom which enables learners to interact with each other in a variety of authentic ways. In promoting EL students' listening and speaking proficiency, ESL teachers need to rely on knowledge of phonology, pragmatics, discourse, and subject area content to help students develop BICS as well as CALP.

Self-Check

1. Can you identify some terms relevant to listening and speaking skills?

2. Can you explain why social interaction is so vital to developing EL students' listening and speaking skills?

3. Can you think of some specific ways in which ESL teachers can integrate listening and speaking opportunities into lessons?

Study Plan

Look carefully at the ELPS sections on listening and speaking. Note how specifically student performance in listening and speaking is described. Knowing those behaviors will help anticipate the types of questions you might see on the test relevant to Competency 004.

- §74.4 (c)(2)—student expectations in cross-curricular listening skills.
- §74.4 (c)(3)—student expectations in cross-curricular speaking skills.

- §74.4 (d)(1)—listening skills across the four proficiency levels.

- §74.4 (d)(2)—speaking skills across the four proficiency levels.

Practice items for Competency 004

Use the information below to answer questions 1 and 2.

All the students at an elementary school are going on a field trip to the zoo. To address ELPS expectations for EL students, the content-area teachers plan to integrate communicative language proficiency activities into this science enrichment opportunity.

1. The Grade 3 teacher, whose class includes approximately 50% beginning EL students, posts pictures of the zoo animals around the classroom. The teacher asks the class to pick their three favorite animals and presents this learning task:

   - Look carefully at the three animals you picked. Pay close attention to what makes each of your three animals special. For example, if you picked a giraffe, you know that its long neck and big spots make it special.

   - Imagine a new animal made up of the qualities that make your three animals special. Draw a picture of this made up animal.

   - Create a name for your creature and put it on your drawing both in your home language *and* in English.

   - When we all finish our drawings, we are going to show our pictures to the whole class and explain how we invented this new animal.

   Which of the following best explains how this instructional activity will promote the student's oral language proficiency?

   A. It shows the teacher using L1 to scaffold L2 learning.

   B. It promotes students' content-vocabulary in science.

   C. It gives students an opportunity to describe and explain in an informal class presentation.

   D. It provides the teacher an opportunity to assess how effectively students can understand instructions.

Response C is correct. This activity, clearly tailored for young EL students, merges science content and oral language proficiency, taking individual differences and distinct abilities into account and integrating an element of linguistic whimsy with the invented names for the creatures. By merging creativity, observation, and artistic range, the teacher is also trying to create motivation and enthusiasm for sharing the paintings and the whimsical names in a whole class, presentational activity. Response A is incorrect because the L1 connection is a minor part of the activity, and since the class is not 100% ESL, the teacher is allowing for linguistic invention rather than scaffolding in naming the creatures. Response B is incorrect because, while some science vocabulary may be involved in identifying the features of the animals, the teacher's set up does not focus on science vocabulary. It seems to be much more aimed at observation of distinctive features of the original animal set. Response D is incorrect because neither the item stem nor the assignment details suggest that the teacher's primary focus is to assess listening or reading skills.

2. The Grade 4 science teacher, who teaches intermediate and advanced EL students, is also creating a field-trip based activity. Which of the following activities would best target development of the students' communicative competence in a science context?

    A. Students listen to the teacher do book talks on several of Rudyard Kipling's *Just So Stories*. Students vote on the one they want the teacher to read to them. On the day before the zoo trip, the teacher reads the winning story aloud to the class and then leads the students in an oral discussion of what makes the story engaging.

    B. Students pick an animal and create an animal trainer blurb that they would present to zoo visitors who stop at their animal's zoo habitat. The teacher requires at least three sources to show research-based information on the animals. On the day before the zoo trip, the students take turns presenting their blurbs to the whole class, using tone and gestures they might use if they were really animal trainers.

    C. Students watch videos of famous zoos in the U.S. The teacher has students create a semantic map of concepts related to zoos. Following the video, the teacher has students do a quick write arguing for the zoo that they think best addresses the animals' needs.

    D. Students vote on five animals they want to research and do a cooperative mini research paper on the animal each group picks. Each group creates a poster presentation of their research results and posts it on the class display wall before the zoo trip.

The correct answer is Response B because it best combines the content-area knowledge (research on an animal) with a communicative task: to address a hypothetical audience of zoo visitors. Response A is incorrect because that activity, although it involves listening and critical thinking about animal features, is better suited for an

English language arts class. Although response C involves active listening skills, the writing follow-up activity moves away from communicative competence and toward literacy. Response D is incorrect because the cooperative work, which would involve communicative competence, is a means to the activity not the focus of the activity. The activity does not include oral presentations of the results of the research.

Competency 005

5

Competency 005: Literacy Development

The ESL teacher understands how to promote students' literacy development in English (Pearson, 2019a).

Competency 005 addresses **literacy development** and is explained through seven descriptive statements (A–G), which cover the following general areas:

- Knowledge of relevant TEKS and ELPS

- Interrelatedness of language domains in promoting literacy

- Connection of phonology and phonics to literacy

- Components of comprehension

- Connections between L1 and L2 literacy

- Impact of diversity on reading and writing proficiency

Literacy is usually thought of as the ability to read. That is a limited definition. Literacy and literacies present a complex set of abilities that pull together not just the four language domains but also suggest possibilities for *using* literacy. Let's start with the definitions as presented by the International Literacy Association:

Literacy: The ability to identify, understand, interpret, create, compute, and communicate using visual, audible, and digital materials across disciplines and in any context.

Literacies: The distinct written and oral language practices evident across varying social circumstances, domains, and classes. As such, literacies are plural, with multiple manifestations, that cover various aspects of human life and social organization (e.g., school literacy, workplace literacy, science literacy).

(ILA, 2019)

Let's add to these definitions James Paul Gee's view that literacy is a sort of "tool" for operationalizing goals:

[R]eading and writing cannot be separated from speaking, listening, and interacting, on the one hand, or using language to think about and act on the world, on the other. Thus, it is necessary to start with a viewpoint on language (oral and written) itself, a viewpoint that ties language to embodied action in the material and social world. (2001, p. 714)

While reading is clearly a component of literacy, reality-centered views of literacy propose that literacy enables us to *do* things with our language. Competency 005 focuses mostly on reading as the prime component of literacy and conflates writing as an element of English language proficiency. If we look carefully at ELPS, we will notice that the descriptors define skills and abilities that EL students demonstrate and use in reading and writing *processes* and *actions*.

Competency 005 Core Content

The full scope of Competency 005 must encompass not just descriptive statements A-G but also the terms, concepts, and teacher expectations presented in the English as a Second Language Educator Standards and the student expectations delineated in ELPS.

The following key terms are compiled from Competency 005 descriptive statements and Standards I and III–VI:

Table 5.1.
Competency 005 Core Content

TEKS applicable to literacy	ELPS proficiency level descriptors for reading	ELPS proficiency level descriptors for writing	interrelatedness of four language domains
strategies for developing literacy	phonological knowledge	reading comprehension skills	transfer from L1 to L2 literacy
individual differences	factors that affect learning	designing instruction	rich language/print environment
conventions of written English	common difficulties	TEKS English Language Arts and Reading curriculum relevant to ESL	responsive instruction
patterns of written discourse	literacy	critical thinking processes	comprehension
fluency	teaching writing	teaching reading	literacy development

Reading and Writing ELPS

Fully understanding the scope of Competency 005 involves close attention to two relevant areas of ELPS (TAC, 2007):

§74.4(c)(4)–(5)   describe student expectations in reading and writing in cross-curricular areas.

§74.4(d)(3)–(6)   present descriptors of student performance in reading and writing in the four proficiency levels, subdivided at Kindergarten-Grade 1 and Grades 2–12 levels.

ELPS describes EL students' observable behaviors using specific, distinct terminology associated with reading and writing learning and pedagogy and which offer clues as to what the descriptors of Competency 005 mean. For example, from the ELPS for beginning level reading, Grades 2–12, terms such as *environmental print, high-frequency words*, and *concrete words that can be represented by pictures* should channel images of classrooms with charts, labels, images, and other vocabulary support for learners. While ELPS focuses on *student* expectations for reading and writing, we can infer what pedagogical practices might be effective strategies for designing and implementing appropriate instruction (from Competency 005.A and B) for supporting EL students' literacy.

Teaching Reading in the Context of ESL

The variable levels of English proficiency presented by any group of learners makes teaching reading and writing a particular challenge. SLA theories hold that L2 acquisition is enhanced by the learner's interdependence on L1, but that assumes a solid grounding in L1 cognitive proficiencies. Very young newcomers may have limited L1 cognitive proficiencies; older students with interrupted schooling may have limited L1 social and cognitive platforms. Full understanding of the parameters of Competency 005 requires strong platforms in basics of reading and writing instruction that can be adapted for teaching ESL. Regardless of EL students' cognitive, social, and affective levels, some teaching practices are foundational for developing literacy skills.

Starting Points: Areas of Reading Instruction

Reading instruction starts at early stages of academic learning with emergent literacy as young learners start recognizing reading basics such as the alphabetic principle, the symbolic nature of language, and the way that meaning is constructed from experience rather than extracted from a text. ELPS expectations for cross curricular proficiencies and reading proficiencies point to content-area teachers' responsibilities in knowing what constitutes effective reading instruction. Principal points in reading instruction include the following:

Alphabetic principle—the understanding that alphabetic symbols represent sounds that are combined into meaning-making structures.

Comprehension—the integration of multiple reading strategies to construct meaning from a text. The strategies include phonemic awareness, vocabulary knowledge, syntactic knowledge, semantic cues, schema construction, and numerous other critical reading abilities.

Context clues—using information embedded in a text to decipher the meaning of a new or unknown word.

Decoding—the ability to "interpret" the words on a page by relying on multiple abilities including knowledge of phonology, semantics, syntax, morphology as well as prior and/or background knowledge.

Drop Everything and Read (DEAR)—a prolific reading appreciation strategy in which teachers set aside a short period for self-selected reading that has no objective other than to allow students free time to read something they want.

Emergent reader—a young learner who is discovering basic elements of reading, such as the fact that sounds and words he/she knows are represented by symbols, that English is read from left to right, that meaning is segmented into words, phrases, and sentences marked with various punctuation.

Levels of comprehension—literal, inferential, and evaluative understandings of the text. Experienced, successful readers rely on simultaneous application of all three levels.

Literal comprehension—literal understanding focuses on what is actually in the text being read, generally providing a limited, rudimentary construction of meaning.

Inferential comprehension—sometimes referred to as "reading between the lines." This is meaning implied by the author, with the understanding that the reader will have sufficient prior knowledge and/or ability to apply context and other clues to derive the intended meaning.

Evaluative comprehension—the "highest" level of reading. The reader may question the ideas or connect them to similar, broader ideas.

Critical reading—reading that engages the reader in significant consideration of the constructed meaning. Critical reading involves inquiry, assessment, evaluation, associations, perhaps even rejection of the ideas.

Vocabulary instruction—instruction focused on helping students learn more words. At early stages of reading, readers need to have sufficient words in their lexicon to support reading. This is why books for very young readers sometimes have a list of words at the back or front of the text to alert readers and teachers to basic vocabulary needed. For content-area learning, ESL or regular, learners must know words relevant to the new content. Additionally, vocabulary can be fortified by frequent required or self-selected reading.

Distinguishing between fact and opinion—the ability to differentiate between observable, quantifiable data and a position or assertion. Fact is something that can be proved with observable or quantifiable data from real experience; opinion represents a position, assertion, or argument which could be based on observable experience but could also be whimsical and/or unsupported. Readers must be able to distinguish between these critical forms of information in a text in order to decode meaning successfully and accurately.

Fluency—reading pace. Effective readers read with ease and understanding when they are working with texts appropriate to their current reading proficiency. Fluency can be cultivated through frequent reading practice, development of vocabulary, and application of metacognitive reading strategies.

Drawing conclusions—using personal experience, prior knowledge, and critical thinking to shape a holistic understanding of the text that extends beyond the literal or inferential meaning. Drawing conclusions can also show the reader's response to a logical framework presented by the writer. Inductive reasoning allows the reader to infer a reasonable conclusion based on the presentation of information in the text; in inductive reasoning, the reader infers or perhaps even guesses intelligently at the writer's intention. Deductive reasoning follows the writer's stated logic to arrive at a conclusion directed by the author of the text.

High frequency words—words that occur frequently in texts and that have specific textual, semantic, and syntactic functions. Words such as *the, is, of, are, were, in, it, has* are considered high frequency words.

Oral reading—a pedagogical practice that views performative reading as a means of promoting a learner's reading proficiency. Oral reading, however, can be anxiety producing for learners who are self-conscious about their language proficiency.

Prediction—a manifestation of the psycholinguistic aspects of reading. Adept readers do not decode individual words as they read. Instead, they "absorb" chunks of text based on semantic, syntactic, and phonological predictions of meaning.

Prereading—a pedagogical strategy for preparing readers to enter a new or challenging text. In academic texts, prereading may involve looking at subheadings in the text or at highlighted words. The teacher can create prereading supports by providing bullet points of what learners should anticipate in reading the text.

Semantic cues—clues within the linguistic elements of a text. Texts are syntactically and semantically redundant, which creates clues and cues as to how decoding should occur, especially when there might be ambiguity in how a segment of the text should be interpreted or decoded.

Sight words—words that occur so frequently or that are so short that they do not need to be decoded by young or experienced readers because they are more or less visually "memorized." There is overlap among sight words and high frequency words, but sight words can also be words that don't follow phonemic and orthographic "rules" such as *are, heard, our, their.*

Sustained silent reading (SSR)—another term for DEAR.

Reading with EL Students

To read effectively, efficiently, and meaningfully, EL students need to demonstrate skills in phonics, vocabulary development, word recognition, comprehension, and fluency. They need to negotiate literal, inferential, and evaluative reading. They need to differentiate among the disciplinary literacies required to comprehend texts in different subjects: they need to know the linguistic markers that distinguish a math text from a literary text from a history text. And they need to use developing L2 skills to learn *in* L2. What can ESL teachers do to support this growth?

- Regardless of the proficiency level, learners need to be in a print-rich environment. Words associated with the content area should be displayed in posters, with image support if possible. Classroom enhancements such as word walls, word mobiles, bulletin boards, word-of-the-day activities can continually enhance EL students' development in content-area vocabulary that will enhance comprehension of discipline-specific texts.

- Reading supports such as chapter or lesson previews, graphic organizers, glossaries, dictionaries, note-taking skills should be integrated into all content areas.

- In-class reading should happen often. Teachers can do read alouds or think alouds to demonstrate cognitive processing of content-area texts. In small groups, students can read text selections aloud to each other and complete targeted collaborative texts. When introducing a new text, whether it's a chapter in a science book or a story for an English class, teachers can do book talks to create anticipation in the learners and activate prior knowledge or schemas.

- Comprehension can be monitored through whole-class discussions, think-pair-share activities, jigsaws, reports based on collaborative group activities, or targeted writing activities such as quickwrites.

- Higher-level cognitive skills such as drawing inferences or reaching conclusions should be supported with teacher modeling, demonstrations, applications, and guided practice before learners are required to create learning products based on these skills.

- Content-area teachers should guide students in recognizing structures, patterns, words, genres, and variations distinct to the discipline.

- Distinctions among literal, inferential, and evaluative reading should be integrated to show students how to read content-area texts deeply and meaningfully. Teachers should demonstrate the limitations of literal reading through activities such as having students identify information that is actually presented in the text. Inferential reading can be presented as expectations based on what the reader is expected to bring to the text from experience and linguistic experience. EL students will need guidance and modeling in constructing inferential meaning because it is often based on cultural or collective knowledge. Evaluative reading involves stepping back from the specific text and contextualizing it in a greater understanding of the content and context. EL students may have limited contextual resources to create robust evaluative comprehension of texts. But teachers can do things such as have anticipation activities or brainstorming to activate prior knowledge when complex texts are being discussed. Teachers can guide students in recognizing schemas in all content areas to support new knowledge.

- Teachers should allow time for self-selected reading in discipline-specific texts. This might mean constructing a class library of math books, science books, or geography books. Students need to see the language of the discipline presented in various genres so that comprehensible input is provided in multiple, meaningful ways.

- Teachers should use oral reading judiciously and carefully. Oral reading can be unnerving, anxiety-producing, and counterproductive for EL students. Literally, oral reading is a *performance* before peers and before a judge (the teacher). In contrast, small group reading aloud sessions allow learners to support each other in non-stressful peer situations. Or teachers can demonstrate oral reading by doing read alouds.

- Although reading falls into the CALP category, reading can be used to develop BICS. The many skills subsets in reading—phonology, word recognition, guessing, establishing literal meaning, testing inferences, inquiry, distinguishing between fact and opinion, finding connections to other disciplinary knowledge—merge basic and academic language skills.

- Foundational to reading skills is the awareness that symbol-based print can be decoded into meaningful content. This is an emergent reading skill traditionally learned at a very young age, but young EL students or older students with limited or no formal education may have to be taught that alphabetic symbols are combined in language-specific patterns to create meaningful strings of text. Older students who have never learned to read in L1 or students whose L1 alphabet is syllabic or non-Roman, will also need to learn directionality of English text. Transference and interdependence of L1 and L2 allows contextualizing L2 sounds within existing L1 phonological knowledge; however, this vital SLA strategy may be limited for students with little or no formal education in L1. Students who have never attended school will have intuitively learned the phonological, semantic, and syntactic systems of L1, but they may not have awareness of the alphabetic principle or orthographic knowledge or sound segmentation that are vital to reading.

- Even when students have a strong L1 literacy foundation, L2 reading **fluency** is likely to be significantly slowed as the learner works through transfer of L1 skills into L2 contexts. In fluent reading, the reader does not read word-by-word; instead, the reader anticipates based on phonological, syntactic, morphological, semantic, and contextual knowledge. The reading input occurs in chunks of about seven words at a time. Thus, reading becomes a fluid, fluent, meaning-construction activity. For EL students, however, reading has to slow down tremendously as they consciously process individual words into sentences and meaning. At very early stages of L2 acquisition, the EL reader may even be "reading" by sounds and syllables. Awareness of where the EL student is in his/her reading proficiency in L2 enables the ESL teacher to devise appropriate instruction and support to guide the learner toward subsequent levels of achievement in reading.

Teaching Writing in the Context of ESL

Because writing is one of the few academic subjects that is taught consistently from the beginning to the end of students' educational journeys, in traditional classes, teachers can expect some prior learning, consistency, and readiness for new learning in writing. However, in ESL teaching, there are many variables that make writing a challenging but also creative teaching opportunity. In the context of ESL, the same variables we mentioned that must be factored into reading instruction are relevant in teaching writing, but perhaps the degree of formal education in L1 is the most salient in creating appropriate instruction for EL writing.

ESL teachers should start with some fundamental understandings about what works in writing instruction.

- Writing can be a way of learning, a way to get learners to think, to explore, to practice. Writing is not just the production of essays or reports for grading or meeting curricular expectations. Writing can be a prolific, versatile tool for engaging learners in immediate preparation for or application of new learning. Writing can be something as practical as creating a word cloud or writing a response sentence. Writing can happen on the whiteboard, on a 3x5 index card, on a spiral page, on a computer screen, on a phone. Writing to learn is "short, spontaneous, unedited, exploratory, personal writing . . . used not to affect an audience but to channel, crystallize, record, direct, or guide [students'] thinking" (Zemelmann & Daniels, 1988, p. 103).

- Writing is a process, something that happens in stages that can be reworked, something that generates thoughts as the writing is happening. Peter Elbow, a classic voice in composition pedagogy, offers an insightful, realistic view of what happens in writing: "Writing is a way to end up thinking something you couldn't have started out thinking" (1973, p. 15). For EL students, presenting writing as a process that is approached in levels or stages is a way of scaffolding their learning. While a lot of things are going on cognitively during the writing process—like decisions about commas, spelling, sentence structure, application of rhetorical strategies, and thinking about what the next sentence might be—if writing tasks are presented in manageable, incremental tasks, instructional tasks can be modulated for developing the literacy skills of EL students.

- Writing is cross-curricular and cross-disciplinary. Writing should not be something that happens only in English classes. While traditional essays such as the type of essays that are required on STAAR writing exams may be the province of ELA teachers, writing can fit productively in all disciplines. For example, a math teacher could promote students' content-area literacy by having them work collaboratively to construct word problems. A science teacher could have students create word clouds posters on key concepts in a chapter. A history teacher could have students construct a dialogue between two historical figures. A social studies teacher could have students write a hypothetical email to a politician. Content-area applications of writing offer the teacher a chance to guide learners into the discourse of the discipline by showing them the linguistic patterns, the thought patterns, the special vocabulary, and the "norms" for writing in that subject area. Knowing how the writing of the discipline works will also support the learner's comprehension of content-area texts.

- Technicalities, conventions, and linguistic expectations require special attention when we work with EL students. Teachers can operationalize knowledge of linguistics (phonology, morphology, semantics, and syntax) to help EL writers understand the causes of errors and the route to solutions. Teachers should use mentor texts to illustrate writing expectations and should construct learning activities that enable EL writers to see the way texts are put together rhetorically. Teachers should be attuned to L1 to L2 confusion over functional and transitional words that can be so similar in meaning but which trigger different semantic ranges and specialized syntactic structures. Consider how confusing it can be for an EL student to understand the differences among words like *therefore*, *thus*, *consequently*, *so* and the accompanying differences in syntactic markers. Younger EL students or students who have had no formal classroom instruction in L1 may be at emergent levels of writing, with limited ability to attempt or complete grade-level writing assignments.

- Effective writing takes time. Writing should not be rushed. Essay-length tasks should be spread over several days, with teacher guidance, mentor texts, conferencing, revision opportunities, and rubrics to guide the learner's progress. Teachers can also adopt the mantra to write smaller (Gallagher, 2006, p. 68) and construct assignments that allow writers to zoom into small moments of experience or understanding to write micro-essays or quickwrites thereby making writing tasks manageable in terms of time and effort.

Principles and Practices in Teaching Writing

ELPS categories in cross curricular writing and the proficiency levels for writing reflect many basic pedagogical practices relevant to general writing instruction. ELPS makes it clear that writing is not just the province of ELA teachers; it is also a vital part of promoting EL students' holistic language proficiency. Let's look at some strategies that are common in writing instruction from K–12:

Brainstorming—a strategy for coming up with preliminary ideas for a writing task. Brainstorming can take the form of lists, mapping, word clouds, oral suggestions, or possibly even outlining.

Collaboration—working with other writers. Networking with other writers as a writing task is being completed stimulates ideas and allows learners to learn from each other.

Conferencing—working individually with learners on a specific writing task. Conferencing can be very short and focused, such as asking learners to identify a focal point or to show an example of a compound-complex sentence. Individualized instruction is considered one of the best ways of teaching writing.

Conventions of written English—traditional and expected ways of producing utterances and writing. Conventions overlap with rules and mechanics. Writers should be reminded about things such as capitalization of the pronoun *I* or the importance of spelling words fully and completely, especially in the age of ubiquitous, truncated communication of social media. The expectations for paragraphing and spacing are considered conventions.

Drafting—writing that includes multiple versions of a writing product. Drafting with opportunities for revision and with feedback from the instructor eases the anxiety that is so often caused by writing tasks.

Revision—going back into a text you've written and making changes and improvements. Revision can be triggered through self-assessment, peer review, or teacher feedback on drafts. Revision should address global, holistic concerns, such as focus and development, as well as surface level features, like word choice and syntax.

Editing—the last stage of writing. At this point, all the holistic concerns have been addressed and the writer can check for conventions and mechanics prior to submitting the piece for assessment.

Mechanics—expectations for the way we present written texts that do not necessarily change the core meaning. Usage rules for apostrophes and quotation marks are considered mechanics. But mechanics also includes expectations about indenting and spacing.

Technological tools—technology-based resources that can be integrated in writing instruction. Word-processing and internet resources can vastly enhance writers' composing experiences and processes. Teachers should take time to show learners how to use word-processing tools available on programs to give learners flexibility in producing their texts.

Assessing student writing—examining the writing that students do to determine how effectively they are meeting expectations. Assessment should include feedback on what the writer has done effectively and what can be done to improve. Teachers should develop a philosophy and approach to assessing student writing. Whenever feasible, teachers should consider creating rubrics to stipulate expectations and performance levels and to give learners a heads-up on what is required.

Genres—the forms in which texts are constructed. Writing occurs in many forms: narrative, explanatory, exploratory, fantasy, analytical, research-based. Teachers should make expectations for each genre explicit to students when a writing task is assigned.

Freewriting—a discovery strategy where writers write in short bursts, in a timed setting, focusing on fluency and simple production rather than on shaping the writing into a type of discourse. Freewriting may start with a topic provided by the teacher or may be completely open-ended with the writer writing on whatever he/she wants to. Freewriting should never be evaluated because that compromises the freedom associated with this type of writing.

Grammar—the "rules" of writing. Students worry about grammar expectations in their writing. Teachers should integrate grammar instruction in the context of writing, for example by showing students how to turn simple sentences in their drafts into longer sentences using strategies for creating complex, compound, or compound-complex sentences. Teachers should also differentiate among "types of grammar," distinguishing among rules, possibilities, and rhetorical choices.

Peer editing—a strategy that involves having students work collaboratively to provide targeted feedback during drafting stages. Peer editing should never encourage students to find errors in each other's writing but instead should guide learners in recognizing good writing strategies in each other's writing.

Prewriting—strategies for discovering ideas and possibilities for a designated writing task. Brainstorming is a form of prewriting but prewriting can also include strategies such as writing kernel essays, coming up with questions, interviewing classmates on idea possibilities, and doing internet research.

Quickwrite—a very short writing task designed to focus students' writing output on a targeted topic. Quickwrites should be low stress, limited in expectations, and frequent.

Stages of writing—the increments of a final written product. Writing should be taught as a multi-stage process that begins with inquiry or prewriting, moves through several drafts, includes feedback from teacher and peers, applies feedback in revision, and culminates in a written or presented product.

Usage—"rules" that govern correct forms and conventions of writing. For example, some teachers do not want their students to use contractions or colloquialisms. But usage also refers to errors that occur by using mistaken forms, such as using *there* instead of *their*, or *affect* instead of *effect*.

Writer's block—not being able to produce evidence that a writing task is being attempted. Writer's block generally occurs when students have not been appropriately "primed" for a task through prewriting activities and collaborative sessions in class. Additionally, assigning topics that show no connectivity to students' knowledge or experience results in writer's block.

Writing workshop—writing in class in extended sessions that include collaboration, reports of progress, and conferencing with the teacher.

Accommodations and Adaptations for Literacy Instruction

Reading and writing are intertwined linguistic skills. Writers learn to write by paying attention to texts. Readers know how to interpret or process texts because they themselves are writers who write for readers. Still, in the context of developing EL students' literacy skills, teachers can shape their pedagogy around understanding of what constitutes effective ESL instruction.

- Transfer and interdependence. Possibly the most powerful SLA tool that EL students have is their dependence on L1 knowledge in moving toward L2 proficiency. That knowledge varies according to learner's level of L1 education, but even intuitively acquired knowledge of L1, as would occur in the absence of formal education, will provide substantive scaffolding for L2 growth. EL writers will use false cognates, approximations, direct translations, L1 syntax with L2 language, and rhetorical patterns from L1. EL readers will pronounce L2 words using L1 phonetic knowledge and L1 syllabic emphasis. ESL teachers should recognize that such errors are evidence of growth as the learner tries to position him/herself in the contexts of L2 literacy. Appropriate accommodations for handling errors include communicating to the learner the correct form, explaining how the form reflects L2 linguistic structures, comparing the correct L2 form to the approximation, asking the learner to say the structure in L1 to detect the writer's intention, directly offering the correct structure.

- Even in a single, time-constrained class session, instruction can be *sequenced*. When instruction is **sequenced**, there is a clear, logical, coherent trajectory from basic to culminating activities. Lessons should start with an activity that activates students' prior knowledge or helps learners construct an appropriate schema. There should be prereading or prewriting activities to serve as cognitive "warm ups" for the lesson input. The lesson should be presented in manageable chunks, ideally in mini-lessons that end with a think-pair-share, reflective, or even quizzing activity. In a guided practice segment, the teacher should circulate and offer one-on-one help to learners as they apply new knowledge in a succinct, focused activity. If there is time, learners can work on an independent application or can be assigned a targeted homework task. Teachers should shape their lessons with the understanding that input, both linguistic and content, must be comprehensible if learning is to occur. Sequencing contributes greatly to promoting comprehensible input.

- In scaffolded instruction, teachers provide cognitive and structural support for reading and writing activities. **Scaffolding** is based on the principle that new learning happens more efficiently and effectively if learners can gradually build new knowledge with the support of the teacher and peers as the lesson gradually moves toward greater complexity. Learners need to have a starting platform for new learning and then gradually work toward the learning goal. Presenting the lesson agenda in enumerated format offers rudimentary scaffolding. But the scaffold can be strengthened if the teacher offers a summary of the upcoming lesson content and provides a list of key terms. During the lesson, the teacher can stop to have students write down definitions of the key terms. In a lesson dependent on reading, teachers can use jigsaw approach to allow learners to focus on designated segments of the text. The lesson can expand to having the learners pull from the jigsaw reports as they read the chapter or story silently on their own in class or for homework. When writing tasks are required, teachers can create stem sentences to serve as triggers for a short writing task and to prevent learner confusion about what is required. Scaffolding operationalizes Vygotsky's zone of proximal development and Krashen's $i + 1$ principle (which we addressed in Chapter 2). Recall that both Vygotsky's and Krashen's constructs explain how new learning is founded on the learner's need to have a mentor or model to guide him/her into the next level of understanding.

Difference and Diversity

The variable literacy levels that EL students bring into ESL and content-area classrooms call for **differentiated,** learner-centered instruction. Teachers should develop a robust repertoire of activities that reflect multiple learning styles. Something as simple as having learners move from their desks to do a gallery walk can change the way learning happens. In writing classes, peer reading of each other's work can be targeted on choices that the writer has made instead of on correctness. For example, students could be asked to highlight the best sentence of their peer's science poster and explain why it stands out. Such an adjustment to peer reading enables learners to focus on how the writer's linguistic and rhetorical choices work in the context of the writing not whether it is right. This type of accommodation celebrates difference and creativity.

Beyond accommodations, there is the day-to-day, sometimes teaching moment-to-teaching moment awareness of what learners need. That is **responsive teaching**. A responsive teacher may see learner confusion and do an immediate teaching intervention. A response teacher may recognize that a planned class activity is failing to engage learners and may change the activity on the spot. Responsive teaching requires immediacy and continual self-assessment of what is happening in the classroom.

Culturally Responsive Teaching

Teachers also need to accommodate learner differences that stem from socio-economic status (SES), immigrant history, cultural distinctiveness, and past educational experience. There should never be a stated or tacit expectation that the learner should know X. Instead, a funds of knowledge mindset recognizes that learner's life experiences offer a rich context for classroom learning. Funds of knowledge is the "totality of experience" from family, culture, outside school peer groups, individual history, and current environment that the learner brings to the classroom (Moll, Amanti, Neff, & Gonzalez, 1992, p. 134). Funds of knowledge can constitute areas of expertise distinct to the learner even if those areas of experience do not seem to reflect traditional literacy. Within the classroom, the learner must feel validated both as an individual with a distinct identity and as a learner who can participate meaningfully in new learning despite apparent lapses in education or experience. Operating from a funds of knowledge approach, teachers see possibilities and potentialities in each learner and are able to work from the learner's experiential repository toward new levels of literacy. Here's how one set of researchers explain it:

> Student knowledge and experience can be joined with the strategies required for reading with understanding different kinds of texts (e.g., literature, science) that involve varied prior knowledge, text structures, vocabulary, and goals. This work can be the beginning of an intellectual journey that is rewarding for both teachers and students. (Risko & Walker-Dalhouse, 2007, p. 100)

Summary, Action Plan, and Chapter 5 Wrap-Up

Competency 005 in many ways overlaps with several other competencies because of the focus on linguistic knowledge in developing literacy. To read effectively, EL students must rely on reinforcement from listening to L2 in social as well as academic contexts. To write effectively, EL students must rely on what they have inferred about writing structures from texts they read. But writing also involves constructing a writing presence. The writer's persona can be influenced by noticing the impact of listening and speaking possibilities. Additionally, ESL teachers must be ever aware that reading and writing proficiencies are assessed in STAAR and TELPAS exams (which we will address in Chapter 7 on Competency 007), so there is an overlay of demonstrable accountability which intensifies the exigency of knowing how to devise instruction that genuinely promotes EL students' developing literacy.

Self-Check

1. How is ELPS connected to the content of Competency 005?

2. What are some core practices for promoting reading proficiency?

3. What are some core practices for promoting writing proficiency?

4. How does learner diversity impact literacy instruction?

Study Plan

1. Make sure you have looked carefully, with highlighter and pen in hand, at the following ELPS sections:

    *   §74.4(c)(4)–(5) Cross-curricular student expectations for reading and writing

    *   §74.4(d)(3)–(6) Proficiency levels for reading and writing

2. Consult sources that establish frameworks for teaching reading and writing extraneous to concerns about ESL pedagogy. To devise instruction that addresses EL students' needs in literacy development, you first have to know best practices for teaching reading and writing. Here are two excellent resources:

    Literacy's Beginnings: Supporting Young Readers and Writers, 6th ed. by Lea M. Mc-Gee and Donald J. Richgels (2012). This book explores children's literacy development from birth through eight years. There are chapters on developmentally appropriate teaching strategies for pre-school through grade 4.

    The English Teacher's Companion, 4th ed. by Jim Burke (2013). This book actually addresses teaching practices in listening, speaking, reading, and writing at middle school and high school levels. Burke integrates actual examples from his own teaching to illustrate best practices.

3. To bolster your understanding of how good teaching practices can be adapted for ESL teaching, you should consult two of the best texts on ESL teaching:

    Reading, Writing, and Learning in ESL: A Resource Book for Teaching K–12 English Learners, 7th ed. by Suzanne F. Peregoy and Owen F. Boyle (2017);

    ESL Teaching: Principles for Success, by Yvonne S. Freeman, David E. Freeman, Mary Soto, and Ann Ebe (2016).

4. Reading and writing are vital parts of the TEKS English language curriculum starting with kindergarten TEKS and spanning through high school. If your initial certification is in an area other than ELA/Reading, you should spend some study time looking through elementary, middle school, and high school TEKS in writing and reading to get a sense of the breadth of literacy expectations in regular classes. Those expectations do not change for EL students; in fact, the expectations are heightened in the context of having to learn literacy skills *in* English while also learning English. Remember that TEKS are available from the TEA website. Look for the Academics tab and then the Curriculum Standards link to Texas Essential Knowledge and Skills.

Practice Items for Competency 005

1. Students in a math class are working on think alouds in groups as a preliminary step in solving a set of fraction problems. While monitoring the groups, the teacher notices that Lin, an EL student, is having trouble pronouncing the terms *numerator* and *denominator* when she talks about the problems in the group. The teacher works with Lin individually to show her how to break up the terms into syllables, models the vowel sounds, and then has Lin pronounce the terms. This teacher activity best illustrates which of the following literacy development strategies?

    A. Authentic assessment

    B. Content-area vocabulary practice

    C. L1 transfer

    D. Linguistic accommodation

    Response D is correct. By showing the student how the word is linguistically structured, modeling the pronunciation, and then listening to the student pronounce the words, the teacher is providing linguistic accommodation to develop her literacy skills in specific math content. Response A is incorrect because the item stem does not indicate that the teacher has constructed the think aloud as an assessment activity. The students are doing a collaborative activity to practice content-area material. Response B is incorrect because content-area practice would most likely involve the entire class in a holistic activity of terms relevant to the current lesson. The student knows the content-area words, so practice is not the focal activity in this scenario. Response C is incorrect because the student's L1 linguistic knowledge does not figure into the specific explanation and modeling that the teacher does to help her master the pronunciation of the content-area terms.

2.   A middle school history teacher has a class that includes 50% EL students. For the past three weeks, the class has been working through a unit on the Texas Revolution. As a culminating unit assignment, students will write a 300-word character sketch of one of five historical figures they have studied. Students signed up for the historical figures on a first come, first choice basis, so everyone now has a designated historical individual with five students working on each historical figure. Which of the following activities would be the best initial activity to support EL learners' literacy development in doing this writing task?

   A.   The teacher has students write a summary of what they know so far about all the historical figures on the basis of the unit activities.

   B.   The teacher asks students to make a list of words they don't understand in the chapters they covered in the unit.

   C.   The teacher has students work collaboratively in groups based on the designated figures to create word clouds that identify the historical person's contribution to the Texas Revolution.

   D.   The teacher has students work individually to construct an idea web that connects the historical figure to other individuals in the Texas Revolution.

Response C is correct. The clue in the item stem is "initial." While all the activities would be appropriate during the process of creating the assigned character sketch, the word cloud is the most appropriate starting activity. Additionally, the word cloud activity is done collaboratively, thereby providing social interaction for students, integrating writing, speaking, and listening skills. Response A is not the best initial activity because it involves students in a different writing task which takes the focus off the designated character sketch task. Response B is incorrect because the list of terms from throughout the unit is not directly relevant to the designated writing task. Listing unit words would very likely have been done throughout the unit. Response D is incorrect because it is not the best choice for starting the writing process. The connections among the historical figures might be relevant, but that activity could be integrated at a later point in the writing process.

CHAPTER

Competency 006

6

Competency 006: Teaching ESL in Content Areas

The ESL teacher understands how to promote students' content-area learning, academic-language development and achievement across the curriculum (Pearson, 2019a).

The broad area addressed by Competency 006 is **content-area teaching.** Four descriptive statements (A–D) in this competency cover the following general topics:

- Linguistic accommodations
- ESL instructional strategies
- Learner diversity

A particular challenge in teaching ESL in content areas is that it requires teaching knowledge and skills typically considered as the province of ELA teachers. Competency 006 extends content-area teachers' domain of pedagogical responsibility into linguistic development. Even though Competency 006 includes only four descriptive statements, the breadth of 006.A and 006.B is expansive because they involve knowing how to make L2 content-area information accessible for EL students.

Competency 006 Core Content

The following key terms are integral to fully understanding the scope of Competency 006 and the aligned Standards I and III–VI. Additionally, many of the terms included in Competency 006 descriptive statements also occur in the cross-curricular ELPS, reinforcing the centrality of these terms in content-area teaching.

Table 6.1.
Competency 006 Core Content

linguistic accommodation	communicated instruction	sequenced instruction	scaffolded instruction
CALP	content-area teaching strategies	prior experience	hands-on learning
experiential learning	visual supports for learning	manipulatives	learner diversity
CALLA	integration of technology	content-relevant genres	demonstrated comprehension
grammar and usage	active listening	learning strategies	textbook structure

Teaching Content Areas in the Context of ESL

To teach ESL effectively in content areas, ESL teachers must know best practices for teaching in each content area; ESL circumstances provide exigencies for intersections of L2 acquisition in the context of specialized disciplinary content. That requires exceptional understanding of how EL students learn English while learning disciplinary content *in* English. To effectively enter and then master the discourse of any given discipline, learners must be guided not just in learning the information relevant to the discipline but also in recognizing the ways of thinking and conversing in the discipline so that they can participate authentically in conversations about and in the discipline (Denstaedt, Roop, & Best, 2014, pp. xii, 2). However, for EL students, the need to learn content-area knowledge *in* L2 adds a cognitive wrinkle to students' learning efforts. L2 language development does not occur only in specialized language classes; it continues into all content-area classes. Competency 006 showcases the content-area teacher's responsibility to guide EL students in acquiring content-area knowledge while also promoting continued development in L2 proficiency. In short, in content-area teaching, the ESL teacher must be a specialist in both basic language teaching *and* in the realm of the academic subject.

CALLA

The Cognitive Academic Language Learning Approach (CALLA) developed by Ana Uhl Chamot and J. Michael O'Malley (1994) provides a learner-centered approach for developing students' academic language skills in a content area while they are also developing their language proficiency. CALLA developers Chamot and O'Malley explain that the complexity of content-area information requires exceptional support systems for EL students. Thus, content-area instruction should include tangible support in activating awareness of how learning happens through three targeted types of learning strategies:

- Metacognitive strategies: EL students anticipate the effort required for a task and monitor and self-evaluate their learning processes by recognizing actions and behaviors that facilitate readiness to learn new information. Examples: previewing new content, recognizing content presentation aids such as headings, key words, and linguistic markers; self-checking throughout the task.

- Cognitive strategies: EL students use specific learning supports to meet the objectives of the task. Examples: summarizing, inferencing, using reference materials relevant to the content area; using notes to reinforce learning; reinforcing content with images; connecting new knowledge to existing knowledge; mentally rehearsing new information.

- Social-affective strategies: EL students enhance and reinforce learning by interacting with other learners. Examples: asking questions; collaboration with peers.

(Chamot & O'Malley, 1994, pp. 61–64;
Chamot & O'Malley, 1989, p. 116–119)

A hallmark of CALLA is the five-part approach to lesson construction which is then operationalized in actual lessons that present content material within a communicative context.

Step 1: Teachers discover what learners already know about the topic in a *preparation* phase. This is a sort of "warm-up" phase where learners are reminded of past successful learning strategies. Or the teacher can model the learning strategies that will be appropriate in the new lesson. Preparation can involve activities to gauge students' prior knowledge, to involve learners in collaborative anticipation activities, to determine what life experiences students can apply to the learning task, and to assess whether their current level of proficiency fits the learning task.

Step 2:   Teachers use best practices in their discipline in the *presentation* stage to convey new content material to learners.

Step 3:   Teachers engage learners in application of the new information through collaborative, inquiry problem-solving, or hands-on activities in the *practice* phase.

Step 4:   Teachers create lesson-specific opportunities for learners to assess their own learning in the *self-evaluation* phase. This enables learners to be conscious of whether they met their learning goals, to recognize what learning strategies work best for them, and to adjust their strategies for future learning. Self-evaluation allows learners to take ownership of their learning processes; furthermore, self-awareness of how success happens can boost motivation.

Step 5:   In the *expansion* phase, teachers guide students in connecting new information to existing knowledge frameworks, such as by thinking of strategies that they've used in past learning, connecting knowledge gained in one class to knowledge gained in other classes, or by planning to use different cognitive strategies in a future learning task.

(Chamot & O'Malley, 1994, pp. 66–71)

CALLA can be applied to all subject areas. It pulls together the best strategies from general pedagogy, inviting teachers to think of creative, learner-centered ways to help EL students access and own learning in content areas.

Content-Area Instruction + Language Development

In the process of concentrating on the information and curricular expectations for content areas, ESL teachers need to remember that EL students require specialized support in negotiating the complex information of content-area material while still learning English. ELPS and Competency 006 identify such support as **linguistic accommodations** because these learning supports enhance EL students' access to content-area information. Recall from Competency 001 that knowledge of basic linguistics is an ESL teacher responsibility; such knowledge enables teachers to provide on-the-spot support for EL students as they create L2 output. Making content-area information and ways of thinking accessible for EL students, however, requires thinking of ways to make content-area material a vehicle for continued language development. Several "principles" are consistently cited as prolific adjustments for ESL teaching across all subjects: hands-on learning, abundant activity that involves *doing* things that illustrate content-area concepts, visual support for new information, demonstrations of content concepts, learner interaction, interrelatedness of all language domains even in content areas, peer and teacher feedback, and prior knowledge (Hudelson, 1989, pp. 138–140; Chamot & O'Malley, 1989, p. 115).

Supporting EL students in developing language proficiency while learning content-area knowledge requires some teaching adjustments. Collectively, most of these strategies constitute *scaffolding*, which is manifested as a variety of activities that support learning.

- Look beyond the textbook for literary or nonfiction presentations of complex concepts. Ideally, content-area teachers should have a small class library of fiction and nonfiction books connected to the content area. Well-chosen storybooks can be used quite productively to introduce learners to challenging topics.

- Create opportunities for pre-lesson engagement. CALLA step 1 establishes the foundational need to help learners position themselves in the context of new learning through prior knowledge, anticipation, background knowledge, or real-world connections.

- Integrate hands-on activities. Hands-on learning is considered one of the most beneficial types of scaffolding for EL students. Also known as *manipulatives*, props, **realia**, and even everyday objects can be used to show learners how to operationalize new knowledge.

- Incorporate a variety of learning activities. While in many classrooms, lecture continues to be the primary vehicle for presenting new knowledge, teachers should experiment with a variety of strategies that activate learners' multiple ways of knowing. Lectures can be segmented into **mini-lessons** focused on a specific, limited learning objective. Learning can happen outdoors as learners apply a new content concept, look for materials relevant to a lesson, or practice kinesthetic applications or demonstrations. In the classroom setting, learners can work at the whiteboard or can draw applications on craft paper. Assessments can be trimmed down to single, open-ended learning checks that can be presented on index cards (and can be scored on-the-spot).

- Provide multiple opportunities for learner interaction. In earlier chapters, we discussed the importance of social interaction in developing language competence. In content-area classrooms, learners need opportunities to talk with each other about new learning. Teachers should integrate paired or group activities with specific learning tasks to encourage learners to share results of learning with each other.

Learner interaction provides opportunities for comprehensible input and output.

- Reinforce learning with content realia. Content classrooms should be sites of focus on the content through posters, illustrations, content-relevant props and objects.

- Reinforce literacy skills from cross curricular experiences (refer to other content areas). In supporting continuing language development, teachers should refer to relevant content that students are learning in other classes. For example, a math teacher can use grammar terminology to unravel complexities of word problems.

- Slow down the teaching pace to allow for processing time. New learning takes time to process. Teachers should not rush to "cover" curricular content but should instead create units and lessons that allow learners time to construct understanding of content.

- Integrate culturally relevant connections. In addition to integrating stories and information that reflect different cultures and languages, teachers should consider culturally-specific ways of learning. In some cultures, family stories are vital sources of new knowledge. In some cultures, facts are the foundation of learning. Stories and examples from other cultures allow EL students to feel comfortable in the L2 environment and expand native speakers' realm of knowledge about the content area.

- Use **read alouds** liberally to present content material. Read alouds allow teachers to present content-area material in an animated, engaging way to emphasize linguistic and rhetorical aspects of a content-relevant text. Read alouds can be material from the class textbook or supplementary material, such as a relevant picture book, a nonfiction passage from a biography of an individual relevant to the content area, an explanatory book. Read alouds are not only for elementary school children. Read alouds are particularly helpful in showing learners how to process complex text, such as science and social studies. (Layne, 2015)

- Illustrate reading scaffolds in textbooks. EL students may be unfamiliar with the structural scaffolds in textbooks such as the list of objectives provided in some chapters, headings, highlighting of key terms, callout boxes with special information, self-check questions at the end, and chapter summaries. Something as simple as showing learners that headings and subheadings are intended to subdivide challenging information into manageable learning chunks can help an EL student feel greater access to content-area information.

- Make room for "the imaginary." *The imaginary* is the realm of experience that enables learners to explore possibilities for creative connections between conscious experience and unconscious possibilities. It is not just "using your imagination"; it involves discovering ways that imagination can be used to promote content-area learning. While content-learning may seem to be necessarily grounded in reality, looking beyond fixed boundaries enables learners to *enjoy* language, discover cross-cultural connections, and draw on resources that fortify identity formation. Guided imagery, for example, involves using linguistic frames to generate content-relevant connections to a lesson. Role-playing positions learners in learner-created representations of scenes relevant to course content. Integrating music that reflects content can reinforce learners' comprehension of complex concepts. Even creating or "finding" poetry in content-area material invites learners to meld content and personal understanding. (Díaz-Rico, 2013, pp. 203–210)

- Take learning styles into consideration. Teachers should integrate visuals, active listening, manipulatives, model-making, performative opportunities, demonstrated problem-solving, kinesthetic learning to allow learners to process new information in a variety of ways.

Cross-Curricular Competencies

Competency 006 pulls us back into the BICS/CALP distinction (Cummins, 1979; Cummins, 2000). BICS, as you should recall from earlier chapters, is learned quickly and almost effortlessly as EL students interact in social, meaningful ways with L2 speakers. BICS enables EL students to talk and listen in informal settings, like the hallways, the playground, the cafeteria, the school bus, but also to participate meaningfully in classroom talk that is more phatic than instructive. A lot of banter and random talk happens in classrooms; EL students need BICS to participate in that aspect of the classroom community. BICS also enables EL students to recognize registers and pragmatics in genuine communicative interactions.

CALP, however, requires concerted attention to critical thinking, construction of abstract thought, moving beyond the concrete, problem solving, innovation, schemas, and multiple intelligences. The most challenging part of CALP is that EL students must continue to develop L2 proficiency simultaneously as they work at mastering complex academic content. CALLA which we discussed in the previous section is an initiative for helping teachers meet the challenge of content-area teaching plus language instruction.

CALP, however, is not a teaching approach but a construct for differentiating between the types of language learning that EL students must engage in.

Developing EL students' cognitive academic language proficiency requires knowing the thinking patterns, linguistic features, ways of learning, rhetorical structures, and broad context of the relevant content area. Teachers need to guide students in connecting prior knowledge within a content area to new learning. EL students, however, especially newcomers or recent immigrants with limited or interrupted formal education, may lack adequate subject area background. Teachers need to offer multiple ways for learners to gain enough background knowledge to participate productively in content-area learning. Chapter 003 addressed the possibilities available via educational technology to help learners bolster background knowledge.

Critical thinking skills that reflect disciplinary ways of thinking can be supported through instruction that guides learners toward higher-order tasks in Bloom's Taxonomy. Learners should have classroom activities that call for analysis, evaluation, and creation instead of just memorization and basic understanding. Critical thinking can be promoted by demonstrating how to construct content-relevant inquiry focused on searching for *how* and *why* answers instead of *who* or *what* or *when*. Critical thinking also involves recognizing opposing points of view and evaluating merits of multiple perspectives. Students should be guided in learning how to use content-area facts to support opinions, positions, and arguments.

Development of cognitive academic language proficiency requires linguistic accommodations such as the scaffolding described in the CALLA section above. Sequencing and segmentation, however, also support EL students' gradual progress through content-area learning. Ideally, new content should be presented incrementally, allowing learners to master contained, defined learning tasks before moving to the next level. Even within a single class session, the lesson for the day should be presented in sequenced tasks that allow learners to move incrementally, logically, and coherently through levels of accomplishment that demonstrate specific mastery of specific learning objectives. Sequencing and the accompanying incremental learning can create and sustain the EL student's motivation in the context of challenging content-area learning.

Diversity, Learner Circumstances, and Differentiation

Even in an apparently homogeneous class of native speakers, learners are different. Every learner has distinct learning needs and represents a different level of learning readiness. Additionally, Competency 006.D pulls us into the extra-curricular environment that impacts how EL students function in classrooms. Factors such as family support, literacy tools at home, the L1/L2 ratio at home, socioeconomic status, and previous educational background all contribute to the learning readiness of the EL student. If we factor in the diversity of EL students' current L2 proficiency, the need for differentiation increases exponentially. The salient question is, "What can ESL teachers do to differentiate content-area instruction so that all learners' needs are addressed?"

A good way to approach a response to differentiated instruction is to ask, "What strategies promote inclusivity and community?" Here are some suggested practices:

- Cultivate a community of learners by celebrating diversity. Learners should be invited to share information bits about themselves in class bulletin boards that allow multi-modal artifacts, such as photos, illustrations, and objects as well as written captions.

- Create opportunities for frequent interaction among learners that supports BICS as well as CALP. For EL students in the beginning and intermediate ELPS levels, interactions with peers will enable them to increase opportunities for comprehensible input and output. Group activities focused on learning goals offer robust strategies for promoting content-area learning while fostering L2 proficiency across all four language domains.

- Construct lessons that integrate cultural background in an egalitarian way. EL students should not be singled out for their difference; instead, teachers should create learning opportunities that allow all learners to recognize differences as a route to creating community.

- Recognize multiple intelligences. Teachers should create opportunities for learners to act and learn within the content area. In-class activities should include reading, speaking, listening, writing, doing, moving, seeing, sharing, and reflecting.

- Consider SES constraints. Students' socioeconomic status can significantly affect learners' ability to participate in activities outside of the classroom. The teacher cannot control the outside environment, but what happens in the classroom or in school spaces can reflect equity and access for all learners. Out-of-class assignments should not depend on technologies, travel, community access, or expenses that exclude some learners. Instead, teachers should create assignments, in and out of class, that allow choice and selection based on student needs and availability of resources.

- Create a culture of high expectations. Students need to know that success is accessible for all learners. Learners should be praised for on-target performance to provide reinforcement for learning behavior that can be repeated or extended in future learning. Expectations should be specific, clear, and attainable.

(Gregory & Burkman, 2012, pp. 19–28)

Summary, Action Plan, and Chapter 6 Wrap-Up

Teaching ESL in content areas presents special challenges for teachers and learners. Teachers have to devise modifications of traditional pedagogy to support EL students' linguistic growth, and learners must negotiate the task of learning L2 while learning *in* L2. As they work with EL students, teachers must keep in mind that knowing two or more languages and being able to listen, speak, read, and write in L2 is an amazing linguistic and cognitive feat. However, to succeed academically, EL students need constant direction and guidance from teachers. ELPS and TEKS offer guidelines that teachers can use in creating comprehensible input for EL students so that they can achieve their learning goals.

Self-Check

1. Can you identify and explain some basic linguistic accommodations to support EL students' learning in content areas?

2. While CALLA is not mentioned in Competency 006, the principles of the Cognitive Academic Language Learning Approach reflect the topics in descriptive statements A and B. Can you identify and explain some instructional strategies for promoting EL students' learning in content areas?

3. How does student diversity figure into teaching EL students in content-area classes?

Study Plan

1. Carefully read the cross-curricular second language acquisition knowledge and skills section of ELPS (§74.4(c)(1)–(5), paying special attention to the specificity of the student expectations in each language domain (TAC, 2007). The specific terms and concepts embedded throughout these ELPS descriptors can help you anticipate test items.

2. To "see" how content area teaching can be adjusted to accommodate the needs of EL students, you should consult these excellent resources:

Strategies for Teaching English Learners, 3rd ed., by Lynn T. Díaz-Rico (2013) presents a broad spectrum of must-have knowledge and skills for successful ESL teaching. The chapters in this book offer a targeted presentation of theory and then move to specific classroom applications.

Academic Literacy for English Learners: High-Quality Instruction across Content Areas by Cynthia Brock, Diane Lapp, Rachel Salas, and Dianna Townsend (2009) presents three detailed lessons in three different content areas. The book starts with a comprehensive, highly informative overview of the issues in ESL teaching. The three content-area chapters describe units in science, math, and history with details that compellingly show how the instructional choices support EL students' content-area learning *and* linguistic development.

The CALLA Handbook: Implementing the Cognitive Academic Language Learning Approach by Anna Uhl Chamot and J. Michael O'Malley (1994) starts with an overview of their signature CALLA model and then moves into specific examples in different content areas. There are abundant tables and applications to illustrate teaching strategies that illuminate content materials for EL students. A clever feature of the book is the use of pencil drawings that show teachers and students enacting learning strategies. The drawings include dialogue bubbles that suggest what learners and teachers are thinking or saying in the scenes.

50 Strategies for Teaching English Language Learners by Adrienne L. Herrell and Michael Jordan (2020) starts with a focused but highly informational overview of theories and practices in ESL instruction. The 50 strategies are presented as short chapters that set up the strategy and then illustrate application in a variety of grade levels. Here's a sampling of the strategies: visual scaffolding, realia strategies, sorting activities, read-pair-share, verb action, multiple intelligence strategies.

Practice Items for Competency 006

Use the information below to answer questions 1 and 2.

Ms. Oliver has an elementary class of beginning EL students. During reading time, she integrates non-fiction picture books that focus on science, history, or social studies topics. In a reading circle, she does an animated read aloud to allow students to familiarize themselves with the content and then rereads it once more, a bit more slowly, taking time to show the illustrations to the students. The teacher allows time for students to comment or ask questions if they want to during the oral readings. After the oral readings, she reads the book one more time.

1. Which of the following activities could reinforce the students' content-area learning following the read alouds?

   A. The teacher administers an objective quiz at the end of the lesson, allowing students to work together to find the correct responses in the text.

   B. The teacher asks for a volunteer to read the book orally.

   C. The teacher stops during the second oral reading to write key vocabulary on the whiteboard, explaining the definition.

   D. The teacher has students draw a picture of their favorite part of the book at the end of the readings.

Response C is correct. The scenario stipulates that the class is a beginning EL class. Reinforcing content-area vocabulary by writing terms on the board and explaining them would promote students' content-area knowledge. Response A is incorrect because the scenario is focused on *learning*; a quiz is an assessment. Response B is incorrect because the class is at the beginning proficiency level; most learners would be unlikely to have the decoding skills necessary to read the book orally. Response D is incorrect because it does not directly promote content-area learning. Drawing a picture of a favorite part of the book would give learners a chance to respond affectively but the activity does not directly support content-area learning.

2. This teaching activity illustrates which of the following types of linguistic accommodation:

   A. Scaffolding

   B. Sequencing

   C. Culturally responsive teaching

   D. Collaborative learning

Response is A correct. The teacher is showing learners how to create a learning platform by reading a text multiple times, learning content-area vocabulary, listening to the words of the text, and interacting with other learners. Response B is incorrect because the item scenario presents a single activity: a read aloud. Sequencing shows a set of incremental activities leading to a culminating learning task. Response C is incorrect but the item scenario does not indicate that the book being read was selected because of cultural features. Response D is incorrect because, while the activity would very likely include comments from the students, the collaborative component is not the focal intention of the activity. The scenario indicates that the teacher's objective is to present content-area knowledge via the read aloud.

Competency 007

Competency 007: Assessment

The ESL teacher understands formal and informal assessment procedures and instruments used in ESL programs and uses assessment results to plan and adapt instruction (Pearson, 2019a).

Competency 007 addresses **assessment procedures and practices** and is explained through six descriptive statements (A–F), which cover the following general areas:

- Connection between state-mandated assessments and classroom instruction

- Texas assessment policies for ESL

- Formal and informal assessment practices

- Use of assessment to support learning objectives

ESL programs in Texas are legislatively mandated through state laws presented in the Texas Administrative Code and the Texas Education Code. Language programs in Texas reflect federal regulations in the current reauthorization of the 1965 Elementary and Secondary Education Act (ESEA). In 2015, ESEA was reauthorized as the Every Student Succeeds Act (ESSA) (U.S. Department of Education, 2017). All information relevant to

ESL programs in Texas is continually updated and presented by TEA on its comprehensive website, tea.texas.gov.

As presented in ESEA/ESSA, assessment is a core component of the full instructional program for English learners (U.S. Department of Education, 2019). Competencies 001–006 describe how learning happens in the ESL classroom and what teachers can do to promote proficiency in basic English and in content areas. Competency 007 reflects ESEA/ ESSA requirements that link instruction to assessment to measurable progress and ultimately to funding for critical language programs.

Competency 007 Core Content

Competency 007 demonstrates the breadth of ESL teacher responsibility in creating and sustaining ESL learning environments that lead to documentable outcomes. The following terms from the descriptive statements indicate the scope of Competency 007 and the alignment of concepts from Standard VI:

Table 7.1.
Competency 007 Core Content

Limited English Proficient/proficiency	Language Proficiency Assessment Committee (LPAC)	Texas English Language Proficiency Assessment System (TELPAS)	Texas Education Code
Every Student Succeeds Act	mandated assessment	testing purposes	test design
classroom assessment	formal assessment	informal assessment	authentic assessment
standardized tests in Texas	LPAC protocols	assessment and learning	integrating assessment results

Mandated Assessment for EL Students

Assessment of EL students in Texas is complex, requiring coordination among everyone from state government officials to classroom teachers to ensure that federally- and state-mandated policies are met. Competencies 001 through 006 establish the knowledge and skills that ESL teachers need to have in using instruction and interactions with learners to develop EL students' language proficiency. Competency 007 adds the responsibility of connecting the many types of mandated assessments to actual classroom activities. The overarching goal of language programs in Texas is to develop EL students' English proficiency sufficiently so that they can enter regular classes. In other words, teachers, administrators, and other campus professionals are working in concert to help EL students *exit* the language programs as a result of demonstrated proficiency in English.

Students in Texas are channeled into a variety of language programs on the basis of a two-item home language survey administered upon the student's entry into the state public educational system (TEC, 1995; TAC, 1996):

1. What language is spoken in the child's home **most of the time**?

2. What language does the child speak **most of the time**?

If the responses indicate that a language other than English is the primary language, a series of additional procedures are initiated starting with diagnostic testing via a state-approved test for determining the student's proficiency level in English.

Statewide Assessment for LEP Designation and Reclassification

Prior to the 2019–2020 academic year, local education agencies could select from a list of tests approved by the state to use results of the home language survey to determine language proficiency status. As of mid-2020, there is a single, state approved English proficiency test: the Language Assessment System (LAS) Battery (TEA, 2019, Update).

TEA also references tests that can be used to *reclassify* EL students as they progress through designated programs. These assessments enable the Language Proficiency Assessment Committee to recommend transferring students to language programs and/or regular classes that best meet their current levels of English proficiency.

ESL teachers should explore the websites for the state approved language assessment tests to note the specificity of the data provided for each student and to note the disaggregated performance information. The LAS website, for example, includes a test overview that shows some of the subskills tested in each of the four language domains. Teachers can use the listed subskills as a self-check on whether they are effectively addressing these skills in their classes. For example, by noting that "following explicit oral instructions" and "responding to idiomatic expressions" are listed as listening subskills, teachers could restructure classroom listening activities to help students practice these skills.

Teachers should familiarize themselves with all materials, links, and assessment information available on the TEA website. While the initial classification occurs before the learner enters an actual ESL classroom, subsequent opportunities for reclassification signal a responsibility for ESL teachers to be attuned to the types of skills that EL students will be required to demonstrate when there are opportunities for moving to different language programs more in line with their developing English proficiency.

The Language Proficiency Assessment Committee (LPAC)

The major driver of the EL student's progress through language programs is the **Language Proficiency Assessment Committee.** The Texas Education Code (Chapter 29. Subchapter B. Sec. 29.063) mandates the establishment of a Language Proficiency Assessment Committee on each campus charged with implementing required laws and overseeing EL students' progress through the language program. Membership includes a professional bilingual educator, a professional transitional language educator, the parent of a student designated LEP, and a campus administrator (TEC, 1995).

Following an LEP designation on the basis of the language proficiency scores on the state-approved exam, the LPAC evaluates the learner's scores and other factors, and the learner is placed in the language program that best meets the learner's language needs (TEA, 2019, LEP/EL). Chapter 008 which addresses Competency 008 (the foundation of ESL education and language programs) will describe and explain the various types of programs implemented in Texas.

The LPAC performs pivotal functions in students' trajectory through mandated language programs. This committee eventually determines when students are ready to exit a language program.

- Holistically, the committee must know what programs are available to learners in the immediate campus and district.

- Viewing each learner as an individual with distinct learning needs, the committee needs to match state-mandated assessment results to potential for success.

- The committee relies on parent and teacher partners to recommend optimal placement for each EL student.

- The committee is the vehicle for securing federally required parental consent for or refusal of language programs and services for LEP students.

- Even after a student exits a language program on the basis of LPAC recommendations, the committee continues monitoring the student for four years based on ESSA in case readmission or supplemental support is indicated by the student's failure to thrive following exit from a language program.

- The LPAC informs parents of a child's progress as determined by state approved language proficiency exams and scores on STAAR exams; the assessment reports to parents include recommendations for continuing in a current language program or transitioning into a program that more adequately meets the learner's current needs.

- The LPAC also coordinates special education requirements for students designated both LEP and special education.

(TEA, 2019, *LPAC Framework Manual*)

TELPAS

The most visible and all-encompassing component of assessment of EL students in Texas is the Texas English Language Proficiency Assessment System (TELPAS), which establishes procedures, processes, and testing protocols for assessing EL students' proficiency in English. TELPAS is fundamentally linked to ELPS with performance criteria in TELPAS reflective of the beginning, intermediate, advanced, and advanced high descriptors that define ELPS. On the basis of annual administration of TELPAS exams, students are assessed in the four language domains using the four performance level descriptors from ELPS. Each student designated as LEP and thereby placed in a language program receives a report similar to the one shown below as part of the LPAC annual review:

Table 7.2.
Alignment of ELPS and language domains in TELPAS

TELPAS				
listening	Beg.	Int.	Adv.	Adv. High
speaking	Beg.	Int.	Adv.	Adv. High
reading	Beg.	Int.	Adv.	Adv. High
writing	Beg.	Int.	Adv.	Adv. High
composite	Beg.	Int.	Adv.	Adv. High

(TEA, 2019, *LPAC Framework Manual*, p. 136)

The listening, speaking, and reading proficiencies on the annual TELPAS exam are assessed using an online multiple-choice test; writing proficiency is assessed holistically. It is important to note that the report shown in Table 7.2 is only part of the comprehensive, annual evaluation of each EL student.

Kept in the loop about student performance on TELPAS and other mandated exams, ESL instructors can use assessment results to inform instructional choices and to create learner-centered instruction that directly guides EL students toward higher levels of proficiency in the four language domains. The most up-to-date TELPAS guide for educators offers abundant insights into the test framework which ESL teachers can use in making instructional choices. For example, the four language domains are defined as follows:

Table 7.3.
TELPAS Definitions of Language Domains

Listening	The ability to understand spoken language, comprehend and extract information, and follow social and instructional discourse through which information is provided
Speaking	The ability to use spoken language appropriately and effectively in learning activities and social interactions
Reading	The ability to comprehend and interpret written text at the grade-appropriate level
Writing	The ability to produce written text with content and format to fulfill grade-appropriate classroom assignments

(TEA, 2018, *Educator Guide*, p. 5)

TELPAS materials available from TEA enable ESL teachers to devise instruction that correlates with ELPS student expectations. Strong, detailed familiarity with ELPS performance levels enables teachers to gauge the progress that EL students are making and to adjust instruction to guide learners toward higher levels of proficiency. TELPAS Educator Guides, available from TEA in the TELPAS section of the Student Testing and Accountability tab, historically include comprehensive overviews of the framework of ESL instruction. Additionally, these guides include helpful examples of the type of items on the reading and writing objective exams and the testing approach that is used in the listening and speaking portions. ESL teachers can use these guides to construct learner-centered instruction that strengthens EL students' listening, speaking, reading, and writing skills and prepares them to perform capably on this high-stakes exam.

Because TELPAS is a *summative* assessment, ESL teachers can implement *formative* assessment measures throughout the school year in preparation for the annual spring semester administration of TELPAS. The underlying principles of L2 learning that shape TELPAS expectations offer robust direction for ESL teachers in connecting assessment to day-to-day teaching.

Assessment-Driven Learning: Aligning Assessment to Classroom Instruction

Fundamentally, classroom assessment focuses on guiding learners to meet clearly articulated learning outcomes. Day-to-day, authentic assessment in the classroom is about continuous improvement. The *formative* assessment that happens minute-by-minute in everyday classrooms enables ESL teachers to offer immediate feedback on spontaneous as well as structured learner performance. Let's consider some fundamental aspects of assessment that enable ESL teachers to enhance student learning:

- Assessment should be continual and authentic. **Authentic assessment** means that feedback, monitoring, and evaluative teaching activities are embedded into the delivery of a lesson or other class activity. When teachers identify on-target behaviors that learners are demonstrating in performing typical class activities, that is authentic assessment. For example, during a class discussion on a word problem, a teacher could say, "Xuan, you just explained how you are paying attention to the suggested operator—multiplying—in the word problem. That shows you are reading carefully." The teacher's comment helps the learner understand what she did effectively.

- Assessment should be focused on continuous improvement. In any given task, learners should understand what they have done effectively and what they need to do to improve.

- Assessment practices should reflect a classroom culture of high expectations. Students should understand that success is possible for all learners. Teachers should create opportunities for learners to revise work following initial assessment to attain higher levels of achievement. Teachers should keep in mind that success creates and sustains motivation in learners.

- Assessment practices should reflect the type of learning task. A learning task that calls for recall should be assessed using different criteria from what would be used on a task that requires that the learner create a product, such as an essay or poster. Even with a simple recall task, however, assessment can be used to guide the learner toward continuous achievement. For example, if a learning task asks learners to jot down the three types of soil described in a reading, and a learner can only recall one, the assessment might ask the learner to go back to the chapter, read carefully, take notes, and perhaps even ask questions during the rereading.

- Assessment should be based on criteria that reflect specific learning objectives. Assessment should be thought of as a way of measuring how learners are meeting measurable learning objectives. Effective assessment looks at learner behavior and performance and offers indicators of how learners are moving toward optimal levels of performance. For example, in a set of 10 math problems, the teacher could set the target performance as 7/10 correct problems and then create opportunities for learners to continue working toward the goal. Measurable objectives show alignment among class activities, practice opportunities, and then independent learner demonstration of new knowledge.

- For constructed products, like projects and essays, assessment should be based on a **rubric**. A rubric is a presentation, usually in chart form, of assessment criteria and performance levels. Rubrics should be made available to learners before a learning product is submitted to allow learners to self-check their work in progress. In constructing task-specific rubrics, teachers should use clear, measurable language so that learners can understand expectations and use those content-relevant expectations to create the assigned learning product. Rubrics are usually associated with writing, but teachers in all subject areas can construct rubrics to guide learners in striving for highest levels of achievement. Additionally, rubrics should reinforce content-area terms. An abundance of rubrics is accessible via internet sites, but teachers should recognize that these free, easily available rubrics are generic and not constructed to meet the specifications of distinct learning tasks.

Feedback

Feedback is the gold standard of assessment. Feedback is written or rubric-based commentary that clearly shows learners what has been done effectively and what needs improvement. Well-constructed assessment includes two types of feedback: formative and summative.

Formative feedback is offered *in progress* throughout the creation of a learning product or as a learning task is being completed. In formative feedback, a teacher *intervenes* to guide the learner toward effective completion of a learning task. This means creating classroom time for guided practice where learners are attempting a task and the teacher is monitoring performance and offering guidance for improvement. Formative feedback can be delivered orally and informally as a teacher is circulating throughout the room as students work collaboratively or independently.

Formative feedback can also be provided in short, in-class conferencing where teachers create opportunities for one-on-one sessions with learners in a designated area of the classroom. Conferencing is considered one of the best ways to help learners improve, especially in challenging tasks.

Formative feedback should also include opportunities for improvement by returning to earlier levels of the learning task, redoing and revising based on feedback, and resubmission.

Summative feedback is delivered at the end of a major learning task. Where formative feedback allows learners to rework a learning product on the basis of clearly articulated suggestions for improvement, summative feedback identifies how the learning product met or did not meet learning objectives. Summative assessment has a place in classroom instruction if the expectations for the summative product are articulated at the beginning of a learning session or unit. A teacher can include summative assessment even in a single classroom lesson. For example, at the beginning of the class session, the agenda can include a list of learner expectations for takeaways at the end of the lesson. The teacher can set up the lesson to include a five-item objective quiz that learners will take at the end of the class session. During the lesson, the teacher can create learner readiness by reinforcing the content, vocabulary, operations, demonstrated understanding, and other evidences of comprehension that might be covered on the quiz.

Assessment in the ESL Classroom

Because ESL teachers have to teach content-area material while they are guiding students toward higher levels of linguistic proficiency, assessment of EL student learning takes on an added dimension. ESL teachers should routinely consult ELPS for cross-curricular skills and knowledge expectations as well as the listening, speaking, reading, and writing proficiency-level descriptors to devise assessments that focus on those student expectations. Let's consider what different types of assessment opportunities may look like in the ESL classroom and how they reflect the language domains and BICS and/or CALP.

Table 7.4.
Examples of ESL Assessment

Language Domain	Activity	Assessment Possibilities	BICS/CALP Support
Listening	Instructions for completing a learning task	Teacher can guide students to develop their listening skills by using markers such as *first, next, then, last*. Teacher can ask learners to repeat key elements of the instructions.	BICS and CALP
Speaking	Small group collaborative activity in heterogeneous, randomly created groups	To provide opportunities for oral language demonstration, the teacher can assign specific tasks within the group that must be completed by individual group members. The teacher can orchestrate in-group reporting by saying something like, "Okay, it's time for #1 to report the key vocabulary. #1, you have one minute to tell the group the three most important words from the paragraph." The teacher would continue until all the assigned tasks have been reported.	BICS and CALP
Reading	Targeted reading practice with designated end-of-reading tasks.	Teacher introduces the reading selection with a short talk to create anticipation, provides key content vocabulary with definitions, and alerts learners to key ideas that are in the passage. The teacher gives learners time to do a preliminary reading to get an overall sense of the content. Then, the teacher gives the class time to reread the passage, this time taking notes and annotating the text, and creating a graphic organizer to show main ideas. At the end, the teacher asks students to share strategies they used to comprehend difficult parts.	CALP
Writing	Students have been assigned a short narrative that recounts a time they learned an important lesson.	After students have completed the first draft, the teacher uses a mentor text to demonstrate variety in sentence structure. The teacher explains how using a variety of clauses to combine sentences improves the quality of the writing. Then students are given a revision task to combine at least two sets of sentences in their draft using the strategies the teacher demonstrated. The teacher circulates around the room to work individually with students as they revise their sentences.	CALP

Language Domain	Activity	Assessment Possibilities	BICS/CALP Support
Integrated	Students watch a film clip that illustrates a content-area concept they are currently studying.	To develop listening skills (including the importance of body language and gestures and facial expressions), the teacher has the students watch the clip with no sound and asks students to identify what they might anticipate learning about the concept when they watch the clip with the sound on. To develop speaking skills, the teacher has students do a think-pair-share activity to identify their major content-area takeaways from the clip. To develop writing skills, students do a quickwrite explaining how the film helps them understand the concept. To develop reading skills, students work in small groups to read each other's summaries. They attach a sticky note to each classmate's quick write expressing what new ideas they got from reading the classmate's quick write.	CALP

In a well-constructed ESL classroom, assessment happens constantly. The necessary integration of content-area material in the context of developing listening, speaking, reading, and writing skills allows for ongoing attention to learner development in all areas.

ELs and STAAR Assessments

EL students must take content-area assessments mandated for all students in Texas public schools through the State of Texas Assessments Academic Readiness (STAAR):

- reading and mathematics, grades 3–8
- writing at grades 4 and 7
- science at grades 5 and 8
- social studies at grade 8
- end-of-course (EOC) assessments in high school for English I, English II, Algebra I, biology and U.S. history

(TEA, 2019, STAAR Resources)

As mandated by ESSA, EL students must meet state standards in content areas. In other words, unless students request and qualify for testing accommodations, EL students take the same content STAAR exams as non-EL students. STAAR Spanish is available in grades 3–5 in reading, writing, mathematics, and science, but this is an accommodation that must be requested and approved by the LPAC. The LPAC is charged with determining whether STAAR testing in Spanish is appropriate for individual learners based on their current performance records. Accommodations for EL students in the STAAR exams are not automatic; the accommodations must be requested and must meet the criteria established by TEC and TEA for accommodations. Other requested accommodations must be accommodations that are already in place for the learner in regular classroom instruction, such as accommodations for special education. Additionally, the LPAC must determine whether requested accommodations are appropriate based on the student's current LEP designation (TEA, 2018; TEA, 2019, Accommodations Resources).

Linguistic accommodations, such as those discussed in earlier chapters and mentioned in ELPS, are pedagogical adjustments intended to enhance EL students' participation in classroom activities, to promote content-area learning, and to continually develop English proficiency. Linguistic accommodations reflect the ESL teachers' knowledge and skills in teaching EL students and thus are managed by the individual classroom teacher. On the other hand, accommodations for exams reflect federal and state requirements intended to provide an equitable assessment environment for all learners and to enhance accessibility to test materials. EL students do not automatically receive accommodations; instead, TEA stipulates that such accommodations are available only to students who routinely require them in daily instruction. Testing accommodations available include the following:

- signing for deaf or hard of hearing students,

- translation, bilingual dictionaries,

- assistance in reading parts of the test,

- assistive tools such as scratch paper, color overlays, amplification devices,

- stress reducing tools,

- individual or small group test administration.

(TEA, 2019, 2019–2020 Accessibility Features)

Summary, Action Plan, and Chapter 7 Wrap-Up

Competency 007 brings into focus the need to align mandated state assessments in ESL with classroom instruction. ESL teachers should consider the descriptors in ELPS as a data-bank of potential teaching activities, asking themselves, "How can I turn this ELPS student expectation into a tangible, assessable classroom activity?" Doing so will demonstrate the ability to connect state-level expectations with day-to-day activities in the classroom. Furthermore, the abundant performance data provided by the LPAC for each student should guide teachers in crafting differentiated instruction to help each learner meet English proficiency goals.

As you move to the end of your Chapter 7 study, a major takeaway should be that assessment is not an add-on to instruction but is instead an integral component of effectively devised instruction that aims to promote content-area learning while fostering continued development of English proficiency.

Self-Check

1.   How are students designated as EL?

2.   What is TELPAS and how does it fit into the education of EL students in Texas?

3.   Why are ELPS important in ESL classroom instruction?

4.   How does content-area instruction in ESL classes impact student expectations for STAAR exams?

5.   What does *assessment* mean?

Study Plan

The realm of state-mandated assessment for EL students is vast, somewhat byzantine, and complex. Competency 007 establishes that ESL teachers should contextualize their classroom teaching within the state system of assessment. To do so, ESL teachers should attempt to construct a coherent understanding of the multiple components, state laws, teaching possibilities, and student expectations that shape the whole picture of teaching

ESL in Texas. To fully understand the teacher responsibilities presented in Competency 007, you should consult these resources:

1. *Supporting English Learners in Texas Web Portal*. This continually updated resource compiles and explains all facts and materials necessary to understand how EL students are supported in Texas public schools. Created by the Texas Education Agency, the site offers links to TEA pages relevant to teaching EL students, to TEC sections that establish state laws regarding the education of EL students, to instructional strategies for targeting ELPS student expectations, to materials for communicating with parents, and to a wealth of other resources vital to teaching ESL in Texas. The site is accessible directly from any search engine: type in Supporting English Learners in Texas.

2. TEA Academics tab, leading to Special Student Populations and then to Bilingual ESL Education sections. The complexity and expansiveness of requirements for ESL instruction in Texas should be an inducement to fully explore TEA materials on how ESL instruction is operationalized in public schools.

3. *Assessing English Language Learners: Bridges to Educational Equity*, 2nd ed. by Margo Gottlieb (2016). This book contextualizes actual classroom assessment activities within theory and best practices. Gottlieb demonstrates the instructional intentionality that should inform assessment practices. She clearly explains how the illustrations of assessment practices provided in each chapter reflect opportunities to foster learner growth in academic content *and* in linguistic proficiency.

Practice Items for Competency 007

1. Which of the following items is not an example of informal assessment?

   A. An entrance ticket to record a student's major takeaway from a homework reading assignment

   B. An end-of-unit exam

   C. Teacher responses to students' comments during whole-class discussion

   D. Teacher monitoring of collaborative classwork

The correct response is B. An end-of-unit exam is a typical example of formal, summative assessment; thus, it is *not* an informal assessment. Ideally, the end-of-unit exam reflects learning objectives articulated at the beginning of the unit, allowing learners to set individual learning goals and teachers to provide formative feedback throughout the activities of the unit. An end-of-unit exam score is also likely to be entered in the grading record for the designated grading period. Response A is incorrect because an entrance ticket *is* an example of an informal assessment designed to provide immediate, targeted feedback to learners on a low-stakes, designated task that could be redone if necessary. Response C is incorrect because teacher comments delivered during class discussion *are* highly informal, designed to offer just-in-time feedback to learners on their responses and general engagement. Additionally, in ESL environments, teacher responses to student comments during class discussion could be consciously constructed to support students' developing BICS. Response D is incorrect because "monitoring" suggests informal, formative assessment designed to promote both BICS and CALP. Response A, C, and D are actually good examples of informal assessment; the stem asks for a response that is *not* a model of informal assessment.

2. Which of the following explanations most effectively explains the role of TELPAS in ESL teaching in Texas?

   A. TELPAS is designed to ensure EL students are college ready when they graduate from high school.

   B. TELPAS implements standards for ESL teaching from the U.S. Department of Education.

   C. TELPAS reflects locally-developed ESL assessments that reflect the percentage of EL students in the district and their specific needs.

   D. TELPAS annually assesses the progress that EL students make in English proficiency in language programs in Texas public schools.

The correct response is D. TELPAS is the state-mandated exam for assessing the yearly progress of students in ESL and other language programs in Texas. TELPAS scores in listening, speaking, reading, and writing are major considerations in determining EL students' readiness to exit language programs and move into mainstream classrooms. Response A is incorrect because TELPAS is not tied to state college and career readiness standards. Response B is incorrect because TELPAS is a state program. Response C is incorrect because local districts do not impact the content or creation of TELPAS.

PART III: DOMAIN III

Foundations of ESL Education, Cultural Awareness, and Family and Community Involvement

Foundations of ESL Education, Cultural Awareness, and Family and Community Involvement

■ Overview of Domain III

Domain III addresses ESL issues beyond the immediacy of the classroom. Domain III enables us to view ESL education in America from a historical lens that sharpens the exigencies of classroom interactions. Domain III completes the full picture of the 10 competencies for English as a Second Language ESL (154) by showing how ESL instruction must reflect the environment beyond the classroom as an integral component of effective learning for EL students.

Domain III Competencies

Domain III includes three competencies that allow ESL teachers to contextualize classroom teaching within the historical, social, and political frameworks relevant to ESL education. Competency 008 includes four descriptive statements (A–D) on the historical and political origins of ESL instruction. Competency 009 includes five descriptive statements (A–E) focused on contextualizing ESL instruction within the egalitarianism of multiculturalism. Competency 010 includes four descriptive statements (A–D) on community scaffolding for EL students and their parents. The competencies of Domain III suggest professional responsibilities that extend beyond the knowledge and pedagogical responsibilities of Domain I and Domain II (Pearson, 2019a).

> **Competency 008:** The ESL teacher understands the foundations of ESL education and types of ESL programs.

Competency 009: The ESL teacher understands factors that affect ESL students' learning and implements strategies for creating an effective multicultural and multilingual learning environment.

Competency 010: The ESL teacher knows how to serve as an advocate for ESL students and facilitate family and community involvement in their education.

Core Content from Domain III Competencies

As you work through Chapter 8, Chapter 9, and Chapter 10, carefully read and annotate these three competencies and descriptive statements in Domain III from your ESL (154) preparation materials. Underline key terms, mark terms you do not know, and pay special attention to the terms in parentheses and terms presented in syntactic series because those provide very specific indicators of the parameters of the competency.

Table D3.1.
Core Content from ESL 154 Domain III

Competency # and General Topic	Core Ideas from Descriptive Statements
008 Historical context of ESL education (4 descriptive statements)	• Policy foundations • Historical and theoretical background of ESL instruction • Types of ESL programs implemented in Texas • Connecting research to planning and instruction
009 Multiculturalism (5 descriptive statements)	• Understandings of the framework of multiculturalism • Connections between learner diversity and instruction • Creation of a multicultural classroom space • Culturally responsive teaching
010 Advocacy in ESL instruction (4 descriptive statements)	• Knowledge of state supports for implementing ESL instruction • Cultivating and supporting family engagement • Integrating community resources

Standard II and Standard VII of the English as a Second Language (ESL) Standards are aligned with Domain III. Standard II reflects the content of Competency 008 and Competency 009. Standard VII reflects the content of Competency 010 (SBEC, 2001, pp. 2, 7).

According to the English as a Second Language Supplemental (154) Preparation Materials website, 30 percent of the exam items will be based on Domain III (Pearson, 2019a).

Competency 008

Competency 008: Foundations of ESL Education

The ESL teacher understands the foundations of ESL education and types of ESL programs (Pearson, 2019a).

Competency 008, subdivided into four descriptive statements (A–D), covers the following general topics:

- The historical framework for ESL education

- Policies relevant to ESL education

- Theoretical frameworks that impact ESL education

- Types of ESL programs

- Connection between research and classroom ESL instruction

Competency 008 allows us to consider how ESL instruction is shaped by the rich history of ESL education in America. Competency 008 guides ESL teachers toward the understanding that nothing about ESL instruction is arbitrary or haphazardly implemented. ESL instruction reflects laws, policies, research, and practice intended to create equity, sustainability, and fairness in education provided to learners whose first language is a language other than English.

Competency 008 Core Content

The following key terms from the Competency 008 descriptive statements and from Standard II are integral to fully understanding the scope of Competency 008.

Table 8.1.
Competency 008 Core Content

foundations of ESL education	ESL history	ESL theory
ESL policy	ESL programs	self-contained
pull-out	newcomer	dual language
immersion	research relevant to ESL education	instructional practices based on research

Historical Framework for ESL Education

The day-to-day teaching we see in Texas ESL classrooms can be traced to a complex history rooted in immigration and civil rights legislation. Currently, language support programs in U.S. schools reflect the 2015 Every Student Succeeds Act (ESSA) which is a reauthorization of the 1965 Elementary and Secondary Education Act (U.S. Department of Education, 2017). Competency 008.A establishes a connection between history, theory, and policy and ESL education. Knowing the provenance of ESL education enables ESL teachers to appreciate the efforts involved in securing special pedagogical rights for students who need to learn English while they are trying to succeed in school.

Through the late nineteenth century into current times, there have been immigration "waves" into the U.S. triggered by homeland economic, environmental, and political crises. As these new arrivals to the U.S. integrated into economic and social systems, immigration acts were imposed to control the influx through immigration quotas, a literacy test, cognitive and physical requirements, and moral "standards" for admission (Gonzalez, Yawkey, & Minaya-Rowe, 2006, pp. 12–21). The Immigration and Naturalization Act of 1965 (subsequently revisited with reform measures in 1986 and 1990) attempted to remedy the discriminatory nature of existing immigration laws by eliminating quota systems. Issues such as the notable impact of immigrants on U.S. demographics, rising numbers of illegal entries, and the immigrant backlash caused after the terrorist attacks on the U.S. homeland on September 11, 2001, have made immigration a politically divisive topic (A&E Television Networks, 2020d).

Regardless of public and political battles over immigration, one constant has remained: the need to educate the children of immigrants and to provide appropriate language support. A number of milestones shape the history of public education of young people whose main language is not English, milestones that clearly link equity in public education to civil and political rights guaranteed by the Constitution:

- *Plessy v. Ferguson* (1896). This case established the separate but equal doctrine that enabled segregation in public settings, including public schools. Homer Plessy, an African American, argued that segregation of public transportation facilities constituted violation of the Equal Protection Clause in the 14th Amendment. Ultimately, the U.S. Supreme Court ruled that separate facilities were not *per se* inferior although they could be perceived as such by individuals. The *Plessy v. Ferguson* decision sanctioned "separate but equal" facilities in interstate commerce, hotels, public buildings, swimming pools, and schools, a circumstance that persisted until the 1950s and 1960s when the advent of the civil rights movement brought the policy under scrutiny. (A&E Television Networks, 2020c)

- *Brown v. Board of Education of Topeka* (1954). This landmark U.S. Supreme Court case reversed the separate but equal doctrine. Brought by Oliver Brown whose daughter had been denied access to all-white schools in Topeka, Kansas, the suit was originally rejected, but Brown appealed. The Supreme Court, in a unanimous decision, found the separate but equal doctrine in schools was a violation of the 14th Amendment. The immediate result of the *Brown v. Board* outcome was a court order mandating desegregation in public schools (A&E Television Networks, 2020a; Gonzalez, Yawkey, Minaya-Rowe, 2006, p. 62). However, the *Brown v. Board of Education* ruling did not result in immediate desegregation of schools; in fact, it triggered resistance to desegregation efforts, fueling the civil rights movement. Furthermore, Brown addressed desegregation; language support, as a right of limited English proficient students in an equitable society, was addressed in later cases.

- Civil Rights Act of 1964. This landmark act was initiated by President John F. Kennedy and brought to completion by President Lyndon B. Johnson. It ended segregation in public places, including schools, and prohibited discrimination on the basis of race, color, religion, sex, or national origin (A&E Television Networks, 2020b). The inclusion of "national origin" in the list of banned reasons for discrimination set the stage for cases that saw failure to provide language programs for students who lacked English proficiency as a form of linguistic discrimination.

- Elementary and Secondary Education Act (1965). Initially passed in 1965, this act has been amended numerous times, the latest revision being the 2015 reauthorization as the Every Student Succeeds Act. The stated purpose of the original act was "to strengthen and improve educational quality and educational opportunities in the Nation's elementary and secondary schools" (U.S. Congress, 1965). Although the initial version of this important legislation did not establish the need for language programs, it recognized that special circumstances for disadvantaged children and other populations of learners had to be factored into efforts to provide educational equity. This act also set up protocols for state educational agencies to receive funds to enact measures in this legislation.

- Bilingual Education Act of 1968 (BEA). This amendment to the original 1965 ESEA can probably be cited as the catalyst for the initiation of formalized language programs in U.S. schools. Title VII of the original act was reconstructed as the Bilingual Education Act and established as U.S. policy funding to:

  > provide financial assistance to local educational agencies to develop and carry out new and imaginative elementary and secondary school programs designed to meet these special educational needs. For the purposes of this title, "children of limited English speaking ability" means children who come from environments where the dominant language is other than English. (U.S. Congress, 1968)

  The BEA included provisions for regions with high concentrations of children of limited English speaking ability, funding opportunities for training teachers, establishing educational programs, and partnering with parents. BEA drew much-needed attention and potential funding to the language needs of children of limited English speaking ability, but critics also saw the language of the bill as creating a culture of deficiency by conflating poverty, social neediness, cultural difference, and limited language ability as situations that needed to be "remedied" by federal funding and regulations (Del Valle, 2003, p. 226–228).

- *U.S. v. Texas* (1971). Originating with a U.S. Department of Health, Education, and Welfare investigation into allegations that several small Texas school districts were in fact segregated, the case ended with a federal court ordering that TEA oversee and report on desegregation in public schools in Texas. Extending to transfer of students from one school site to another, busing routes, delineation of school boundaries, hiring of faculty, extracurricular activities, and mandates for language programs, this case is considered one of the most extensive desegregation orders in legal history. The original court decision stated that

TEA and Texas as a whole was violating the Civil Rights Act of 1964 (Del Valle, 2003, pp. 233–234; United States v. State of Texas, 1971; Kemerer, 2017). This case has undergone numerous challenges, resulting in a reversal in 2010, but according to the most recent TEA website statement on the case, the details of the reversal decision are still being legally determined:

> Texas has been subject to a federal court statewide desegregation order since 1971. Over the past several years, several interventions have resulted in trials before the court relating to student transfers under the order and the provision of services to limited English proficient students. Pursuant to an order of the Fifth Circuit Court of Appeals in March of 2010, all Texas school districts except the original nine defendant districts have been released from the Court's order. On October 31, 2012, the Texas Attorney General's Office and the United States Department of Justice jointly moved to dismiss the part of the case involving the 1971 order eliminating a dual school system, which was granted by the Court. Texas school districts are no longer subject to the order. The state has moved to dismiss the remaining intervention in the case involving bilingual education and is awaiting the Court's ruling. (TEA, 2019, Civil Action 5281)

- *Lau v. Nichols* (1974). *Lau v. Nichols* was a class action suit that started as a suit by a specific Chinese American student in San Francisco but extended to a whole community who contended that "equal" facilities, curriculum, and materials did not afford equal opportunity to succeed for students who could not speak English. Drawing on segments of the Civil Rights Act of 1964, the Supreme Court ruled that school systems were obligated to equalize the educational field by addressing the language needs of non-English speakers to allow them to participate meaningfully and equitably in educational experiences (U.S. Department of Education, 2019, Developing Programs; Del Valle, 2003, pp. 236–240). *Lau v. Nichols* is considered a landmark ruling in the history of language-support education because it called attention to the ingrained inequities in education. At the heart of this case was the plaintiffs' contention that expecting students to meet graduation standards without providing language support for non-native speakers of English constituted discrimination. Additionally, after the ruling, the U.S. Department of Education Office of Civil Rights (OCR) implemented "Lau remedies" intended to direct school districts in meeting the needs of LEP students; however, those remedies were not universally or readily implemented (Wright, 2015, p. 84).

- Equal Educational Opportunities Act (1974). The EEOA primarily addressed the inappropriateness of using busing as a tool toward desegregation. One condition of the bill was seen as a mandate for bilingual and other language programs. However, subsequent court challenges demonstrated the broad legal interpretation possible for the phrase "appropriate action," essentially giving school districts the flexibility to present almost any program as "appropriate" or, conversely, to read the phrase as a requirement for bilingual education programs (Haas, 2019; Del Valle, 2003, p. 243; Wright, 2015, pp. 84). The actual wording of the "appropriate action" clause is as follows:

  §1703. Denial of equal educational opportunity prohibited

  No State shall deny equal educational opportunity to an individual on account of his or her race, color, sex, or national origin, by (f) the failure by an educational agency to take appropriate action to overcome language barriers that impede equal participation by its students in its instructional programs. (United States Code, 1974)

- *Castañeda v. Pickard* (1981). This case originated in Raymondville, a small South Texas town about 50 miles from the U.S.-Mexico border. The "Castañeda test" has become a measuring stick for determining the viability of language programs. This case centered on the de facto segregative outcome of classes based on "ability grouping" determined by achievement test scores. The plaintiffs argued that test scores skewed groupings such that Hispanic students were segregated into classes based on low scores while white students with higher scores went into the top level classes. Furthermore, the suit contended that the testing system that determined the ability category did not take into account the fact that Spanish-dominant children could not adequately demonstrate *ability* on a test administered in English; thus, the ability grouping was based not on ability but on language proficiency which ultimately demonstrated the district's racial and language-based discriminatory practices. And, the suit included, if students were segregated in order to offer language instruction, the grouping would be appropriate; however, the district was not using the ability grouping to support and develop language proficiency. The upshot of the 1981 Supreme Court decision, which found in favor of the plaintiffs, was the now famous three-pronged Castañeda test: (1) Is the program based on sound educational theory? (2) Are sufficient resources and personnel expended to implement the program? (3) Are evaluative measures in place to assess efficacy of the program in developing students' proficiency in English? While the decision seemed to favor the needs of language minority children, the three prongs have proved to be fluid and easy to negotiate and interpret to meet district propensities in language program initiatives (Del Valle, 2003, pp. 245–247; *Castañeda v. Pickard*, 1981).

- *Plyler v. Doe* (1982). This case also originated in Texas after the state legislature enacted a policy to deny public school enrollment to immigrant children who were not "legally admitted" to the U.S. and when some school districts set up enrollment restrictions requiring immigrant children to produce documentation that they were legally in the U.S. or in the process of acquiring legal status. The final Supreme Court decision, based on the 14th Amendment, established that immigrant children could not be denied public school education. The court also explored the argument that resources expended on educating immigrant children harmed the overall functionality of school districts, finding instead that *not* educating immigrant children would cause greater harm to the children and to U.S. society as a whole. School districts in many states have enforced the *Plyler v. Doe* decision by collecting information on immigrant school children which has the effect of absenteeism or complete withdrawal from the school system (American Immigration Council, 2016). In response to apparent school district efforts to circumvent the ruling, many state and federal agencies and organizations provide material and other support to immigrant families to ensure they know their children's educational rights.

- No Child Left Behind Act (2002). This reauthorization of the 1965 ESEA is notable for requirements that schools offer specific programs to equalize the educational field for students, including immigrant children with linguistic, economic, and/or other special circumstances, that highly qualified teachers be in classrooms, and that districts document average yearly progress toward supporting all students meet required state academic standards. Title III of NCLB (formerly Title VII), Language Instruction for Limited English Proficient and Immigrant Children, was marked by a focus on helping students with linguistic needs meet state academic standards, but as some researchers point out, created a deficit view of students from different language backgrounds (NCLB, 2002; Wright, 2015, pp. 73–75). This legislation emphasized the teaching of English without making reference to other programs like bilingual or dual language instruction.

- Every Student Succeeds Act (2015). In 2015, ESSA is the 50-year reauthorization of the 1965 ESEA. Title III, retitled as Language Instruction for English Learners and Immigrant Students, is highly focused on instruction for helping students meet proficiency in English, including identifying proficiency levels (U.S. Department of Education, 2017). TEA documents and presentations on implementation of ESSA focus on the new flexibility that this act provides in enabling states and local districts to integrate statute requirements into the state vision of education for all children and young people. TEA's state strategic plan includes four strands that reflect ESSA: (1) recruit, retain, and support teachers and principals; (2) build a foundation of reading and math; (3) connect high school to career and college; (4) improve low-performing schools (TEA, 2017).

The History of ESL Education in the U.S.

Holistically, the story of ESL education in the U.S. appears to be a series of milestones toward recognition that speaking a first language other than English is not a deficiency or a fault in the learner. Many of the early legal cases were triggered by challenges to deeply entrenched English-only or white-dominant policies that marginalized or completely ignored the educational needs of L1 learners in an L2 environment. For most of the court cases, the arguments hinged on rights guaranteed by the 14th Amendment and civil rights legislation. Unfortunately, the language of many of the court decisions cited above in our historical timeline of ESL education in the U.S. included language that reinforced stereotypes about students whose first language is not English, about poverty, about underrepresentation, and about socioeconomic status. Additionally, many court decisions and subsequent federal policies were initially interpreted as mandates for *bilingual* programs, with dual attention to literacy in two languages. However, periodic reauthorizations of ESEA via NCLB in 2002 and ESSA in 2015 mandate programs to support English proficiency that leads to academic success, but the laws do not stipulate support in the native language (Wright, 2015, pp. 84–87). In Texas, ESL teachers have a vast, comprehensive system of research-based language programs for EL students, supported by specific state laws in the TEC and TAC and prolifically operationalized by TEA.

Types of ESL Programs

The scope and breadth of bilingual and ESL programs in Texas clearly indicate the state's commitment to fully support EL students' journey through the state's public education system. Requirements for bilingual and ESL education are codified in the Texas Administrative Code and the Texas Education Code, in great detail, and are implemented by TEA. Furthermore, the TEA website offers continually updated materials on all aspects of EL education in Texas. Teachers have access to resources from TEA that address every aspect of teaching ESL.

As mandated by TAC §89.1210. Program Content and Design and by TEC Subchapter B. Bilingual Education and Special Language Programs Sec. 29.066, Texas schools offer two broad language programs for students identified as English learners: (1) bilingual programs delivered in four distinct models and (2) ESL programs delivered in two distinct models:

Table 8.2.
Language Programs in Texas Public Schools

Bilingual Programs	
Transitional bilingual/ early exit	• Instruction in both English and another language • Goal: meet reclassification criteria for English-only instruction no earlier than two years or later than five years after student enrolls • Teacher is certified in bilingual education instruction in assigned grade level and content area • Instructional delivery method: students use L1 while acquiring full proficiency in English • Program provides instruction in literacy and academic content in L1 and targets L2 development through academic content
Transitional bilingual/ late exit	• Instruction in both English and another language • Goal: meet reclassification criteria for English-only instruction no earlier than six years or later than seven years after student enrolls • Teacher is certified in bilingual education instruction in assigned grade level and content area • Instructional delivery method: students use L1 while acquiring full proficiency in English • Program provides instruction in literacy and academic content in L1 and targets L2 development through academic content
Dual language immersion/ one way	• Bilingual/biliteracy program • Instruction in both English and a language other than English • Classes composed only of students identified as LEP • Goal: meet reclassification criteria for English-only instruction no earlier than six years or later than seven years after student enrolls • Instruction in another language is delivered by teacher certified in bilingual education • Instruction in English is delivered by teacher certified in bilingual education or by a teacher certified in ESL • Instructional goal: students attain full proficiency in English and another language • Program provides instruction in literacy and academic content in English and another language • Non-English/English delivery ratio: at least half of the instruction in the non-English language

(continued)

Bilingual Programs	
Dual language immersion/ two way	• Bilingual/biliteracy program • Instruction in both English and another language • Classes composed of students identified as LEP and students proficient in English • Goal: LEP students meet reclassification criteria for English-only instruction no earlier than six years or later than seven years after student enrolls • Instruction in a language other than English is delivered by teacher certified in bilingual education for the assigned grade level and content area • Instruction in English is delivered by teacher certified in bilingual education or by a teacher certified in ESL for the assigned grade level and content area • Instructional goal: students attain full proficiency in English and a language other than English • Program provides instruction in literacy and academic content in English and a language other than English • Language delivery ratio: at least half of the instruction in non-English program language
ESL Programs	
ESL/ content-based	• English acquisition program for students identified as EL • Goal: students acquire full proficiency in English • Teacher is certified in ESL instruction • Instructional delivery method: linguistically and culturally responsive instruction in English language arts and reading, mathematics, science, and social studies
ESL/ pull-out	• English acquisition program for students identified as EL • Students participate in mainstream content-area classes • Goal: students acquire full proficiency in English • Teacher is certified in ESL instruction • Instructional delivery method: linguistically and culturally responsive instruction in English language arts and reading in pull-out or inclusionary delivery

(TAC, 1996, Chapter 89.1210 TEA, 2018, Supporting English Learners)

Language Program Points to Remember

- The home language survey is the starting point in channeling a student into the appropriate language program. When parents indicate that the primary language spoken at home and used by the child is a language other than English, the language program identification protocol is activated for the learner.

- Students identified as LEP on the basis of the state-approved English language proficiency test administered within four weeks of entry into a Texas school are evaluated by the LPAC to determine the appropriate bilingual or ESL program for the student's individual language learning needs.

- Bilingual programs are dual language programs, meaning that instruction is delivered in L1 and L2 with the goal of biliteracy and proficiency in both languages upon exit from the program and reclassi-fication as non-EL.

- ESL programs are aimed at developing students' English proficiency to a point where they can exit the language program and be mainstreamed into content-area classes. In Texas, exit from an ESL program depends on being assessed at the advanced high ELPS level via the TELPAS and the other assessment measures overseen by LPAC.

- In ESL programs, whether content-based or pull-out, English is the language of instructional delivery. ESL programs rely on L1 for lin-guistic accommodation when appropriate.

Program Distinctiveness

Within the state-mandated, legislatively-defined language programs, there are other dis-tinctions that allow teachers to further tailor instruction to meet student needs.

- Newcomer programs allow teachers to factor into instruction the spe-cial needs of recently arrived immigrant school-aged children gen-erally at elementary and middle school levels with acculturation as a pivotal goal of the program (Echevarria & Graves, 2010, p. 7). The U.S. Department of Education subdivides newcomers into catego-ries that include English learners, asylees, students with interrupted formal education, unaccompanied youth, and foreign-born (2017, pp. 1–3). Individual schools and districts sometimes construct new-comer programs in cases where newcomer populations are extensive and resources allow specialized attention to recent immigrant students. Newcomer programs can be housed within schools or in separate loca-tions. In the absence of specialized newcomer programs, newcomers are integrated into existing language programs. Language learning spe-cialists recognize that beyond language proficiency skills, newcomers, especially when their immigration to the U.S. reflects traumatic home-land circumstances or limited education, need substantive support in socialization and acclimating to an entirely new land, new home, new culture, and new language. To address the needs of newcomers at the high school level, in 2017, the state implemented a high school level language development and acquisition course "to provide instructional opportunities for secondary recent immigrant students with little or no English proficiency" (TEA, 2017, §128.36).

- The TEC/TAC sanctioned learning programs for bilingual education in Texas are classified as dual language/immersion programs. "Immer-sion" typically refers to language programs in which students are learning L2 while also learning content in L2. Immersion programs are aimed at supporting bilingualism and biliteracy which means that instruction and classroom experiences occur in both languages. Immersion programs clearly rely on L1 support and transfer as natural routes to L2 literacy and learning. The efficacy of immersion programs seems obvious when contrasted with "submersion" approaches, "sink-or-swim" approaches where learners are provided no support in their linguistic, academic, and affective language learning efforts. Federal laws such as ESSA ensure that students in need of language support in U.S. schools are never subjected to this approach. (Diaz-Rico, 2013, pp. 316–323)

- The ESL programs established by TAC and TEC are both content-based and pull-out programs. In content-based classes, EL students receive content-area instruction delivered by a content-area specialist (a teacher certified in the subject, such as math or social studies) who is also certified in ESL. Ideally, the teacher uses a sheltered instruction approach (which we describe in the next section of this chapter) or other research-based approaches that support learners' comprehensible input linguistically and academically. In pull-out approaches, students are literally "pulled out" of mainstream content-area classes for targeted instruction in English intended to support their learning of academic content. The two ESL models support different EL student needs.

Competency 008.B, C, and D underscore the importance of having comprehensive understanding of ESL program and instructional approaches so as to construct the best, most effective classroom experiences for EL students.

From Research to Effective ESL Programs

A consistent point in the court decisions and federal laws regarding language programs for students of limited English ability is the requirement that education programs be research-based. The instructional strategies presented in the Domain II competencies which focused on content-area teaching, communicative and literacy development, and assessment all reflect research-based teaching. Research-based teaching of EL students reflects some pillars of ESL teaching.

- Transfer. In SLA, transfer refers to the learner's ability to use L1 linguistic and cognitive abilities to construct new learning in L2. Research shows that learners who have strong L1 academic backgrounds learn L2 academic content more readily. Communicative or conversational L2 learning is promoted by high levels of meaningful interaction with L2 speakers. Research, such as the work of Cummins and of Krashen, shows that the intuitively-acquired L1 communication and interaction skills have a high-level of transfer in L2 learning. For ESL teachers, these research findings suggest that opportunities for listening and speaking should be supported through informal and formal group learning, through on-going teacher-student conversation in class interaction, and through astute pedagogy that recognizes times when L1 support may facilitate the learning activity. Research also shows that strategies that integrate L1 vocabulary, translations, or texts are robust, prolific linguistic accommodations.

- Interlanguage. The construct of interlanguage, which we discussed in Chapter 2, posits that learners construct idiosyncratic forms of "mid" or "bridge" language systems as they acquire more and more L2 proficiency. Interlanguages are learner-specific and constantly changing as new knowledge is acquired. Selinker and Corder, the researchers associated with this classic concept, saw interlanguages as approximations that clearly point to the learner's competence as new L2 forms are acquired. For teachers, this puts a highly positive cast on error, which comes to be seen not as misses but as linguistic risk-taking that demonstrates growing knowledge (Bartholomae, 1980). Chapter 1 covered the basic linguistic knowledge that enables teachers to recognize what a learner is doing linguistically and offer guidance toward accessing and producing the targeted form. Knowledge of the interlanguage construct enables teachers to create activities such as sentence frames and models that accommodate learners' current knowledge and guide them toward the next level in application of Vygotsky's ZPD and Krashen's $i + 1$ concept where "expert" speakers serve as models and mentors for the learner.

Sheltered Instruction

To guide EL students toward comprehension and achievement in content areas, classroom instruction must be constructed adeptly around activities that support the learner's needs. In **sheltered instruction**, the EL student learns content-area material while also acquiring increased proficiency in L2. Echevarría and Graves, the researchers and practitioners who developed the sheltered instruction model, point out that the approaches associated with sheltered instruction are generically strong pedagogical practices which are seen in all classrooms, ESL or regular. This holistic model of instruction for ELs is known as the Sheltered Instruction Observation Protocol (SIOP), a framework that includes eight components: lesson preparation, building background, comprehensible input, strategies, interaction, practice and application, delivery, and assessment (Echevarría & Graves, 2010, pp. 51–53).

The sheltered instruction approach reminds us that EL students can easily be excluded or marginalized when content-area material is incomprehensible. Using sheltered instruction as an approach to ESL learning enables teachers to consistently create instructional scenarios that enable EL students to have meaningful, inclusive, comprehensible learning experiences in content-area classrooms:

Table 8.3.
Sheltered Instruction Examples

Teacher Activity/Plan	Impact on EL Learner
Content *and* language objectives for each lesson	Learner knows specific behavioral objective for the lesson
Supplementary materials such as models, graphs, technology support	Learner receives scaffolded instruction
Teacher talk is reduced to allow greater interaction with learners	Learner is able to demonstrate understanding, to ask questions, to interact with teacher and classmates
Teacher speech reflects simpler vocabulary, simpler syntax, reiteration of content-specific concepts, slower delivery pace, gestures, movement, and reinforcement with visuals	Learner is able to follow a content-area lecture
Teacher uses interactive techniques such as modeling, hands-on applications, visuals	Learner participates actively in constructing new knowledge
Teacher presents and defines key vocabulary and uses overhead or board to reinforce vocabulary and definitions in writing	Learner acquires terminology foundational to the content area
Teacher uses appropriate wait time during discussions	Learner anxiety about "right" answers is reduced and learner is given adequate time to process a response
Teacher paces the lesson through learner-appropriate segmenting, guided practice, application, group activities, and independent work	Learner has time to process new learning while working actively with classmates
Teacher introduces new content using visual supports, prior knowledge	Learner enters the realm of new content with accommodations to support acquisition of new knowledge
Teacher makes appropriate linguistic accommodations such as providing sentence frames, models, relevant supporting materials, realia, and manipulatives	Learners participate actively in constructing content knowledge as they acquire higher levels of English proficiency

(adapted from Echevarría & Graves, 2010, pp. 51–60)

TEA supports the sheltered instruction approach as is shown by the extensive training available for teachers through the Sheltered Instruction Training Series offered through Texas Gateway for online resources (TEA, 2019). This is the explanation of sheltered instruction offered as an entry point to the extensive training materials and courses webpage available through the Supporting English Learners in Texas web portal:

Sheltered instruction is an instructional approach that uses various strategies to ensure that grade-level instruction provided in English addresses both content and language objectives. Through sheltered instruction, students master the required essential knowledge and skills and become proficient in the English language. (TEA, 2018)

Summary, Action Plan, and Chapter 8 Wrap-Up

Competency 008 covers an extensive body of information necessary for effective construction and delivery of ESL instruction. Individual ESL teachers may not know all the details of federal laws related to ESL instruction, but TEA offers abundant support to ensure that all federal and legal requirements are met. Teachers, however, should be fully aware of the continuing evolution of support for civil and educational rights for students whose primary language is not English. Additionally, although federal and state laws regarding ESL programs are enforced by TEA and local administrators, individual teachers are the ones who actually operationalize ESL theory and research in day-to-day classroom practice.

Self-Check

1. Think about constructing a timeline of the history of ESL in the U.S. Try doing this using your general understanding of the dates when the ESL milestones happened. Then, go back and fill in the details that you need to remember. Keep in mind that the dates and cases and federal laws matter in charting the route of where things started and where we are now in ESL education.

2. Can you explain the significance of key court cases such as Lau, Castañeda, Plyler, cases and decisions which have significantly influenced language programs in the U.S.?

3. What ESL programs are in place in Texas as stipulated by the Texas Administrative Code (TAC) and the Texas Education Code (TEC)?

4. Can you explain the difference between bilingual and ESL instruction?

5. Explain why research matters in devising sound instructional approaches and strategies for ESL instruction?

6. How is TEA involved in implementing federal regulations relevant to language programs in Texas public schools?

Study Plan

1. Spend some time exploring the U.S. Department of Education web pages on ESSA, NCLB, and other laws relevant to ESL instruction. The U.S. Department of Education offers almost unending links to additional information from top quality organizations and agencies that fully explain terms, concepts, and policies in ESL.

2. Check out TEA's Supporting English Learners in Texas web portal. It includes up-to-date information and links to just about every aspect of working with EL students in Texas. This prolific site is accessible via TEA or by doing a search using your search engine.

3. You should recognize how the legal language of ESSA and court cases is "translated" into robust teaching practices. With your knowledge of federal requirements in mind, look carefully at comprehensive presentations of ESL teaching in books such as the following:

    Strategies for Teaching English Learners, 3rd ed. by Lynne T. Diaz-Rico (2013) contextualizes ESL classroom practice within teaching and learning theory and research. The chapters that focus on what ESL teaching *looks like* in the classroom include abundant graphics and examples to clearly show how to turn theory and research into practice.

    In *ESL Teaching: Principles for Success,* by Yvonne S. Freeman, David E. Freeman, Mary Soto, and Ann Ebe (2016), each chapter starts with extended examples of real students in real learning environments. The authors then backtrack and clearly link the example to relevant theory and research.

    English-as-a-Second-Language (ESL) Teaching and Learning by Virginia Gonzalez, Thomas Yawkey, and Liliana Minaya-Rowe (2006) is a good source for intensifying your understanding of the history of language education in the U.S. The first two chapters contextualize the evolution of language programs within immigration history and demographics.

Practice Items for Competency 008

1. Which of the following statements correctly represents a key aspect of ESSA?

    A. ESSA gives Local Educational Agencies (LEA's) significant autonomy in implementing the bill's requirements for language instruction.

    B. ESSA is a complete revision of the Bilingual Education Act of 1968.

    C. ESSA requires that bilingual education be taught in at least 10% of school districts in every state.

    D. ESSA requires that states implement language programs to help language learners prepare for high levels of achievement in academic programs.

The correct response is D. ESSA places responsibility for implementing language programs in the hands of state agencies; furthermore, ESSA, unlike NCLB, focuses on high levels of achievement in academic programs. NCLB language was geared toward meeting state standards and providing documentation of average yearly progress. Response A is incorrect because ESSA places responsibility for implementing the act with state educational agencies. In Texas, that means that TEA has responsibility for guiding districts to appropriately and fully implement ESSA. Response B is incorrect because ESSA is a reauthorization of the full Elementary and Secondary Education Act of 1965; the Bilingual Education Act refers to a limited segment of ESEA. Response C is incorrect because ESSA does not mandate bilingual education.

2. Which of the following correctly explains the English-L1 instructional ratio in ESL programs?

   A. In ESL classes, there is no set ratio for English-L1 instruction; instead, state documents refer to linguistically and culturally responsive instruction.

   B. In ESL classes, where English is the language of instructional delivery, teachers are not allowed to use L1 in instruction.

   C. In ESL classes, teachers devote at least 50% of instructional delivery to L1 instruction and practice.

   D. In ESL classes, teachers start with 90% instruction in L1 and gradually move to 100% instruction in English.

Response A is correct. While state descriptions of dual language programs state that at least 50% of instruction must be in the non-English language, ESL programs do not include ratios for integrating L1 support. Instead, the TAC §89.1210 states that ESL instruction should be "linguistically and culturally responsive," indicating that the individual teacher has significant discretion in using L1 support. Response B is not supported in any aspect of state documents relevant to content and design for language programs. Additionally, B contradicts a principle of linguistic accommodation: that L1 support can be used productively to make L2 input comprehensible for learners. Response C is incorrect because at least 50% instruction in L1 is a requirement for the dual language bilingual programs not for the ESL programs. Response D is incorrect because in ESL programs in Texas public schools, the integration of L1 support in the context of L2 teaching is modulated by the instructor's responsive teaching, not by a ratio.

Competency 009

9

Competency 009: Multicultural Environment

The ESL teacher understands factors that affect ESL students' learning and implements strategies for creating an effective multicultural and multilingual learning environment (Pearson, 2019a).

Competency 009 addresses teacher actions, attitudes, and behaviors that contribute to constructing a multicultural environment in ESL classrooms. Five descriptive statements (A–E) in this competency cover the following general topics:

- Factors that create learning diversity

- Connection between a multicultural classroom environment and learning

- Factors that can impede creation of a culturally responsive environment

- Demonstrating awareness of diversity

- Fostering respect for cultural diversity

One of the most amazing, enduring things about teaching—regardless of what students you are teaching, what subject you are teaching, or where in the U.S. you are teaching—is that when you step into a classroom, every single learner represents a different, unique life story. Competency 009 reminds us that out of that difference we can forge community. Multiculturalism is about helping learners find commonalities out of their diverse experiences.

Linguistic diversity such as is represented by the demographics of Texas public school students is a pillar of multiculturalism. TEA's Supporting English Learners in Texas web portal offers the following "snapshot" of multilingualism/multiculturalism in the state:

- Over 120 languages are represented in Texas public schools

- 90.25% (911,680) of the 1,010,756 English learners in Texas are Spanish speakers

- 1.61% (16,262) speak Vietnamese

- 1.17% (11,835) speak Arabic

- .51% (5,130) speak Urdu

- .47% (4,735) speak Mandarin Chinese

- .37% (3,749) speak Burmese

(TEA, 2018)

This data is from the 2016–2017 PEIMS but it gives us a strong indication of the diversity in Texas public school classrooms. This data focuses on EL students, those students who have been officially classified as LEP and are in language programs. The diversity is likely far more extensive when the entire school population of public school students is considered—students designated LEP as well as those who have diverse cultural and linguistic backgrounds but are not designated LEP. Competency 009 looks at affective factors that can substantively impact EL students' linguistic and academic learning.

Competency 009 Core Content

The following key terms reflect the core ideas in Competency 009. The seriations (the items in a series and the parenthetical statements) in the competency descriptors offer insights into the specifics that shape the core of this competency. Integrated in this list are terms from alignment with Standard II.

Table 9.1.
Competency 009 Core Content

multicultural learning environment	multilingual learning environment	cultural diversity	linguistic diversity
age	developmental characteristics	academic strengths	academic needs
learning styles	personality	sociocultural factors	home environment
attitude	exceptionalities	affective needs	linguistic needs
cognitive needs	stereotyping	prejudice	ethnocentrism
culturally responsive teaching	socioeconomic background	awareness of diversity	respect for diversity

Fostering Multiculturalism

Let's start with a working definition of multiculturalism.

> Multiculturalism is the mindset of inclusivity and diversity aimed at creating equity among all learners. Multiculturalism can be manifested in many aspects of teaching, from the way a classroom community is created to the types of materials that are used in teaching. Multiculturalism is not unique to ESL classrooms; in fact, multiculturalism can be fostered in classes comprised of 100% native speakers of English. However, the inherent linguistic, social, cultural, and demographic diversity of ESL classrooms suggests that multiculturalism is an essential aspect of ESL instruction.

Multiculturalism in the classroom exists as opposition or balance to traditions of main or dominant culture centrism. While it is recognized that English is the language of the United States, that schools operate primarily on delivery of instruction in English, and that curriculum reflects centuries of Anglocentric culture and experience, educators now realize that things have to change in order to promote equity for all learners. Multicultural education attempts to eliminate inequities that may be traced to social, ethnic, racial, linguistic, or cultural differences. Multicultural education also aims to eliminate or at least reduce discrimination, intentional or inadvertent, that is connected to such differences (Banks, 2019, pp. 1, 4).

Multiculturalism is a manifested feature of classroom *ambiance*. Multiculturalism falls into the realm of the affective aspects of ESL teaching. It's not something you teach; instead, multiculturalism is an environment that you can construct, foster, and sustain as an ESL teacher. Multiculturalism in the classroom is an attitude or mindset that ESL teachers can operationalize through creatively constructed classroom activities that actively engage learners in forging a community of inclusivity by recognizing the diversity of interests, contributions, and possibilities represented by the immediate classroom and the larger community beyond the classroom.

Beyond the immediacy of classroom community, multiculturalism creates a macro view of how students will operate in the realm of globalism. What happens in the classroom prepares students for the realities of cultural and linguistic negotiations, integration of multiple perspectives, understanding of historical context, and development of voices, skills, and mindsets that will enable all learners to participate equitably and successfully in society, whether it's a local community or much broader global context. Teachers can promote multiculturalism by integrating cultural information that "fills in" gaps in existing curricula, by recognizing contributions to content areas by individuals from different cultures, by showing students that multicultural thinking leads to social justice, and by creating opportunities for students to explore inequities that reflect a lack of cultural inclusivity (Wright, 2015, pp. 20–21).

Earlier in this book (Chapters 3–7), we explored Domain II, which focuses on how teaching happens in ESL classrooms. Whereas Domain II addresses issues of class environment, learner difference, and learning styles in constructing instruction, Competency 009 focuses on how ESL teachers can construct a multicultural community of learners supported by learner difference and individuality.

The EL Student's Affective Needs

Creating an effective multicultural classroom environment requires that the ESL teacher look at the classroom space from the EL student's perspective:

- EL students might feel "identified" by their current ELPS designation. The elaborate, ongoing LPAC documentation keeps teachers, parents, and students fully aware of their current ELPS level. Being in an ESL class means that learners have not yet attained the advanced high ELPS level required to exit the program.

- EL students in content-area classes may be transitioning from one language program to another, thereby changing their current class and peer environment.

- Exiting into mainstream classes with pull-out ESL can make EL students feel out of place or possibly unready for full participation with native English-speaking classmates.

- EL students may practice cultural and linguistic autonomous segregation in social settings, but in classroom settings, there is the
  expectation of full collaboration among learners. It does not happen
  automatically.

- EL students face the challenge to continually work at developing
  English proficiency. Teachers need to realize that this means more processing time, likely misunderstanding, insufficient content-area background, and the silent period of internalized processing without output.

- EL students may feel deficient because of their current L2 proficiency
  and, as a result, may appear to be unmotivated or resistant to full class
  participation.

EL students may experience "language shock" and "culture shock" when they realize
that their output, especially when they make linguistic errors, may be seen as comical by
L2 speakers or when they cannot coordinate L2 behavioral expectations with L1 cultural
norms. The result is disorientation and/or anxiety in the EL student, attitudes that can shape
the learner's participation in the class community (Gass, 2013). Consider how discomfort-
ing it can be for a young person to be required to make eye contact, to participate in class
discussions, to construct and share opinions, and to relate to a non-parent authority figure
when these are not part of his/her cultural norms.

ESL teachers need to devise classroom techniques that ensure EL students are not unintentionally excluded from class interactions. The disengagement and apparent non-com-
municativeness manifested by cultural mismatches and linguistic insufficiencies can be
alleviated by using *total participation techniques* that engage all learners in a vibrant class
community. ESL teachers can construct classroom activities for linguistic support and academic learning that keep EL students from shrinking into corners of non-participation and
that instead invite all learners to join equitably and confidently in creating new knowledge
(Himmele & Himmele, 2009, pp. 143–147).

Activities that Promote Multiculturalism and Community

In a multicultural class community, individual learners feel comfortable and accepted
in a space shaped by celebration of difference. Teachers can create this sense of belong-
ing, participation, and acceptance by using lessons and other class activities to orchestrate
learner interaction and mutual acceptance of difference. Creating a multicultural learning
community can also reflect the powerful strands of CALLA (Chapter 6) and sheltered
instruction (Chapter 8) as is suggested in these activities designed to forge community:

- Math class: In word problem "stations" or centers, students work independently or in small groups or pairs to solve the problems set up at each station. If they need help, they can raise a "flag" (students have created the flags in a quick pre-lesson activity). The flags denote different types of help requests, for example a blue flag might mean "we need language or math term or operation help," a green flag, "we need help understanding," a red flag, "we're totally lost." The teacher tells the students that they can respond to the flag calls, going over to the group that needs help to try to help out. The teacher lets the students help each other instead of intervening.

- Social studies: Students work in groups to draw scenes from a jigsawed lesson. Their scenes have to include short captions or bubble comments that integrate key terms from the lesson. When the scenes are completed, the groups work as panelists to present their scenes to the class. This activity allows an alternate form of product creation—drawing instead of testing or writing—and allows learners to discover how to collaborate to create the group project in a low-stress, creative venue.

- English: Students pick "golden lines," their favorite lines from a literary text, write them on craft paper sheets, use illustrations to reinforce the images in the lines, and post the sheets on the walls to create a gallery walk. Students walk around the gallery and leave comments on the sheets. This activity allows full-scale participation from all learners in a low-risk, low-anxiety format.

- Science: Students explore the construction/science of a typical item like a pencil or a lollipop or a popular candy bar. The teacher selects an item that is more complex than it appears to be and that will allow learners to discover fun facts as they research independently and collaboratively. This activity would allow integration of technology in a research activity. Depending on available time, students could construct a simple multimodal project or a poster, allowing all learners to participate by contributing their own levels of expertise.

- Class gallery: The teacher can post pictures of students working on class activities and post bubble comments that show the teacher's response to how they are contributing to class community. Students could be encouraged to add their own class photos to showcase learning takeaways and even funny class moments.

- Showcasing individuality. From the first day of class, ESL teachers should strive to encourage learners to tell their stories. Even for high school ESL students, a wall or bulletin board that shows artifacts of each learner's individuality is a valuable community-shaping strategy. Young learners can share info bits about favorite foods or pets or siblings; older learners can share details about hobbies, career goals, things they are experts at. Teachers need to be proactive about keeping learners' differences in plain sight so that the difference becomes a bonding element for the class community.

A multicultural environment is supported through responsive teaching. Responsive teaching means paying attention to what individual learners need, especially when an assigned activity is a mismatch with what the learner is able or willing to do. For example, a learner who feels unready to participate in round-robin oral reading could be asked to be the class notetaker with the task of creating a list of key terms on the board. An EL student, however, would very likely need assistance in hearing and noting key words, so the teacher could assign a note-taking "team" composed of the EL student and one or more other students.

Culturally responsive teaching involves integrating lesson materials that reflect a variety of cultures. In English classes that involve reading and writing, it is relatively easy to integrate readings that reflect a variety of cultures, but in other content areas, it might be more challenging. Science, math, and social studies teachers need to be familiar with stories, books, and events that reflect cultural diversity in discoveries, pivotal events, and diverse individuals relevant to the subject area. In just about every content area, teachers can find current events that reflect issues and concepts directly connected to the subject. In all content areas, it would be very easy to keep a current events bulletin board that reflects news items from around the world that allow learners to connect classroom content to the real world, all around the world.

A classroom that includes even a small number of EL students should look culturally inviting and culturally diverse. There should be posters, realia, illustrations, props, and other materials that extend beyond mainstream, hegemonic culture to include connections to a variety of cultures.

Learner Diversity

In a class of EL students of different abilities or a mainstream class made up of English speakers and language learners, there will be many sources of student difference. The linguistic level of EL students may cause feelings of deficiency for the language learners and may raise barriers between the traditional students and the EL students. For the EL students, home circumstances may be less than optimal if their parents do not speak English or do not provide a home environment that welcomes working at home on school matters. Socioeconomic circumstances may prohibit EL students from participating in extracurricular activities or may limit access to technology.

Cultural differences may be so vast that EL students have trouble blending into the class community. Limited levels of past educational experience may reduce EL students' background knowledge on content-area topics. English may be the language of the classroom while L1 remains the language of "real" life. For students who are designated LEP *and* special education, there will be multiple "markers" of their distinctiveness as members of the class community.

Whatever the source of learner difference or distinctiveness, the ESL teacher needs to work to shape and sustain a multicultural community of learners where each learner respects and values every other learner and where each individual learner feels safe, confident, and accepted.

Summary, Action Plan, and Chapter 9 Wrap-Up

Competency 009 epitomizes the pedagogy and teacher mindsets presented in Competencies 001 through 008. Multiculturalism is not a separate component of ESL instruction; it is *integral* to all teaching practices. What happens in the ESL classroom, whether it is a self-contained or pull-out classroom, should serve as a "bridge" for ensuring EL students' success once they exit the program and move fully and independently into mainstream classrooms (Himmele & Himmele, 2009, p. 146). The importance of fostering a multicultural environment as an aspect of the affective domain ESL instruction is underscored by TAC §89.1210. Program Content and Design:

> English learners in an ESL program shall be provided instruction using second language acquisition methods in English to introduce basic concepts of the school environment, which instills confidence, self-assurance, and a positive identity with their cultural heritages. The program shall be designed to incorporate the students' primary languages and learning experiences and shall incorporate the cultural aspects of the students' backgrounds in accordance with TEC, §29.005(b). (TAC, 1996, Chapter 89)

A multicultural mindset enables teachers to discover how every learner's individual story can enrich the whole class environment and contribute to shaping a community of learners where every learner respects the individuality, distinctiveness, and difference of every other learner.

Self-Check

1.   Make sure you are able to define *multiculturalism*.

2.   Explain how multiculturalism can be fostered in an ESL classroom.

3.   How can teachers integrate content-area instruction with multicultural teaching strategies?

Study Plan

Here are a few resources that you can consult to help you see how multicultural teaching strategies are operationalized in classrooms:

*   *The Language-Rich Classroom: A Research-Based Framework for Teaching English Language Learners* by Pérsida Himmele and William Himmele (2009) is structured on the authors' C-H-A-T-S approach to teaching ESL (C = content-area reading strategies, H = higher order thinking skills, A = assessment, T = total participation techniques, S = scaffolding strategies). The T section of their approach illuminates the intention of Competency 009. The authors delve deeply into the affective mindset of EL students and offer numerous examples of classroom activities designed to address connections among culture, learning, and community.

*   *Academic Literacy for English Learners* by Cynthia Brock, Diane Lapp, Rachel Salas, and Dianna Townsend (2009) is a collection of detailed explanations of units in science, history, and math showing how teachers enrich content-area teaching by integrating cultural elements and by responding to specific learners' immediate linguistic and academic needs.

*   *An Introduction to Multicultural Education* by James A. Banks (2019) connects the politics of educational reform to what can be done in day-to-day classroom activities. Banks sees multicultural education as a leveling force that eliminates the "otherness" associated with difference; instead, as Banks sees it, multicultural education enables all learners to be better prepared to function and succeed in the diverse global society.

Practice Items for Competency 009

Use the following scenario to respond to the next two items.

An elementary school ESL teacher gives her students the following directions.

"We are starting a unit on folk stories—stories that you learn from your family or stories that you know from your culture. A lot of times, stories like these are supposed to keep you from doing something dangerous. Or they might explain how or why something happens. We are going to start out by reading a folk story from a Native American tribe in Texas and then you will bring folk stories from your own culture."

To illustrate what a folk story is, the teacher reads Tomie DePaola's *Legend of the Bluebonnet* which offers a native American explanation for the apparent overnight appearance of bluebonnets in Texas in the spring.

1. When the students bring in their folktales, the teacher hands out construction paper booklets for the students to write and illustrate the stories they brought. The teacher creates a Folk Story Gallery for the students to post their booklets. When all the booklets are done, the students read each other's booklets and then have a class discussion about similarities and differences they found in their own stories and their classmates' stories. This activity best addresses which of the following ESL teaching strategies?

    A.   The activity integrates several academic and non-academic skills.

    B.   The activity allows the teacher to promote students' oral language proficiency.

    C.   The activity creates a culturally responsive learning environment.

    D.   The activity promotes students' creativity by asking students to think like authors and to imagine how their story would be best presented through illustrations.

The correct response is C. While all of the responses represent strong pedagogical strategies, Response C most directly addresses the stem focus of identifying similarities and differences. To create a multicultural learning environment, learners need to be aware of how differences can shape community. Response A is incorrect because it offers an oversimplified assessment of the objective of the activity as presented in the stem. The stem suggests the teacher is targeting affective aspects of ESL education rather than academic strands. Response B does not fully represent the instructional objective suggested by the stem; while the students would need to use oral language skills to discuss their responses, the focus of the activity is to get learners to recognize cultural similarities and differences. Response D is incorrect because it does not focus on the objective suggested by the stem. While students would have to use creative, artistic skills and demonstrate audience awareness, the activity is focused on recognizing cultural connections.

2. The teacher wants to expand the folk story unit in order to promote students' awareness of linguistic and cultural diversity. Which of the following activities would best meet this goal?

   A. The teacher collaborates with the school librarian to identify books that present children's versions of folk stories from around the world. The teacher has each student pick a book from this collection and bring it to class to read and to present in reader's theater.

   B. The teacher assigns each student a specific country to research. The students create small posters presenting the following basic facts about the country: the language spoken, one story from that country, and a picture of a typical scene from daily life in that country.

   C. The teacher integrates the folk story unit into a geography lesson. The teacher brings in pictures of scenes from countries throughout the world and tells students a few facts about each country as the students look at the scenes.

   D. The teacher gives each group a picture of a scene from a foreign country. Each group has to write a folk story triggered by the scene.

Response A is the correct answer because it allows learners to contextualize the original bluebonnet story with their own stories and then with stories from around the world. Furthermore, in letting the students pick a story and then present it, the teacher is fostering autonomy and active participation in the diverse performances elicited in reader's theater. Response B is incorrect because the research assignment isn't clearly connected to cultural diversity; it seems to be focused on research skills. Response C is incorrect because the geography lesson veers away from cultural diversity. Response D is incorrect because it invites students to invent a story that is not likely to be connected to cultural awareness and that is triggered only by an uncontextualized image.

Competency 010

10

Competency 010: Advocacy

The ESL teacher knows how to serve as an advocate for ESL students and facilitate family and community involvement in their education (Pearson, 2019a).

Competency 010 brings together categories of advocacy that extend beyond the classroom, beyond pedagogy, and toward areas outside the classroom where teachers can support EL students' learning, social, personal, and post public school goals. The four descriptive statements (A–D) of Competency 010 cover these topics:

- ESL teacher participation in committees that assess student progress and evaluate site contributions to state educational goals

- Support for family engagement through communication and collaboration

- Knowledge of community resources

Competency 010 Core Content

While Competencies 001 through 009 address skills and knowledge that ESL teachers need to be effective teachers, Competency 010 integrates factors that are external to the classroom but that impact the decisions and actions teachers make in classrooms. Competency 010 also reminds us of the highly politically charged nature of language programs in the U.S. Our discussion of Competency 008.A, which included a timeline of court cases and federal acts relevant to the rights of students whose first language is not English, established that language support programs exist in U.S. schools today because they have been mandated by federal actions. Generations of parents, politicians, and advocacy groups have had to stake legal fights to seek educational and social equity for ELs. Competency 010 shows how the ESL teacher advocates for students and parents as part of the long-fought struggle for equity.

This list of terms combines Competency 010 and Standard VII content.

Table 10.1.
Competency 010 Core Content

advocacy	educational equity	social equity
LPAC	Admission, Review, and Dismissal Committee (ARD)	Site-Based Decision Making
family engagement	communication with families	collaboration with families
community resources	ESSA and parent support	communicative bridges with families

What Advocacy Means

At the end of the book *English-as-a-Second-Language (ESL) Teaching and Learning: Pre-K–12 Classroom Applications for Students' Academic Achievement and Development*, authors Virginia Gonzalez, Thomas Yawkey, and Liliana Minaya-Rowe offer their ideas on what it means to be a "committed advocate" for ESL students. Instead of *defining* what advocacy means, they identify actions and habits of mind that illustrate advocacy (2006, pp. 352–356):

- ESL teachers serve as "cultural mediators" helping students and families adjust to the culture of school and community.

- ESL teachers partner with parents to discover what is best for the student.

- ESL teachers educate parents about federal and state policies that impact their children.

- ESL teachers should be able to guide parents toward community resources like health service availability, school programs that can help their children, and even housing or day-to-day living resources.

- ESL teachers should develop awareness of cultural expectations and norms that can clash with what is expected in the school environment.

- ESL teachers need to develop empathy toward students' cultures by learning about their culture, by observing the students, by consciously avoiding stereotyping.

These observations about advocacy opportunities show that teaching is a holistic venture that encompasses spaces outside the classroom as well as the immediacy of the classroom space.

ESL Teacher as Advocate for EL Student Success

The overriding target goal of ESL programs in Texas is the student's exit from the program which happens when the learner has achieved the required proficiency level and the required scores on mandated state content-area exams. From the time a student enters an ESL program to the time of exit, ESL teachers are the prime advocates in helping learners meet linguistic and academic goals. Competencies 001 through 009 describe pedagogical practices that promote learner progress toward these goals. However, teachers also demonstrate attitudes and understandings that inform how they interact with EL students.

Let's look at two powerful comments from two different teachers that show the centrality of teacher attitudes in cultivating advocacy. The first quote is from a teacher writing about lessons she learned in her first year of teaching. The second is from a teacher who reconstructed her view of her students during a Multiliteracies Teacher Institute Program early in her teaching career:

Lessons learned in early teaching:

The first [lesson] is that, for many students, the teacher is the only source of encouragement in their lives; we need to appreciate the importance of this. Another critical lesson I learned is that there really is no such thing as a "model student." We cheat ourselves and our students out of many extraordinary moments if we persist in believing that the ideal student looks or acts a certain way. We must try to know all of our students as individuals. (Hanson, 2003, p. 33)

Comments on perceptions of students by Helen, first-year teacher in Reno, Nevada:

> We see what we believe. To challenge my own mental paradigm, I need to change my perception. . . . When I believe that my students are future scholars, doctors, dentists, lawyers, [scientists]—whatever their hearts and minds desire, then I will see it. I will see them. When I believe that they can do anything, then I will see it. . . . It all has to do with expectations. (Brock, Pennington, Oikonomidoy, & Townsend, 2010, p. 328)

Let's consider how these insights about seeing students as people with needs impacts how ESL teachers advocate for their students. Consider that ESL students arrive in ESL classes with a string of labels attached to them as students. First, they have been identified as LEP on the basis of a home language survey and then a language proficiency test. Next, the LPAC committee has determined whether they are bilingual or ESL program students. ESL students are further classified on the basis of their readiness to be in pull-out programs or their need to develop further proficiency in a full ESL class. Every student in an ESL class also has ELPS level labels for each language proficiency category. And there are test scores for each year of TELPAS. If the teacher's instructional goal is to help EL learners attain the advanced high proficiency level, it might be easy to forget that underneath the labeling there is a real, vibrant learner who has cultural, linguistic, personal, social, academic, and developmental needs. The teaching strategies and mindsets suggested by Competencies 001 through 009 are designed to help ESL teachers create learner-centered, nurturing classroom environments that enable the teacher to truly serve as an advocate for each learner.

State and Federal Policies

Advocacy extends to knowing how individual teachers factor into enforcement of federal and state policies for English learners. In Texas, that includes knowing the LPAC protocols for placing and reassigning EL students, knowing when the Admission, Review, and Dismissal process (ARD) is relevant, and participating in site-based decision making groups and processes.

The Language Proficiency Assessment Committee, mandated by the Texas Education Code and the Texas Administrative Code, is charged with initially placing students in the appropriate language program, then reviewing and monitoring their progress, and considering reclassification on the basis of their progress. While individual teachers are not directly involved in the committee decisions, ESL teachers are directly involved in helping EL students meet scoring expectations on TELPAS and STAAR exams. The content of Competencies 001 through 009 presents the scope of teacher advocacy as mentor, coach, instructor, and guide in ensuring that students are progressing in linguistic proficiency and academic competence. Additionally, ESL teachers offer valuable support for EL student learning as they make the appropriate linguistic accommodations for learners based on observations and daily class interactions. Additionally, ESL teachers can prepare students for success on the TELPAS by integrating into class activities and assignments the student expectations listed in ELPS for cross-disciplinary, listening, speaking, reading, and writing proficiencies.

ESL teachers are obligated to follow the **Individualized Education Program (IEP)** created by the ARD for students who are designated LEP and are also special education students. The student's LEP status is considered a "special factor" in the development of the IEP. Thus, the ESL teacher has advocacy opportunities in ensuring that the student's special ed needs are met in the context of linguistic accommodations for the language program.

Site-based decision making processes, instituted by the Texas Education Code, offers teachers direct opportunities for input regarding how programs are working, what adjustments could be made to better meet student needs, and how students are progressing toward meeting performance expectations for linguistic proficiency and academic achievement. While every ESL teacher is not a member of site-based decision making committees, the provisions for operations and procedures for SBDM committees include opportunities for committee members to meet with groups of teachers, such as ESL teachers, to get input and suggestions on needed changes in programs.

Supporting Families

Parent support is a starting point for EL students' participation in language programs in Texas public schools. Even if students are designated as LEP on the basis of the mandated language proficiency testing, they cannot be channeled into ESL or bilingual programs without official parental approval. Parents have the right to refuse language services for their children. The LPAC is obligated to obtain parental approval as a pre-condition to integrating a student into a language program; if parents elect to refuse the programs, they can discuss other options for addressing their children's academic and language needs (TEA, 2019, *LPAC Framework Manual*, pp. 76–79).

Once students are in a language program, ESL teachers frequently serve as liaisons or intermediaries in procedures involving EL students. Just as in all other academic programs,

ESL teachers should follow best practices for staying in contact with parents and encouraging parental involvement. Working with parents who may not be fluent in English does present special challenges. That is why teachers should be highly attuned to how the LPAC can support instructional efforts. Starting with the parent's choice to channel LEP students into language programs, parents have a pivotal role in determining how their children's language learning needs are met. The LPAC committee is obligated to send parents a detailed account of their child's performance on TELPAS, STAAR, and other exams. Teachers, who are not directly involved in LPAC actions, can serve as liaisons or "interpreters" of these performance reports.

Family engagement efforts should include ongoing communication about class activities, student progress, and teacher-parent conferences. Teachers may need to translate class communication for parents, but translation programs and administrative support systems can help ESL teachers stay in steady contact with parents. When appropriate, teachers can enlist the help of students to ensure that parents understand that forms, such as permission forms or forms related to class information, are completed and returned. Additionally, teachers should inform parents about the information available through the Supporting English Learners in Texas web portal. This web portal includes a tab with information and links for parent services, such as brochures in English, Spanish, and Vietnamese on bilingual and ESL programs, information about adult language programs in the education service center region, and information on testing. Users can select the portal language from English or seven other languages.

Because teachers are the point of immediate contact between parents and the school, ESL teachers should work diligently to be informed about policies relevant to ESSA, TELPAS, STAAR, possible accommodations for mandated testing, and ongoing circumstances that impact what happens in the classroom. For example, parents might need information on the rights of immigrant children in American schools, such as the American Federation of Teachers information pages on *Plyler* rights (you might want to refer to Chapter 8 if you don't remember *Plyler v. Doe*). Or teachers may need to show parents, right at a computer, how to access TEA websites that include information relevant to their children's current educational status.

Teachers can also guide parents toward community resources that can help students acculturate. Teachers can share information about soccer leagues, after-school programs, the public library, arts and performance activities, swimming lessons, and other activities sponsored by city organizations. Even from early elementary grades, teachers can partner with parents and community resources to build excitement and anticipation in young learners about potential careers. In districts that are close to universities, there may be a Pre-K to college initiative that links college of education faculty and students to public schools. As students get close to graduation, teachers can guide students and parents in filling out applications for colleges and finding financial aid opportunities.

ESL teachers will quickly learn that their EL students come from a broad spectrum of family support systems and cultural expectations. For some students, school will be an entirely separate enterprise from home, with parents participating minimally in their child's educational endeavors. Other families may lack the financial resources to support students in simple things like providing school supplies or discretionary reading materials. Nonetheless, research shows that regardless of sociocultural and SES variables, the family contributes richly to students' developing literacy. Home literacy experiences and opportunities vary in extent and quality, but they serve as a bridge between school activities and the home environment. Research suggests that such bridging has positive outcomes for EL students. This critical support system provided by family is sometimes overlooked as a component of helping EL students meet their language proficiency goals (Goldenberg, Rueda, & August, 2006, pp. 256–258). Literacy experiences that may be set in L1 in the home environment can support transfer and interdependence between L1 and L2 , which we explored in Chapter 5 as important aspects of developing proficiency in English.

The political realities of immigration decisions made in Washington, D.C., may be played out in actual events in classrooms, especially in Texas with its 1200-mile border with Mexico. ESL teachers may have to deal with circumstances that involve parents not knowing what their or their children's rights are. Teachers may not know the answers, but they can serve as conduits in guiding parents to find answers in the community and in state and federal agencies.

A great thing about being a teacher, whether ESL or traditional, is that you become deeply involved in the stories and circumstances of learners and their families. Parents come to see teachers as much more than "just" teachers. For parents of EL students, teachers can facilitate access to information and services that schools and communities offer to support the learning and achievement journey of their children.

Summary, Action Plan, and Chapter 10 Wrap-Up

Advocacy is not a mandated requirement of ESL teaching. However, advocacy is a remarkable side effect of working with students and families who are trying to become productive members of American society. For ESL teachers, it is likely that every class session enables advocacy as learners demonstrate what they know, as learners take risks that show their affinity for their new language, as learners struggle to overcome the stigma of being labeled LEP, as learners deal with language and culture shock in their trek toward proficiency in English. In *ESL (EL) Literacy Instruction: A Guidebook to Theory and Practice*, the authors talk about EL students' *resilience*, the ability to overcome the stress of a multitude of risk factors. These risk factors include being a learner of a language other than your first language, living in a country that is not your country of origin, and interacting with peers who are not really your peers because you speak a different language than they do. They assert that student success rests to a large extent in the hands of teachers and administrators: "They are role models, coaches, advisors, mentors, caregivers, healers and counselors" (Gunderson, D'Silva, & Odo, 2014, pp. 259–260).

Self-Check

1. Explain what *advocacy* means in the context of ESL education.

2. Can you provide core details about how ESL teachers are involved in LPAC, ARD, and site-based decision making endeavors?

3. How can ESL teachers support parents in ensuring that EL students have productive classroom and school experiences?

4. Explain how the teaching guidelines and strategies presented in Competencies 001 through 009 enable teachers to be advocates for their EL students.

Study Plan

1. Spend some time carefully looking through the Supporting English Learners in Texas TEA web portal, especially the Parents and Families tab. Click on some of the other languages to see how TEA is trying to meet the needs of families by offering crucial information in languages in addition to English.

2. Study the LPAC process which is described through multiple links and documents in the TEA website section on Special Student Populations—Bilingual/ESL Education tab. Actually looking at what this committee does, how the results of student achievement are reported, and how parents are informed of their child's progress will demonstrate why ESL teachers need to be advocates for their students and their families. Reading and understanding the Parent Notification on Student Progress requires an advocate to interpret and explain the data and results presented.

3. Spend some time navigating through ¡*Colorín Colorado!*, a website with the subtitle "a bilingual site for educators and families of English language learners" (2019). Users can select a Spanish presentation of the materials. The menu tab for parents includes sections on helping children read, on supporting children's learning, on fostering success in school, on knowing when to contact a teacher, and many other areas that show parents how to be advocates for their children in ESL programs.

Practice Items for Competency 010

1. An upper elementary ESL teacher decorates the classroom with motivational reading posters, borrows grade-appropriate fiction and nonfiction books from the library, and invites parents to a read aloud demo in class. After the teacher does the read aloud, the teacher gives the parents a reading log, which the children have decorated with stickers and their own illustrations, on which parents and children are supposed to record at-home oral reading time. The teacher suggests several at-home reading scenarios, such as reading to a younger sibling, the whole family, or an individual parent. This instructional activity primarily supports which of the following ESL teaching goals?

   A. The reading log reconstructs reading homework as self-selected reading time, with the goal of improving student attitudes about reading.

   B. The reading log allows the teacher to collect quantitative data for the end-of-year subjective report on the students' reading proficiency.

   C. The reading log fulfills state requirements for out of school literacy experiences.

   D. The reading log creates collaboration among the teacher, the parents, and the students in promoting students' academic success.

The correct response is D. Reading logs monitored by parents are considered a good strategy for fostering collaboration with parents in developing EL students' literacy skills. The reading log does not require that parents actually involve themselves in the literacy activity but it does create an opportunity for parents to support a home opportunity for students to practice their reading. Response A is incorrect because the stem sets up the activity as a parent engagement opportunity. While it is likely that students' attitudes about reading would improve via the autonomy embedded in the activity, that is not its primary goal. Response B is incorrect because reading proficiency in Texas is not assessed subjectively by teacher observations. Additionally, Response B veers away from the parent engagement focus of the stem. Response C is incorrect because there are no "state requirements" for out of school literacy experiences. Proficiency in reading is assessed by TELPAS and the STAAR exams.

2. At the school's parent night, a teacher with an ESL class where 100% of the students speak Spanish as their first language distributes 4 x 6 cards and invites parents to write *una cartita,* a "Little Letter," a few lines describing their child, in English or in Spanish. The teacher explains that every three weeks, the parents will be sent a "Little Letter"/*cartita* written by the teacher with a few sentences about the child's classroom experiences. The "Little Letter" will include a blank card so that the parents can write a return note to the teacher. This activity best addresses which of the following essential components of ESL instruction?

A. Improving parents' L1 and L2 literacy skills

B. Establishing communication and collaboration with parents

C. Keeping parents informed about their children's developing L2 proficiency

D. Compiling information about students' home life

Response B is correct. The "little letter" strategy promotes communication between parents and teachers in an informal, child-centered way. Significantly, the teacher is establishing a two-way route: ordinarily, letters from school do not require a response, but this activity invites parents to write back. Response A is incorrect because this is not a realistic goal for ESL programs. ESL programs foster parent-teacher communication, but improving the parents' literacy skills is not a direct program goal. Response C is incorrect because the LPAC is in charge of informing parents of students' current L2 proficiency with data from TELPAS, STAAR, and class grades. Additionally, activity does not focus on assessment of L2 proficiency; as set up in the stem, the activity is aimed at fostering parent-teacher communication. Response D is incorrect because it would be inappropriate to probe into a student's home life. While the *cartitas* activity may result in parents sharing details about home life, the intent of the activity is to partner with parents as participants in the student's school experiences.

PRACTICE TEST 1

TExES English as a Second Language Supplemental (154)

Also available at the REA Study Center *(www.rea.com/studycenter)*

This practice test is also offered online at the REA Study Center. We recommend that you take the online version of the test to simulate test-day conditions and to receive these added benefits:

- **Timed testing conditions**—helps you gauge how much time you can spend on each question

- **Automatic scoring**—find out how you did on the test, instantly

- **On-screen detailed explanations of answers**—gives you the correct answer and explains why the other answer choices are wrong

- **Diagnostic score reports**—pinpoint where you're strongest and where you need to focus your study

1. Ⓐ Ⓑ Ⓒ Ⓓ
2. Ⓐ Ⓑ Ⓒ Ⓓ
3. Ⓐ Ⓑ Ⓒ Ⓓ
4. Ⓐ Ⓑ Ⓒ Ⓓ
5. Ⓐ Ⓑ Ⓒ Ⓓ Ⓔ Ⓕ
6. Ⓐ Ⓑ Ⓒ Ⓓ
7. Ⓐ Ⓑ Ⓒ Ⓓ
8. Ⓐ Ⓑ Ⓒ Ⓓ
9. Ⓐ Ⓑ Ⓒ Ⓓ Ⓔ
10. Ⓐ Ⓑ Ⓒ Ⓓ
11. Ⓐ Ⓑ Ⓒ Ⓓ
12. Ⓐ Ⓑ Ⓒ Ⓓ Ⓔ
13. Ⓐ Ⓑ Ⓒ Ⓓ
14. Ⓐ Ⓑ Ⓒ Ⓓ
15. Ⓐ Ⓑ Ⓒ Ⓓ
16. Ⓐ Ⓑ Ⓒ Ⓓ Ⓔ
17. Ⓐ Ⓑ Ⓒ Ⓓ
18. Ⓐ Ⓑ Ⓒ Ⓓ Ⓔ Ⓕ
19. Ⓐ Ⓑ Ⓒ Ⓓ Ⓔ
20. Ⓐ Ⓑ Ⓒ Ⓓ
21. Ⓐ Ⓑ Ⓒ Ⓓ
22. Ⓐ Ⓑ Ⓒ Ⓓ
23. Ⓐ Ⓑ Ⓒ Ⓓ
24. Ⓐ Ⓑ Ⓒ Ⓓ
25. Ⓐ Ⓑ Ⓒ Ⓓ
26. Ⓐ Ⓑ Ⓒ Ⓓ Ⓔ
27. Ⓐ Ⓑ Ⓒ Ⓓ

28. Ⓐ Ⓑ Ⓒ Ⓓ
29. Ⓐ Ⓑ Ⓒ Ⓓ
30. Ⓐ Ⓑ Ⓒ Ⓓ
31. Ⓐ Ⓑ Ⓒ Ⓓ
32. Ⓐ Ⓑ Ⓒ Ⓓ
33. Ⓐ Ⓑ Ⓒ Ⓓ
34. Ⓐ Ⓑ Ⓒ Ⓓ
35. Ⓐ Ⓑ Ⓒ Ⓓ
36. Ⓐ Ⓑ Ⓒ Ⓓ
37. Ⓐ Ⓑ Ⓒ Ⓓ Ⓔ
38. Ⓐ Ⓑ Ⓒ Ⓓ
39. Ⓐ Ⓑ Ⓒ Ⓓ
40. Ⓐ Ⓑ Ⓒ Ⓓ
41. Ⓐ Ⓑ Ⓒ Ⓓ
42. Ⓐ Ⓑ Ⓒ Ⓓ
43. Ⓐ Ⓑ Ⓒ Ⓓ
44. Ⓐ Ⓑ Ⓒ Ⓓ
45. Ⓐ Ⓑ Ⓒ Ⓓ
46. Ⓐ Ⓑ Ⓒ Ⓓ
47. Ⓐ Ⓑ Ⓒ Ⓓ
48. Ⓐ Ⓑ Ⓒ Ⓓ Ⓔ
49. Ⓐ Ⓑ Ⓒ Ⓓ
50. Ⓐ Ⓑ Ⓒ Ⓓ
51. Ⓐ Ⓑ Ⓒ Ⓓ
52. Ⓐ Ⓑ Ⓒ Ⓓ
53. Ⓐ Ⓑ Ⓒ Ⓓ
54. Ⓐ Ⓑ Ⓒ Ⓓ

55. Ⓐ Ⓑ Ⓒ Ⓓ
56. Ⓐ Ⓑ Ⓒ Ⓓ
57. Ⓐ Ⓑ Ⓒ Ⓓ
58. Ⓐ Ⓑ Ⓒ Ⓓ
59. Ⓐ Ⓑ Ⓒ Ⓓ
60. Ⓐ Ⓑ Ⓒ Ⓓ
61. Ⓐ Ⓑ Ⓒ Ⓓ
62. Ⓐ Ⓑ Ⓒ Ⓓ
63. Ⓐ Ⓑ Ⓒ Ⓓ
64. Ⓐ Ⓑ Ⓒ Ⓓ
65. Ⓐ Ⓑ Ⓒ Ⓓ
66. Ⓐ Ⓑ Ⓒ Ⓓ
67. Ⓐ Ⓑ Ⓒ Ⓓ
68. Ⓐ Ⓑ Ⓒ Ⓓ
69. Ⓐ Ⓑ Ⓒ Ⓓ
70. Ⓐ Ⓑ Ⓒ Ⓓ
71. Ⓐ Ⓑ Ⓒ Ⓓ
72. Ⓐ Ⓑ Ⓒ Ⓓ
73. Ⓐ Ⓑ Ⓒ Ⓓ
74. Ⓐ Ⓑ Ⓒ Ⓓ
75. Ⓐ Ⓑ Ⓒ Ⓓ
76. Ⓐ Ⓑ Ⓒ Ⓓ Ⓔ Ⓕ
77. Ⓐ Ⓑ Ⓒ Ⓓ
78. Ⓐ Ⓑ Ⓒ Ⓓ
79. Ⓐ Ⓑ Ⓒ Ⓓ
80. Ⓐ Ⓑ Ⓒ Ⓓ

TIME: 4 hours and 45 minutes
         80 multiple-choice questions

Directions: Answer each question by selecting the correct response or responses. Most items on this test require that you provide the one best answer. However, some questions require that you select one or more answers, in which case you will be directed to respond with either a specific number of answers or all answers that apply.

Use the following scenario to respond to the next two items.

A teacher is reviewing classroom data reflecting EL students' performance in a middle school science class. The teacher reviews the following notes about a recent immigrant currently categorized as an intermediate EL.

> • Never asks questions when I introduce a new assignment; instead, speaking in Spanish, turns to ask a classmate.
>
> • During informal class activities, interacts comfortably with classmates but speaks in Spanish.
>
> • When asked a question during class discussions, responds monosyllabically.
>
> • In group work, sits quietly, non-participatory, but seems to understand what her group members are saying.
>
> • When asked about incomplete homework assignments, she shrugs her shoulders. If I ask for details, she usually says, "Didn't do it."

1. This teacher's notes will be useful in making an informal assessment about the student's proficiency in which of the following areas?

    A.   Academic language proficiency
    B.   Listening and speaking
    C.   Content-area knowledge
    D.   General language proficiency

2. Which of the following adjustments should the teacher make in teaching activities to promote EL students' language development?

    A. Whenever EL students are speaking in Spanish, the teacher should interrupt them, tell them they have to speak in English, and have them come up to the desk for reteaching.

    B. During lectures, the teacher should stop occasionally and ask an advanced EL student to translate the information for classmates who are having trouble understanding the content.

    C. The teacher should model think alouds that illustrate how to express understanding, confusion, questions, need for more explanation, and other responses to typical class situations.

    D. The teacher should have a question and answer session at the end of each lecture, requiring every student in the class to ask one question.

3. A high school biology teacher is starting a unit that addresses state assessment standards on knowledge of interactions among biological systems in plants. Which of the following instructional activities would most effectively promote EL students' achievement in this area?

    A. The teacher assigns a group project: each group identifies a specific plant and uses visuals and props to demonstrate how various systems contribute to growth.

    B. The teacher has students fill in a graphic that identifies parts of a plant's ecosystem.

    C. The teacher takes his students on a walk around the campus to point out different types of plants growing on the school grounds.

    D. The teacher shows students the state assessment standards in biology and explains the concepts and defines all the content-specific terms in each standard.

4. Which of the following statements best summarizes the way an ESL teacher can use results of mandated assessment to improve student achievement in the classroom?

    A. Although scores on mandated state exams provide summative assessment data, teachers can use information about performance in discrete areas of the exams to devise formative assessments embedded in day-to-day class activities.

    B. Because mandated state exams create a great deal of anxiety among teachers and students, the teacher should concentrate on improving students' comprehension of academic content instead of integrating state testing requirements.

    C. Because state exams are high stakes for students and teachers, teachers should revise their curriculum to cover only material included on the mandated exams.

    D. Teachers should adapt all course content to reflect the format of state assessments and administer benchmarks every few weeks.

5. Which THREE of the following conditions explain how students in Texas are identified as LEP/EL students?

    A. The student does not meet English proficiency requirements as indicated by the state-approved English language proficiency test.

    B. The student is unable to respond readily to instructions in English.

    C. The parents provide written approval for entry into the recommended language program.

    D. The home language survey indicates that a language other than English is the primary language.

    E. The student has had no classroom instruction in the United States.

    F. The student does not know English even at a rudimentary level.

Use the following information to answer the next two items.

A middle school science teacher is reading a set of student lab reports. The following sentence is in Remi's report:

I knew that if I just had too more minutes, I could of finished.

6. Remi's sentence demonstrates difficulty in which of the following areas?

   A. Using past tense forms correctly
   B. Distinguishing between the oral and written forms of homonyms
   C. Using modals correctly
   D. Spelling

7. In response to the last report item, "Explain your major understandings about lab procedures in completing this experiment," Remi writes:

You should never feel bad just cuz u didn't finish.

Which of the following feedback strategies should the teacher use to help Remi understand how to present his content-area knowledge in completing the science experiment report?

   A. The teacher should mark an X through *cuz* and *u* and write "misspelled" in the margin.
   B. The teacher should use Remi's sentence in the next day's Daily Oral Language exercise and have students try to correct the sentence.
   C. The teacher should affirm the learner's frustration over not completing the experiment, explaining that next time, he should use science terms to explain why he didn't finish.
   D. The teacher should leave the sentence as is since writing is not the focus of the science class.

8. A fifth grade teacher's class includes beginning and intermediate ESL students. The teacher has students keep a section in their writing notebooks to jot down words that they encounter in their independent reading. The teacher calls these "Wow Words." There are only three "rules" for Wow Words: (1) jot down new words that you want to learn; (2) jot down words you already know but have never used and you want to use in your writing or speech; (3) jot down the sentence in which you found the word. This activity focuses on which of the following areas of language?

   A. Phonology
   B. Lexicon
   C. Morphology
   D. Pragmatics

9. Which THREE of the following strategies represent effective practices in delivering instruction in a content-based math class?

   A. The teacher has students write a summary of the class lesson at the end of each class.
   B. The teacher defines key vocabulary at the beginning of the day's lesson.
   C. The teacher writes key vocabulary words on the whiteboard, breaking them into syllables, and asking learners to repeat the words as he pronounces them.
   D. The teacher administers a quiz based on a problem from last night's homework to determine the students' weak areas.
   E. The teacher picks a problem from last night's homework and has three student volunteers do a think aloud to demonstrate how they solved the problem.

10. Which TWO of the following scenarios illustrate why ESL teachers need a strong foundation in the structure of English?

   A. A math student is having a lot of trouble in pronouncing *quadrilateral*.
   B. A science teacher administers homework quizzes at the beginning of each class period, but 90% of the students consistently fail.
   C. A history teacher wants students to memorize the names of the presidents of the United States.
   D. A social studies teacher wants students to write sentences that show cause-and-effect outcomes triggered by runoff in areas with limited vegetation.

11. Beginning EL students in an elementary math class are having a lot of trouble doing simple problems, but they do not tell the teacher what they find difficult about the problems. The teacher has a short discussion after each math problem is explained, but the students do not respond. Which of the following L2 acquisition concepts probably explains what is going on?

   A. Silent period
   B. Limited Basic Interpersonal Communicative Skills
   C. Interlanguage
   D. Limited Cognitive Academic Language Proficiency

12. Which THREE of the following instructional strategies promote students' content-area achievement?

   A. The teacher identifies and defines roots relevant to content-area vocabulary.
   B. The teacher has students identify subjects, verbs, and adjectives in sentences from the chapter they are studying.
   C. The teacher guides students in doing interactive vocabulary activities focusing on key words from the lesson.
   D. The teacher helps students write sentences that reflect important content-area knowledge by creating stems that the students can complete working in pairs or independently.
   E. The teacher has students copy sentences from their content-area textbooks in order to learn correct punctuation.

Use the following scenario to respond to the next three items.

A teacher is starting a unit on local plants in a middle school science class. Most of the students are beginning and intermediate EL students. The teacher wants to make sure the activities in the new unit help students understand science content but also promote their language proficiency.

13. The teacher gives each student three plastic zippered bags and asks them to collect leaves from three different plants they see each day on the school grounds or in their neighborhoods. How does this introductory strategy demonstrate a recommended strategy for content-area teaching in ESL environments?

   A.   Students can have fun while completing the assignment.
   B.   New content acquisition will be reinforced through hands-on activities.
   C.   Students will not need to use language strategies in completing this assignment.
   D.   Students will demonstrate the extent to which they can follow basic instructions.

14. When they bring in their three leaves, the teacher gives the students this assignment:

   Each of you is going to present your three leaves and explain where you found them. As you show them to the class, try to identify some of the features that make each leaf distinct from the others or features that the leaves have in common.

   How does this instructional activity demonstrate effective strategies for promoting EL students' understanding of content-area information?

   A.   The oral language activity forces students to speak in L2 without relying on L1 vocabulary.
   B.   The activity reinforces new science vocabulary for this unit.
   C.   The activity creates a non-academic environment which should reduce students' anxieties over participating in class discussions.
   D.   The activity integrates oral language and prior knowledge as a beginning point for new content-area learning.

15. As a culminating activity for this unit, the teacher asks students to interview one family member about a favorite or special plant. The students are to create a construction paper poster with a drawing of the plant and a short written account of the interview. The teacher displays the posters on the wall outside the classroom. How does this instructional activity promote the EL students' content-area learning?

   A.   Students will use family connections and language background to support new content-area learning.
   B.   Students will integrate new science vocabulary into their written accounts of the interview with a family member.
   C.   Including a drawing of the family member's favorite plant will allow the teacher to test the students' understanding of basic unit information.
   D.   After reading all the interviews, the teacher will be able to determine if reteaching is necessary in this unit.

16. Which THREE of the following scenarios best depict application of sheltered instruction?

    A. A history teacher is beginning a unit on women politicians in Texas. He starts the unit by posting illustrations with bio blurbs about each woman.
    B. A math teacher wants students to solve a volume problem involving the number of jelly beans that fit in a 1 × 1 cube. He gives each group a bag of jelly beans to experiment with the formulas.
    C. A literature teacher is about to start a lesson on a story that students were assigned for homework. The teacher administers a pop quiz before the start of the discussion.
    D. A social studies teacher is starting a unit on rivers in Texas. Students are divided into groups and each group is assigned the task of coming up with the names of at least three rivers in Texas.
    E. An English teacher is about to start a lesson on a commonly taught short story. The teacher asks for a volunteer to do a think aloud on the first three paragraphs of the story.

17. Which TWO of the following strategies represent how EL students might rely on L1 knowledge?

    A. Translating challenging L2 passages into L1
    B. Pronouncing L2 words using sounds of L1
    C. Asking L2 speakers to explain challenging text
    D. Looking up new L2 words in an L2 dictionary

18. In an elementary-level ESL class, the teacher starts the day by saying "Good morning" to each child, greeting each one by name. The morning greeting is followed by a 10-minute SSR (Sustained Silent Reading) period. The teacher signals the end of SSR by ringing a small bell. Then the teacher says, "Group leaders, it's time to get the math workbooks." Which THREE of the following ESL teaching strategies are reflected in these activities?

    A. Routines keep EL learners from getting bored when they don't understand directions.
    B. Routines reinforce EL students' understanding of content-area material.
    C. Routines help EL students feel that they are a part of the classroom community.
    D. Routines enable EL students to participate meaningfully in classroom activities.
    E. Routines support EL students' understanding of the order of classroom procedures.
    F. Routines simplify time frames for EL students, thereby improving cognitive processing of complex subject-area content.

Use the following scenario to answer the next two items.

Abel is an EL student in a high school history class. His essay on the beginnings of slavery in America includes the following sentences.

(1) The slavery begins in 1619.

(2) A ship bring to the shore a lot of African captive.

(3) In the beginning, the business man trade food for the Africans.

19. Which TWO of the following L1 to L2 errors are shown in the passage?

    A. Verb tense
    B. Interference
    C. Spelling
    D. Plural formation
    E. Word choice

20. Sentence (3) in Abel's draft reflects which of the following structures?

    A. Fragment
    B. Simple sentence
    C. Complex sentence
    D. Compound sentence

21. Mr. Nyugen has a Grade 10 class with intermediate and advanced ELs. He wants students to understand how context impacts language choices. In a short pre-assessment activity, he does a quick poll to see how many students are familiar with the popular video game Fortnite. He sees that everyone in the class has either played or knows of the game. The teacher hands out two passages: (1) a transcript of a short conversation among several students as they talk during lunch about their latest Fortnite gaming session and (2) a paragraph from a student process essay explaining how to play Fortnite. Mr. Nyugen asks students to work in groups to create a T-chart comparing the language in the two samples, focusing on the differences they can identify. This activity primarily addresses which of the following areas of language study?

    A. Semantics
    B. Syntax
    C. Non-verbal communication
    D. Registers

Use the following scenario to answer the next five items.

A junior high school English teacher wants to support EL students' writing proficiency by developing higher-level vocabulary. The teacher breaks the students into groups, gives each group a high-bounce rubber ball, and has the students bounce their balls. The task is for each group to come up with five different synonyms for *bounce* based on what they observed when they bounced their ball.

22. This activity illustrates which of the following ESL instructional approaches?

    A. Classroom activities that use Total Physical Response
    B. Classroom activities that rely on the Immersion Approach
    C. Classroom activities to develop Basic Interpersonal Communicative Strategies (BICS)
    D. Classroom activities to develop Cognitive/Academic Language Proficiency (CALP)

23. Which TWO of the following evaluations of the activity best illuminate how it supports EL students' language proficiency?

    A. The activity promotes ELPS writing expectations focused on vocabulary that adds detail to writing.
    B. The activity introduces an element of play into an academic learning task.
    C. The activity enables students to rely on multiple ways of learning to complete the academic task.
    D. The activity allows students to use their L1 knowledge to create new L2 learning.

24. Which of the following descriptions best explains how the activity integrates opportunities to develop communicative competency?

    A. Students will practice using a dictionary to look up synonyms for *bounce* and learn new words they can integrate into their lexicon.
    B. Students will be able to act out scenes involving bouncing as they search for new verbs.
    C. Students will have an authentic opportunity to use oral language skills in completing the activity with their group.
    D. Students will engage in kinesthetic activities to reinforce their understanding of the new words.

25. After the groups present their set of five synonyms for the verb *bounce*, the teacher asks students to pick one verb, draw a picture that shows a character doing something that shows the verb in action, and write one sentence using the verb. The students read their sentences to the class. Then the teacher circulates throughout the class to help students revise their sentences if they used the verb incorrectly. This activity best illustrates which of the following instructional activities?

    A. Integration of art into a grammar lesson
    B. Authentic assessment
    C. Informal presentation
    D. Critical thinking skills applied in a writing task

26. Which THREE of the following instructional delivery practices are illustrated in this vocabulary development activity?

    A. Using realia
    B. Experiential learning
    C. Preteaching key vocabulary
    D. Scaffolding
    E. Culturally relevant pedagogy

27. Which of the following statements correctly expresses understandings about EL students' acquisition of listening and speaking competencies in L2?

    A.   In order to read and write in L2, students must first acquire L2 communicative competency skills at a relatively high proficiency level.
    B.   EL students generally acquire communicative competency more easily than literacy competencies, usually demonstrating proficiency in about two years.
    C.   For EL students, proficiency in the reading, writing, speaking, and listening domains develops simultaneously rather than sequentially.
    D.   To help students succeed academically, teachers should focus on reading and writing proficiency because literacy scaffolds communicative competency.

28. A high school EL student routinely says *supposably* instead of *supposedly*. What does this construction indicate about this speaker's current oral language proficiency?

    A.   The student does not know how to spell *supposedly*.
    B.   The student's pronunciation suggests she is approximating the sounds she hears when other speakers utter the word *supposedly*.
    C.   The student is not using her monitor in oral language production.
    D.   The word *supposedly* is not in the student's lexicon; this explains why she is mispronouncing it.

29. A Grade 3 teacher introduces new content vocabulary to her beginning EL students each Monday. To reinforce their initial understanding of the new words, she posts labeled pictures of the words throughout the classroom. She wants to promote their listening and speaking proficiency in the context of content instruction. Which of the following instructional activities most effectively addresses the teacher's goal?

    A.   The teacher puts up the lists of new content words, pronounces each one, asks for volunteers to pronounce the words, and then leads the class in choral response to pronounce each word.
    B.   Working in groups, students pick one of the new words to explore by looking in their books, using the dictionary, and using other class resources. Each group does a short presentation to introduce the class to the new word.
    C.   The teacher gives students two days to learn the words. They spend a few minutes each day pronouncing the words out loud in unison. On the third day, they have a spelling test on all the new words.
    D.   The teacher shows an animated video in which animal characters introduce the new words on the list. After the video, the teacher gives students a short test to determine which words they seemed to understand best.

30. A Grade 2 EL teacher asks her students to bring a special object from home (like a toy, a photograph, a book, a gift, etc.). On Storytelling Day, the students take turns describing their object and telling the story of why it is special to them. Which of the following English Language Proficiency Standards (ELPS) expectations for speaking is best addressed through this instructional activity?

    A. Narrating and explaining
    B. Distinguishing sounds and intonations in English
    C. Integrating new vocabulary into day-to-day language
    D. Using grade-level content area vocabulary

31. To promote her Grade 5 EL students' academic language proficiency, a science teacher takes her students to the school library once a week and has them check out books on topics related to the unit they are currently studying. The teacher notices that in the library, students talk constantly, showing each other their books, and reading each other's books. She recognizes this as an opportunity to promote her students' communicative language development with a follow-up activity after the library session. Which of the following instructional activities best addresses the teacher's intent?

    A. Assigning students book reports on the book they pick and posting the reports on the class Writing Wall
    B. Having each student do a book talk on his/her book
    C. Having each student post the title of his/her book on the Class Notes Wall
    D. Having students do internet research to find information on the authors of their books

32. In assigning listening and speaking class activities, an ESL teacher needs to take into account individual differences in language and culture because

    A. students' diverse cultural and linguistic backgrounds can interfere with assimilation.
    B. culturally-based behavioral and social norms impact oral language interactions in the class environment.
    C. most ESL students are very uncomfortable about speaking in public.
    D. rates of oral language acquisition vary significantly among individual students.

33. The following sentence occurs in a student essay describing lessons learned in a physical education class.

    From jumping rope to doing many crunches were just some of the many things you could do in this class.

    Which of the following descriptions correctly analyzes the syntactic problems in this sentence?

    A. The sentence starts with an introductory prepositional phrase.
    B. The sentence is a run-on because the comma after *crunches* is missing.
    C. Two prepositional phrases are used in the subject position, creating a sentence that lacks a grammatical subject.
    D. The sentence has a compound subject.

Use the following scenario to respond to the next four items.

A middle school teacher assigns her class of intermediate ESL students a short essay on the topic "How we learn," but her students tell her that they don't know what to write. The teacher tells her students, "We find the best writing by thinking about what we know from our own lives." Then the teacher puts the following graphic on the board with examples from her own experiences, explaining the lesson she learned with each "zone." The teacher then has students create their own graphic in their notebooks.

My Learning Zones

Watching my mother	Watching my father	Something I learned when I went on a trip
Something I learned when I did something I wasn't supposed to	Spending time with my grandparents	A surprise lesson
A hard lesson	A lesson I learned by doing my chores	A lesson I learned on the playground

34. In creating her own Learning Zones chart, the teacher is implementing which of the following linguistic accommodation strategies?

    A. Scaffolding
    B. Segmenting
    C. Modeling
    D. Graphic presentation

35. In creating the Learning Zones graphic, the teacher is demonstrating reliance on which of the following teaching concepts?

    A. Culturally relevant pedagogy
    B. Funds of knowledge
    C. Learner-driven syllabus
    D. Process writing

36. When the students are creating their own Learning Zones graphic, the teacher encourages students to work in pairs as they come up with events to put in their cells. After five minutes, the teacher asks each pair to present one story from their charts. This activity is likely to promote which of the following language competencies?

    A. Oral communication
    B. Collaborative work
    C. Metacognitive strategies
    D. Content-area vocabulary

37. The teacher also wants to use this activity to support students' literacy development. Which TWO of the following additional activities would support this learning goal?

    A. Students draw images of a scene from their Lesson Zones.
    B. Students do internet research to find a video that illustrates one of the activities they put in their zones.
    C. Students do a quickwrite of one of the events they put in their Learning Zones graphic.
    D. Students pick one of their Learning Zones events and create a word cloud of ideas and details they remember from the event.
    E. Students work in pairs to ask each other questions about the events in the zones.

38. Which of the following statements best explains why idioms pose particular challenges for ESL students?

    A. Idioms frequently are based on sophisticated allusions that EL students are not likely to recognize.
    B. The meaning of idioms cannot be derived from the literal meaning of the component words in the expression.
    C. Idiomatic expressions can be understood only if the speaker knows the genesis of the expression.
    D. Idioms usually have ambiguous meanings.

39. The following verb forms occur in an essay written by a Grade 5 ESL student.

haded	knowed	eated
thinked	knewed	runned
breaked	broked	broughted

    What do these forms indicate about the student's current English language proficiency?

    A. The writer is overgeneralizing in use of the past morpheme.
    B. The writer has limited understanding of verb tense forms in English.
    C. The writer has not yet internalized rules for irregular verb forms in English.
    D. The writer lacks phonological understanding to recognize that the –ed suffix sounds "wrong" when attached incorrectly.

40. Which of the following passages shows the correct use of verb tenses and verb forms?

    A. He got his first pen when he was eight. He wrote his first story and felt he had grown up. He felt the story or the words he wrote won't be erased.
    B. He got his first pen when he was eight. He wrote his first story and felt he had grown up. He felt the story or the words he wrote will not be erased.
    C. He got his first pen when he was eight. He wrote his first story and felt he had grown up. He felt the story or the words he wrote would not be erased.
    D. He got his first pen when he was eight. He wrote his first story and felt he had grown up. He feels the story or the words he writes won't be erased.

41. An EL student writing a story about an experience when he was in ninth grade includes the following sentence in his draft:

     Because we wanted to end the course with excellent grades, we all assisted class every day.

     The writer's use of *assisted* instead of *attended* is an example of which of the following common L2 acquisition difficulties?

     A.   Approximation
     B.   False cognate
     C.   Generalization
     D.   Interference

42. A teacher is conducting a read aloud session in a Grade 6 language arts class, with the students sitting in a circle, each student taking a turn to read a few lines aloud. George is a newcomer ESL student. The teacher notices that George is following along closely in his storybook, tracing the words with his finger. When it's his turn, George says, "Cannot." George's response might be explained by which of the following SLA concepts?

     A.   L1 dependence
     B.   Lack of comprehensible input
     C.   Monitor hypothesis
     D.   Interlanguage

43. A teacher is presenting a mini-lesson on figurative language. Students are shown the following passage.

     Instead of starting the new lesson like we did every day, she asked us what we thought could make our science class more fun. That's when an explosion of comments erupted out of us <u>like lava flowing from a volcano</u>.

     Which of the following terms is the best label for the underlined phrase?

     A.   Hyperbole
     B.   Imagery
     C.   Simile
     D.   Alliteration

Use the scenario presented below to answer the next five items.

Janie is a middle school student whose family recently emigrated from Nicaragua. On the first day of class, she told her teacher that she had to drop out of school in her native country a year ago; she has had no tutoring or formal schooling in the interval. She has the following conversation with her science teacher.

Janie:	Is because loss . . . uhmmmm . . . oosbi. No finish . . . uhmmmmm . . . the home-work. . . the speermen.
Teacher:	You were unable to complete your lab experiment, Janie? You lost your USB? So you could not do your lab report? [speaking slowly and clearly enunciating and making eye contact with Janie]
Janie:	No.
Teacher:	Do you think you could complete your homework during your study period? [speaking slowly and clearly enunciating, still looking at Janie]
Janie:	Uhmmmmm . . . Estoody time. Finish. *Si.*
Teacher:	That's great, Janie. I hope to get your science report later today. [teacher smiling and giving Janie a thumbs-up]
Janie:	[smiles and returns the thumbs-up]

44. Based on this brief exchange, which of the following statements offers the best description of Janie's L2 development at this point?

   A.   Janie has virtually no understanding of English grammar.
   B.   Janie's syntactic and phonological output point to interference from Spanish grammatical structures.
   C.   Janie is not capable of completing a logical utterance in English.
   D.   Janie is unable to use her L1 competence as scaffolding for her L2 development.

45. Which of the following statements best explains her teacher's responses during the conversation about homework?

   A.   The teacher seems to be encouraging Janie's oral language competence by responding to her in complete sentences that reflect Janie's communicative intentions.
   B.   The teacher is more interested in having the assignment completed than in helping Janie improve her language proficiency.
   C.   Because of Janie's limited English proficiency, the teacher probably does not understand what Janie is saying; consequently, she makes no effort to correct her.
   D.   The teacher thinks Janie does not understand what she's saying to her, so she repeats and exaggerates her responses to Janie.

46. This conversation between Janie and her teacher best reflects which of the following aspects of second language acquisition?

    A.   Cognitive/Academic Language Proficiency (CALP)
    B.   Filter
    C.   Basic Interpersonal Communicative Skills (BICS)
    D.   Interlanguage

47. Janie's pronunciation of USB as *oosbi* is indicative of which of the following L2 acquisition strategies?

    A.   Transfer
    B.   Incorrect translation
    C.   Risk taking
    D.   Inactive filter

48. Which THREE of the following assessments of the teacher's holistic response best illustrates the teacher's understanding of L1 to L2 acquisition?

    A.   The teacher seems focused on making sure Janie understands how to correctly pronounce the words she has mispronounced.
    B.   The teacher offers affective support for Janie's communicative efforts.
    C.   The teacher wants Janie to understand that missing an assignment is not a problem.
    D.   The teacher is focused on establishing meaningful communication with Janie.
    E.   The teacher seems to understand that Janie is struggling with L2 structures but is using L1 support to express herself.

49. A high school ESL teacher has students ranging from intermediate to high advanced in his class. He assigns the following project.

    > Pick a movie in your native language. Create a poster that includes information about the basic plot elements (the characters, the key events, the conflict, and the outcome). Your poster should also include information about how this film is a good presentation of your country and/or culture. Each of you will have five minutes to present your movie poster to the class and explain why this is your favorite film. Workdays: Two class periods followed by two presentation periods.

    Which of the following teaching goals does this assignment best address?

    A.   To create an opportunity for students to develop writing skills
    B.   To test students' ability to do a formal class presentation
    C.   To teach students critical viewing skills in the context of international films
    D.   To integrate listening, speaking, and writing skills in an authentic, multicultural context

50. Mr. Hodges teaches U.S. history in a content-based ESL program. The class is made up of intermediate and advanced ESL students. To promote students' understanding of history content when he presents a lesson, he writes key words and focal points on the board as he lectures. Which of the following additional strategies would most effectively promote students' understanding in this content-based ESL class?

    A. The teacher starts each class with a pretest and ends with a quiz on the material covered that day.
    B. The teacher asks students to read aloud from the history book and corrects any mispronunciations.
    C. At the end of the class, the teacher asks students to submit questions about anything they didn't understand from the lesson.
    D. The teacher stops every 10 to 15 minutes to conduct a "state-of-the-class" session during which he poses questions about key points and encourages students to explain what they understand and identify what they don't understand.

51. A high school English teacher plans a unit focused on a frequently taught short story from American literature. Because half of his students are intermediate to advanced ESL students, he needs to provide appropriate accommodations to create comprehensible input. Which of the following instructional activities should the teacher select to meet this goal?

    A. Before starting the unit, the teacher writes 20 vocabulary words on the board and gives students a class period to look them up.
    B. Students watch a film on the author's novels and stories, focusing on the shared thematic elements.
    C. The teacher begins the unit with a "book talk" in which he introduces the characters, the initiating event, and touches on the conflict, and then reads a few pivotal passages from the story.
    D. For homework prior to the first unit day, students are required to read the story and answer a set of questions.

Use the following scenario to answer the next three items.

Ms. Pierce teaches Grade 7 intermediate EL students. During their language enrichment period, she hands out the following exercise. Her students are clustered into base groups, but she instructs them to work independently for five minutes and then network with their group members to complete the exercise.

Read the following passage carefully. Fill in the blanks with words that make sense in those slots. Remember that to make sense, the words need to fit both in meaning and grammatical form. In addition, you can put only *one word* in each blank.

The playground can _____ kids how to work hard to _____ anything. Whether kids are trying to swing by _____, go down the big slide, or go _____ the monkey bars, they are out there every day trying to _____ the task. Once they go down the big _____ for the first time, they _____ that when they work at something, they can _____ their goal. I still remember the _____ time I was able to slide down by myself. _____ I was able to do something on my own!

---

52. What is the label generally given to this type of exercise?

    A.   Cloze exam
    B.   Daily Oral Language
    C.   Sustained Silent Reading
    D.   Read aloud

53. This type of learning activity is primarily intended to promote proficiency in which of the following areas?

    A.   Metacognition
    B.   Syntax and semantics
    C.   Comprehension
    D.   Vocabulary

54. Ms. Pierce discovers that some of her students are frustrated because they can't figure out the "right answers." Which of the following modifications should she make to support students' efforts to complete this activity effectively?

    A.   She provides a list of possible choices for each blank, including some alternatives that are inappropriate for the context of the blank.
    B.   She asks for volunteers to read the passage aloud in front of the class, saying "blank" every time they come to a blank and having the class call out a possible word.
    C.   She tells students who are frustrated to look up words they don't know in the passage.
    D.   She provides picture books and elementary-level story books on the general topic of the passage and tells students to read several of these books if they don't understand how to fill in the blanks.

Use the following scenario to respond to the next three items.

Mr. Sauls teaches a high school biology class made up of native speakers and intermediate to advanced ESL students. A good bit of the course work involves conducting experiments in class by following written directions provided by the teacher. Students work collaboratively on each experiment.

55. Mr. Sauls notices that each time a new experiment is assigned, the EL students turn away from their assigned groups and talk in their native language with EL students in other groups. Which of the following strategies would most effectively support the teacher's goal to use collaborative work to promote his EL students' language competence?

    A.   The teacher tells the EL students that to learn science content, they must speak in English rather than in their L1.
    B.   The teacher restructures the groups to include two or more EL students in each group.
    C.   Using an internet translation tool, the teacher translates the experiments into the students' L1.
    D.   The teacher moves from group to group and reads the instructions orally to each group.

56. Which of the following teaching activities would enable Mr. Sauls to promote his EL students' understanding of science content?

    A.   To help the students understand the scientific concepts addressed by the hands-on experiments, he has the EL students read elementary-level books on the relevant science concepts.

    B.   Before the next experiment, the teacher schedules a computer lab period so that EL students can search for information on the experiment on websites in their native language.

    C.   Before the next experiment, the teacher models a similar experiment and posts illustrations throughout the room to reinforce the EL students' understanding of the procedures.

    D.   Before the next experiment, the teacher administers a pre-test to predict areas in which students may have comprehension problems.

57. As part of each experiment, each student has to write a report explaining the results of the experiment. Because he wants to ensure that his teaching strategies address English Language Proficiency Standards (ELPS) for writing, Mr. Sauls invites an English teacher colleague to conduct a writing workshop as the students complete their reports. Which of the following strategies would best enable Mr. Sauls to meet ELPS expectations for writing?

    A.   During the workshop, the English teacher reviews each report and marks all errors in spelling, punctuation, and word choice; the students then rewrite the reports reflecting the corrections made by the English teacher.

    B.   As part of the workshop, students exchange reports for peer editing; Mr. Sauls tells students that they need to find at least five errors in each report they read and correct them for their classmates.

    C.   Because the ESL students probably lack sufficient vocabulary to write their reports correctly, the English teacher encourages the ESL students to write their reports in L1 first and then translate their writing into L2.

    D.   The English teacher and Mr. Sauls use directive and non-directive strategies in conferences with the students to help them craft well-written sentences using terminology that reflects their understanding of the science content.

58. A middle school history teacher has noticed that the EL students in the class misuse prepositions frequently in their written responses to class readings. The students rely on basic prepositions (like *on, in, to, of*). The teacher wants to encourage the students to start using prepositions like *beyond, beneath, concerning, underneath*. Which of the following activities might best address the instructional objective to promote EL students' ability to integrate a variety of prepositions into their writing?

    A.   The teacher administers a quiz consisting of paragraphs from the latest chapter. The directions are to circle every preposition in the passage.

    B.   The teacher puts a list of 50 prepositions on the board. The students are divided into groups, and each group is given the task to look up five of the prepositions and write the meaning next to the words on the board.

    C.   The teacher writes 25 prepositions on the board. The teacher distributes visuals showing scenes from the chapter the class is currently studying. The directions are to generate a list of 10 prepositional phrases (using 10 different prepositions) describing the scene in the photograph.

    D.   The teacher returns the students' last graded chapter response and has students work with partners to integrate more prepositional phrases into their essay.

59. A high school history teacher decides that instead of delivering a lecture, she will have students act out key scenes from the historical events in the unit they are currently doing. Working in groups, students will conduct some internet research on the historical figures involved, write a script for a three-minute scene, and present their scene to the whole class using props that they have made themselves. Which of the following statements best explains how this activity demonstrates effective ESL teaching methods?

   A. Because history content tends to be challenging for EL students, this activity will enhance student learning by introducing an element of fun into an otherwise routine academic environment.
   B. This activity will foster a higher level of content mastery by forcing students to read the chapter multiple times.
   C. Because the assignment is a departure from the usual lecture format, students will work harder to understand the content on their own.
   D. This highly interactive, collaborative assignment will encourage students to work at higher cognitive levels by integrating reading, writing, speaking, and listening domains.

60. Which of the following descriptions defines two-way dual language/immersion education?

   A. An educational approach that separates EL students from native English speakers in order to immerse learners in the L2 environment by providing intensive, targeted instruction in English with supplementary scaffolding from L1.
   B. An educational approach that integrates native English speakers and EL students in a context that provides language and content area instruction in L1 and English.
   C. An educational approach that brings together EL and native English language students in a supplementary class where all students learn both English and L1.
   D. An educational approach that integrates native English speakers and EL students in a self-contained classroom; all instruction is in English, with "immersion" referring to allowing students to learn the two languages naturally using their first language acquisition skills.

61. Which of the following explains the L2 (English) to L1 instruction ratio in Texas dual language immersion programs?

   A. The ratio is always left up to the instructor's discretion since the instructor is best able to determine learners' needs.
   B. At least half of the instruction is delivered in L1.
   C. The ratio is 50/50 from kindergarten through Grade 4 when it becomes 90% English/10% L1.
   D. The ratio is 100% L2 from kindergarten through Grade 2 when it becomes 90% English to 10% L1.

62. Specifications for ESL programs in Texas are mandated by which of the following?

   A. The Texas Education Agency
   B. The U.S. Department of Education
   C. The Texas Education Code
   D. Every Student Succeeds Act

63. A school district establishes an ESL program for young students who have recently arrived in the United States and who have limited or no academic background in their native language or in English. The program addresses acculturation, language, and affective and academic aspects of the children's educational experience. The program is a temporary "stopover." The goal is to transition these students into a traditional ESL program. What label is typically applied to this type of program?

    A. Transitional ESL program
    B. Initial Language program
    C. Assimilation program
    D. Newcomer program

64. The fundamental purpose of federal and state regulations regarding ESL education is which of the following?

    A. To provide equal educational opportunities for all learners
    B. To develop a citizenry that is fluent in English
    C. To promote English as the official language of the United States
    D. To promote assimilation of immigrants by reducing students' dependence on L1 in everyday social and academic activities

65. A Grade 3 teacher in a two-way dual language/immersion program is conducting a geography lesson in her class. She has large pictures of geographical sites such as volcanoes, rivers, rain forests, deserts, canyons, etc. She gives each group a picture and directions for the geography assignment. Which of the following directions for further class activity would best reflect the characteristics of a two-way dual language/immersion program?

    A. Each group collaborates in writing a paragraph in English describing their picture.
    B. Each group creates a T-chart showing words that describe the picture with L1 words on one side and L2 on the other.
    C. The teacher creates a master list of English words that describe geographical sites. Each group selects the words that fit their picture.
    D. Each group collaborates in writing a paragraph in L1 describing their picture.

66. Research on ESL instruction shows that use of multiple scaffolds promotes young learners' social adjustment and academic learning. Which of the following descriptions provides the best examples of learning scaffolds?

    A. The teacher reinforces daily instruction with a quiz at the end of the school day; students score each other's quizzes and ask questions about the right and wrong responses.
    B. The teacher uses props and pictures to support new learning in all subjects, makes extensive use of print throughout the room, and structures lessons to integrate cooperative learning.
    C. The teacher uses short, animated videos to introduce every lesson in content areas and asks students to summarize their understanding of each video.
    D. The teacher uses instructional materials which offer L1 and L2 versions of every lesson to create a learning environment that addresses the affective needs of all the students.

Use the following scenario to respond to the next two items.

A high school teacher presents a unit on the 1960s civil rights movement in a sheltered social studies class. The lesson includes film clips, news stories and magazine pictures published in the 1960s, and excerpts from speeches from key civil rights leaders, as well as textbook chapters.

67. Additionally, the teacher creates a Civil Rights Around the World bulletin board and adds a first entry on Nelson Mandela. She tells students that each group needs to contribute a picture and short explanation of civil rights activists from other countries or cultures to add to the bulletin board. She integrates computer-assisted instruction and tells students they may do their computer work in their L1 if they choose. Which of the following explanations best addresses the connection between this instructional strategy and EL student learning?

    A.   The integration of technology with the option to use internet resources in their L1 will promote students' content-area knowledge and language acquisition.

    B.   By integrating materials other than the traditional textbook, the teacher demonstrates how history books present limited views of historical events.

    C.   The students will be able to create multimedia products to connect knowledge of this important period in American history to historical events in cultures throughout the world.

    D.   By integrating electronic resources, the teacher creates a class environment that reduces the effort that learners need to expend and reduces anxiety over required class work.

68. As a culminating activity, the teacher organizes the class into a large circle for a round-robin discussion. Each student completes the sentence, "I admire _____ (the historical figure the student chose) because _____." Then, the teacher has each student write a letter to the historical figure they mentioned. This activity best reflects which of the following ESL instructional strategies?

    A.   The teacher creates an assignment that EL students can complete effortlessly.

    B.   The teacher creates a learning environment in which students find meaningful connections to content-area knowledge presented in a multicultural setting.

    C.   The teacher creates an assignment that allows for authentic assessment in contrast to the traditional end-of-unit test.

    D.   The teacher makes an assignment that will encourage students to do additional research in order to complete the letter satisfactorily.

69. An English teacher reads aloud a chapter from a novel to her middle school EL students. The chapter is about Rey, a Hispanic boy, who jumps out of a tree to prove to his friends that he's a man. The chapter includes quite a few sentences that show code-switching between English and Spanish as the narrator muses about how he has to jump to fulfill cultural expectations. At the end of the read aloud, the teacher asks, "How many of you have done something similar to what Rey did?" She invites students to share their stories. This teaching activity creates a multicultural learning environment primarily by

    A.   showing students that even a simple childhood event can be turned into a story.

    B.   encouraging ESL students to talk comfortably in a classroom oral language activity.

    C.   showing students connections between shared common childhood experience and culturally driven behaviors.

    D.   showing students how integrating L1 is essential to effectively presenting an experience in L2.

70. A middle school teacher shows her ESL class film clips of people from different countries and cultures greeting each other. This instructional strategy primarily focuses on

    A. showing students that shaking hands is not a universal greeting.
    B. developing students' awareness of cultural diversity.
    C. emphasizing the need to watch videos set in other countries.
    D. reinforcing students' understanding of body language in communicating.

71. A high school teacher has his ESL class listen to excerpts from several types of music: a classical piece, a popular rap song, a country-western song, a classic rock song, a K-pop song, and a Mexican *corrido*. Each group picks a song and completes the following sentences about the person who might listen to that song:

    My listener's favorite food is _____.

    My listener usually wears _____.

    My listener drives a _____.

    My listener would never, ever _____.

    My listener's hobby is _____.

    This activity is likely to help students understand that cultural bias is connected to

    A. different preferences.
    B. limited understanding of a language.
    C. conflicts between old and young persons.
    D. stereotyping.

72. Early in the school year, a middle school ESL teacher gives each student a 4 × 6 card and makes the following assignment:

    On the blank side, please write in large letters a single word that you think describes you perfectly. On the ruled side, write a little story or just a paragraph explaining how and why that word fits you. The word you pick can be either in English or in your native language.

    After the students complete their cards, the teacher has each student read his/her statement. Then, the teacher posts all the cards, word side showing, on the Class Community Board.

    This activity primarily promotes which of the following components of creating and maintaining an effective multicultural learning environment?

    A. By sharing information about themselves, the students will work more effectively in groups.
    B. By sharing information about themselves, students will develop awareness of and respect for each other's cultural diversity.
    C. By displaying the cards on the board, the teacher will have readily available examples of L1 and L2 words for grammar and writing lessons.
    D. By having students read their statements orally, the teacher will establish a baseline for tracking students' speaking skills throughout the year.

73. A teacher in a newcomer program has a "Parents Are Stars" segment every Friday. The teacher invites parents to offer demonstrations and instruction in L1 culture-specific topics. This strategy primarily addresses which of the following ESL teaching recommendations?

    A. The teacher is demonstrating that learning takes place at home as well as at school.
    B. The teacher is providing downtime to keep students from being overwhelmed by the linguistic and academic content of the ESL program.
    C. The teacher is fostering meaningful parent participation in their children's school activities.
    D. The teacher is partnering with parents in order to fulfill requirements of the Texas English Language Proficiency Assessment System (TELPAS).

74. The math and science teachers at a large urban high school with a high number of EL students are concerned that they are not sure about how to promote their EL students' communicative language development. They want to integrate strategies that will support content-area learning while also developing listening and speaking skills. Which of the following strategies would best address the math and science teachers' concern?

    A. The teachers form a subcommittee to find information on the TEA website. Then, the teachers have a follow-up meeting with all the science and math teachers to share information about TELPAS.
    B. The teachers ask the principal for guidance in finding materials to prepare students for success on the communicative language components of TELPAS. The teachers show the principal their class performance on the latest TELPAS exam to support their request.
    C. The teachers do some research on teaching communicative competence in content-area classes and implement those strategies. The teachers observe each other and offer feedback on strategies that seem to best address communicative proficiency needs.
    D. The teachers ask the campus speech teachers for guidance in teaching students to do oral presentations. The teachers then assign each science and math class a multi-modal project as the culminating assignment for the current grading period.

75. An elementary school with a large number of students identified as EL is aiming for 100% parental approval for placing students in the district's language programs. Which of the following strategies would best address the school's goal to facilitate family involvement in EL students' educational experiences?

    A. Inviting families to a meeting where several teachers do a class demonstration showing how L1 instruction and ESL methods are integrated into daily instruction
    B. Sending parents an information brochure on the benefits of ESL education
    C. Sending a letter to the impacted families explaining the ESL program guidelines stipulated by the Texas Education Code and the Every Student Succeeds Act
    D. Inviting parents to a special Parent-Teacher Organization meeting where a question-and-answer session on ESL education is the only item on the agenda

76. Which THREE of the following entities are officially included in the Language Proficiency Assessment Committee (LPAC)?

    A. A member of the local school board
    B. A member of the school's parent-teacher association
    C. A parent of a student participating in a language program
    D. Teachers certified as bilingual or ESL teachers
    E. A campus administrator
    F. The bilingual coordinator for the region's Education Service Center

77. Which of the following best describes the individual teacher's role in the LPAC's decision regarding students' readiness to exit a language program?

    A. To inform parents of each student's progress in language acquisition and core course performance at the end of each semester
    B. To evaluate a student's readiness to exit a language program based on the student's classroom performance and potential
    C. To work closely with the LPAC to determine EL students placement options at the end of each academic year
    D. To serve as an advocate for each learner by providing research-based ESL instruction to guide students toward success on high-stakes assessments

78. Parental notification that a student has been classified as an EL and is recommended for placement in the school district's bilingual or ESL program comes from which of the following entities or individuals?

    A. The Language Proficiency Assessment Committee
    B. The student's English Language Arts teacher
    C. The school principal
    D. The school district's ESL Coordinator

79. A teacher new to the ESL program in a school district in Texas wants to learn the state-mandated responsibilities for teachers in bilingual and ESL programs. Which of the following resources would provide the most thorough, up-to-date information for this new teacher seeking information on ESL teacher responsibilities?

    A. The Language Proficiency Assessment Committee Framework Manual
    B. The Texas Education Agency's Supporting English Learners in Texas web portal
    C. The Texas Education Code
    D. The English Language Proficiency Standards

80. Two elementary school ESL teachers are talking about preparing students for the upcoming state-mandated exams in writing, reading, and math. They have this conversation in the lunchroom.

Teacher 1: Now that it's crunch time, I'm focusing everything on the English speakers.

Teacher 2: And your EL kids?

Teacher 1: At this point, I'd be wasting valuable class time on them. Everyone knows they're not going to do well regardless of what we do. So, I say, focus on the English speakers; at least, we know they'll do okay. But the LEP's . . . well, they're going to fail no matter what.

Which of the following terms best describes the attitude reflected by Teacher 1's comments?

A. Bias
B. Cultural insensitivity
C. Results-driven pedagogy
D. Teaching to the test

PRACTICE TEST 1 ANSWER KEY

1. (B)	21. (D)	41. (B)	61. (B)
2. (C)	22. (D)	42. (C)	62. (C)
3. (A)	23. (A), (C)	43. (C)	63. (D)
4. (A)	24. (C)	44. (B)	64. (A)
5. (A), (C), (D)	25. (B)	45. (A)	65. (B)
6. (B)	26. (A), (B), (D)	46. (C)	66. (B)
7. (C)	27. (B)	47. (A)	67. (C)
8. (B)	28. (B)	48. (B), (D), (E)	68. (B)
9. (A), (B), (E)	29. (A)	49. (D)	69. (C)
10. (A), (D)	30. (A)	50. (D)	70. (B)
11. (A)	31. (B)	51. (C)	71. (D)
12. (A), (C), (D)	32. (B)	52. (A)	72. (B)
13. (B)	33. (C)	53. (B)	73. (C)
14. (D)	34. (C)	54. (A)	74. (C)
15. (A)	35. (B)	55. (B)	75. (A)
16. (A), (B), (E)	36. (A)	56. (C)	76. (C), (D), (E)
17. (A), (B)	37. (C), (D)	57. (D)	77. (D)
18. (C), (D), (E)	38. (B)	58. (C)	78. (A)
19. (A), (D)	39. (A)	59. (D)	79. (B)
20. (B)	40. (C)	60. (B)	80. (A)

PRACTICE TEST 1 ANSWER EXPLANATIONS

1.   **(B)**   The correct response is B. The teacher's notes mention the learner's questioning skills, participation, and oral responses, all of which reflect diagnosis and assessment of the student's listening and speaking skills. Response A is incorrect because the notes reflect Basic Interpersonal Communicative Skills (BICS) not Cognitive/Academic Language Proficiency (CALP). Response C is incorrect because the teacher's notes do not address the learner's understanding of content areas. Response D is incorrect because the teacher's notes mention only the learner's oral language.

  Competency 007: Assessment in ESL contexts

2.   **(C)**   The correct response is C. The broad topic of Competency 007 is assessment, which includes using the results of classroom assessment to address learner needs. The teacher's notes about the student's non-participation indicate a need for adjusting instruction in order to promote learning and participation. Response C shows a possibility for demonstrating how to use language skills to be an active participant in class. The think aloud is a prolific, versatile strategy for demonstrating how to think through a problem. In this case, the teacher is demonstrating how to construct class participation comments. Response A is incorrect because it marks EL students as problematic. Speaking in L1 is a legitimate SLA strategy. Response B is incorrect because other EL students should not be put on the spot to translate or interpret what is going on in the classroom. Response D is incorrect because it adds a punitive edge to class participation by requiring everyone to ask one question. Additionally, the ask-one-question requirement is likely to lead to meaningless, disingenuous questions.

  Competency 007: Assessment in ESL contexts

3.   **(A)**   The correct response is A. The stem establishes that the teacher is focused on state standards that drive the mandated assessment. Response A describes an activity that calls for a great deal of learner participation in a collaborative project that will take individual interests and abilities into account as well as provide hands-on learning. Response B is incorrect because filling in a graphic is a simple identification activity not aimed at addressing the state standard mentioned in the item stem. Response C is incorrect because identifying the plants does not lead to an understanding of how the biological systems work. Response D is a borderline "teaching to the test" activity. Understanding the knowledge measured in each standard may help students connect classroom activities to testing requirements; however, the hands-on activity of option A is more practical as a strategy for promoting student performance on the standards.

  Competency 007: Assessment in ESL contexts

4.   **(A)**   The correct response is A. Because state exam score reports include holistic as well as discrete information, teachers can create class activities that help learners develop greater understanding in areas that the scores suggest are challenging or problematic. Response B is incorrect because it suggests that there is a mismatch between what is being taught in the classroom and what state exams assess. Response C is incorrect because state exams should not be the driving force behind the curriculum. Teachers should use best practices to present the most current information in content areas. Response D is incorrect because it reflects what some researchers refer to as "impoverished teaching": teaching that 100% reflects mandated testing instead of focusing on best practices and student-centered teaching. While benchmark examinations may help students prepare for the exams, teaching should be focused on promoting students' understanding of content-area materials.

  Competency 007: Assessment in ESL contexts

5.   **(A), (C), (D)**   Responses A, C, and D correctly reflect some of the state-mandated processes for the admission of ELs into ESL programs. Response A correctly references the state-approved test used to determine students' English proficiency levels. Response C correctly cites the need for parental approval for students to be placed in language programs. Response D correctly references the home language survey administered to all students upon entry to a Texas public school. Response B is incorrect because assessments about a student's English proficiency are based on the state-approved language exam. Response E is incorrect because prior educational experiences are not a requirement for entering a Texas public school. Response F is incorrect because the student's LEP status is determined by the home language survey and the results of the language proficiency exam.
   Competency 007: Assessment in ESL contexts

6.   **(B)**   The correct response is B. The learner's use of *too* instead of *two* and *of* instead of *have* indicates difficulty in differentiating words that sound similar or completely alike but are spelled differently. Recognizing the error as a homophone error reflects the teacher's knowledge of semantics. Response A is incorrect because there is no problem with the verb tenses. Response C is incorrect because *could* is used correctly. Response D is incorrect because there are no misspelled words in the passage; the incorrect forms are spelled correctly but used incorrectly. Marking homophones as spelling errors is a problematic teaching strategy in working with ELs. Instead, the teacher should devise class lessons to help students overcome confusion caused by homophones.
   Competency 001: Linguistic knowledge

7.   **(C)**   The correct response is C. The item stem focuses on feedback so the response should demonstrate an appropriate feedback strategy. Response C shows the teacher providing affective support to the student and explaining how to improve next time. Response C shows the teacher using feedback to promote the learner's achievement. Response A is incorrect because, technically, the words are not misspelled; instead, the use of *cuz* and *u* shows a mix up of registers. Response B is incorrect because using the student's incorrect forms in a Daily Oral Language exercise does not help the learner understand how to integrate science-related terms into future experiments. Response D is incorrect because it reflects a failure to recognize the interrelatedness of literacy and content-area knowledge.
   Competency 007: Assessment in ESL contexts

8.   **(B)**   The correct response is B. The Wow Words activity is designed to build up students' repertoire of words, which is their *lexicon*. Response A is incorrect because the activity does not focus on the sounds or spelling. Response C is incorrect because the activity does not focus on segmenting the word into syllables or roots or affixes. Response D is incorrect because the activity does not include using the new words to modulate intention and outcome in an utterance, which is the focus of pragmatics.
   Competency 001: Linguistic knowledge

9.   **(A), (B), (E)**   Responses A, B, and E describe three strategies that can bolster EL students' understanding of content. Response A, writing a summary at the end of the class, allows learners to record the core points of the lesson; the writing aspect will reinforce the listening and speaking that occurred in class as the instructor delivered the lesson. Response B, defining new key words, is a pillar of EL teaching in content-based classes. Response E, having students do think alouds, will put learners in a performative stance and will allow the teacher to see what needs to be reinforced through additional teaching. Response C is incorrect because knowing how to pronounce new words is less important than knowing what they mean. Response C does not indicate whether the teacher is defining the new words as he breaks them into syllables. Response D is incorrect because it focuses on areas of needed improvement. This is more of an assessment than teaching activity.
   Competency 003: General pedagogy in ESL context

10.   **(A), (D)**   Responses A and D show that content-area teachers need a firm foundation in linguistics in order to help students enter the discourse of the content area. Response A is correct because to help learners pronounce a challenging content-area word, like *quadrilateral*, the teacher needs to show the learner how to break it into syllables and how to use knowledge of roots (morphology) to master the meaning and pronunciation. Response D requires knowledge of how to construct sentences using appropriate connecting words (conjunctions) to demonstrate cause and effect. Response B is incorrect because the science quiz described in the response would not require knowledge of specialized areas of linguistics. Response C is incorrect because memorization is a rote activity that can be done without correct pronunciation or knowledge of what words mean. We are able to memorize strings of words in foreign languages with no understanding of their linguistic significance.
   Competency 001: Linguistic knowledge

11.   **(A)**   Response A is correct. The silent period is an initial period of second language acquisition when a learner has not yet acquired sufficient proficiency and accompanying confidence to interact in L2; thus, the learner stays quiet. This does not mean that the learner is not learning; instead, the silent period construct suggests that the learner is taking in L2 data and waiting until he/she feels comfortable enough to participate. Response B is incorrect because the context is academic rather than BICS. Response C is incorrect because, with the learners not participating in oral language interactions, it is impossible to determine their interlanguage status. Response D is incorrect because the learners' silence makes it difficult to determine how extensive or limited their Cognitive/Academic Language Proficiency is.
   Competency 002: L1 and L2 acquisition

12.   **(A), (C), (D)**   Responses A, C, and D identify strong content area teaching strategies. Response A, identifying roots of important content vocabulary words, will illuminate the meaning of the words. Response C, interactive vocabulary practice, reinforces learners' mastery of content area words. Response D, guiding students to write sentences using content-relevant stems, helps students understand the discourse of the discipline. Response B is incorrect because simply identifying sentence elements does not promote learning in specific content areas. Response E is incorrect because copying sentences is a meaningless drill that does not promote active content-area learning.
   Competency 006: Teaching ESL in content areas

13.   **(B)**   The correct response is B. Hands-on learning is considered one of the most productive strategies for shaping new learning. Response A is incorrect because, while fun is an important part of learning, it should not be the core objective in learning activities. Response C is incorrect because all learning involves using cognitive, metacognitive, and communicative language strategies. Response D is incorrect because the activity is set up as a science project not a test of following instructions.
   Competency 006: Teaching ESL in content areas

14.   **(D)**   Response D is the correct response. The teacher has clearly set up this initial activity as an oral language activity that requires learners to use prior knowledge about general classification to identify similarities and differences in the leaves they collected. Response A is incorrect because limiting L1 transfer is not a valid ESL teaching goal; learners need to be able to rely on their L1 knowledge to shape new L2 learning. Response B is incorrect because there is no indication in the stem that the teacher is expecting students to use new terms in this initial activity. The activity is set up to allow learners to use prior knowledge. Response C is incorrect because the environment *is* academic—the students may have done their work outdoors but they are in a science class.
   Competency 006: Teaching ESL in content areas

15.   **(A)**   The correct response is A. Asking students to interview family members about a favorite plant offers a family connection to classroom learning and engages family in the learners' academic endeavors. Response B is incorrect because integrating new science vocabulary is not the goal of the activity; the interview is likely to be presented as a narrative or as a series of quotes. Additionally, the family member may not have relevant science vocabulary or may introduce concepts that the learner is unfamiliar with and can describe but not present in science terminology. Response C is incorrect because this is not an assessment activity; it is clearly an activity designed to engage family members in the learner's school endeavors. Response D is incorrect because the family member interview is not an assessment activity.
   Competency 010: State and federal guidelines, family engagement, and advocacy

16.   **(A), (B), (E)**   The correct responses are A, B, and E, all of which show learners actively engaged in constructing new learning. Response A is correct because the teacher provides visual scaffolding to introduce the historical figures. Response B is correct because the math teacher provides manipulatives to help learners work through a volume problem. Response E is correct because the teacher creates a learner-led think aloud to show how a reader could enter the story. Response C is incorrect because pop quiz over homework creates anxiety and does not directly promote learning. Response D is incorrect because the brainstorming-names-of-Texas-rivers activity might lead to frustration if learners have no prior knowledge of Texas rivers.
   Competency 008: History of ESL instruction

17.   **(A), (B)**   Responses A and B correctly designate two common transfer and interdependence strategies. Response A is correct because EL students commonly translate passages that are too challenging in L2. Response B is correct because unfamiliar L2 sounds can be pronounced through approximation by relying on similar L1 sounds. Response C is incorrect because asking for help from an L2 speaker does not involve L1 interdependence. Response D is incorrect because looking up L2 words in an L2 dictionary does not depend on L1 knowledge.
   Competency 002: L1 and L2 acquisition

18.   **(C), (D), (E)**   Responses C, D, and E show the importance of creating and sustaining classroom routines as a way of helping EL students integrate into the class community. Response C shows the role of routines in shaping inclusivity for EL students who may not yet have developed communicative competence. Response D shows how the predictability of routines enables EL students to participate in class community activities successfully regardless of current language proficiency. Response E reflects the importance of establishing classroom procedures for all learners. Response A is incorrect because routines are not intended to diminish or offset potential boredom. Response B is incorrect because class routines typically are logistical and organizational and do not directly impact content-area learning. Response F is incorrect because routines do not directly impact cognitive processing of new content-area knowledge.
   Competency 003: General pedagogy in ESL context

19.   **(A), (D)**   Response A and D are correct. Response A is correct because the draft shows consistent errors in verb tense (the writer uses present instead of past tense). Response D is correct because the plural form is not used in *captives* in Sentence (2). Response B is incorrect because the errors appear to be not interference but simple English grammar errors that can be easily corrected through morphological rule application. Response C is incorrect because no words are misspelled. Response E is incorrect because the problems reflect difficulties in rule application not word choice. In fact, the writer's word choice shows understanding of the content-area vocabulary.
   Competency 001: Linguistic knowledge

20. **(B)** The correct response is B. The sentence has only one subject and one verb, so it is a simple sentence. Response A is incorrect because the sentence is grammatically complete. Response C is incorrect because with only one clause, the sentence cannot be considered a complex sentence. Response D is incorrect because the sentence does not include two complete clauses.
   Competency 001: Linguistic knowledge

21. **(D)** The correct response is D. The scenario is designed to help the EL student understand how *registers* are used in different rhetorical circumstances. There is a sharp contrast in the two scenarios. One is a casual conversation among students where speakers would be likely to use colloquialisms, truncated comments, and phatic sounds (such as "hmmm"). The other is a formal academic essay where a student would very likely be observing grammar rules, writing conventions, and genre expectations. Response A is incorrect because while the T-chart will likely include contrasting word choices, the words alone do not show the main difference between the passages. Response B is incorrect because the syntactic choices will not reflect the participants' awareness of the register. Response C is incorrect because nonverbals cannot be detected in written passages.
   Competency 001: Linguistic knowledge

22. **(D)** The correct response is D. The opening line of the scenario shows that this activity is a content activity intended to develop students' vocabulary by learning synonyms for *bounce*. Response A is incorrect because TPR primarily involves following directions that demonstrate basic understanding of L2 by correctly completing simple instructions. While the students have been asked to bounce a rubber ball, the main activity is to complete an academic task: creating a list of verbs, so TPR is not an adequate descriptor of the activity. Response B is incorrect because immersion refers to a holistic approach to language study; the scenario shows only a limited, specific task, in a specific classroom lesson. Response C is incorrect because the students are completing an academic task not primarily a BICS task, although clearly the students will have to talk with each other as they decide on the synonyms.
   Competency 005: Literacy (reading and writing) proficiency

23. **(A), (C)** Responses A and C are correct. These responses show the teacher constructing a language-learning activity that integrates multiple learning styles. Response A correctly reflects the ELPS writing expectations to use details for meaningful explanation. The kinesthetic activity of bouncing the ball should enable the groups to see the ball moving in different ways. The activity would enable students to think of words such as *careen*, *ricochet*, *hurl*, *shoot*, *streak*, and similar synonyms that could be incorporated into writing that illustrates higher levels of ELPS writing expectations. Response C is correct because the task requires multiple types of learning: kinesthetic, collaborative, communicative, and cognitive. Response B is incorrect because insertion of play is not the primary focus of the activity. Response D is incorrect because the task is established within the realm of L2 vocabulary development; however, students might use L1 to identify words they do not know in English.
   Competency 005: Literacy (reading and writing) proficiency

24. **(C)** The correct response is C. This activity will require a high level of communicative interaction among learners. Response A is incorrect because looking up words is an independent activity; however, consulting a dictionary might be triggered by students' communicative interaction if they do not know how to express a certain word. Response B is incorrect because the instructions do not include acting out scenes as part of the activity. Response D is incorrect because, while the activity will require kinesthetic response, moving about is not considered evidence of communicative competence.
   Competency 004: Listening and speaking proficiency

25. **(B)** The correct response is B. The teacher circulating throughout the room and offering feedback on how to revise sentences is an example of authentic assessment that occurs as part of a learning activity. Response A is incorrect because the use of art is a platform for the main activity: the teacher's feedback on the written text. Response C is incorrect because the informal presentation of the group sentence was a lead-in to the assessment opportunity. Response D is incorrect because the activity does not focus on how the students construct the sentences but instead on the follow-up feedback from the teacher.

   Competency 007: Assessment in ESL contexts

26. **(A), (B), (D)** Responses A, B, and D correctly identify the instructional delivery practices seen in the rubber ball activity: the rubber ball is an example of *realia*, the students are creating an actual experience to discover new verb forms, and the multiple activities serve as scaffolding for the culminating short writing activity. Response C is incorrect because there is no preliminary vocabulary to teach since the activity is intended to help students discover new words. Response E is incorrect because culturally relevant pedagogy does not figure prominently in this relatively egalitarian collaborative activity.

   Competency 006: Teaching ESL in content areas

27. **(B)** The correct response is B. Research consistently shows that communicative competencies are acquired relatively easily and quickly, usually in about two years, whereas academic skills take up to eight years. Response A is incorrect because it suggests an acquisition hierarchy with communicative competence as a precondition for growth in other areas of proficiency. While communicative competence is acquired more readily and quickly than competence in academic areas, it is not a precondition for linguistic growth in other areas. Response C also misrepresents the interrelatedness of the language domains by setting up a false dichotomy between sequential and simultaneous acquisition. Neither of these correctly represents the interrelatedness of linguistic skills in SLA. Response D is incorrect because literacy proficiency is not a precondition for communicative proficiency.

   Competency 004: Listening and speaking proficiency

28. **(B)** The correct response is B. Response B correctly explains why L2 mispronunciations occur: the speaker does not "hear" the L2 sound and instead approximates a structure that is close to the actual phonological structure. Response A is incorrect because the item focuses on oral language; we do not know how the student spells the word. Response C is incorrect because the monitor would include the student's knowledge of the correct structure. Response D is incorrect because the word does in fact exist in the student's lexicon since the student is using it.

   Competency 004: Listening and speaking proficiency

29. **(A)** The correct response is A. The scaffolded presentation and practice explained in Response A shows the teacher guiding students in oral language activities to learn new vocabulary. Response B is incorrect because while oral language is involved in the skit, the task also integrates dictionary usage and research and thus deviates from the teacher's learning objective. Response C is incorrect because testing, not oral language development, is the core of this response. Response D is incorrect because the students do not have an opportunity for oral language development in this option.

   Competency 004: Listening and speaking proficiency

30. **(A)** The correct response is A. The activity is described as "Storytelling Day," which clearly reflects ELPS expectations for narrating, describing, and explaining. Response B is incorrect because phonological practice is not the core of the storytelling activity. Response C is incorrect because the scenario does not include specific instructions about integrating new vocabulary. Response D is incorrect because the task does not include stipulations about using content-area vocabulary.

   Competency 004: Listening and speaking proficiency

31.   **(B)**   The correct response is B. A book talk will enable each student to share information about the self-selected book in an oral language context. Response A is incorrect because a written book report does not support oral language development directly. Response C is incorrect because posting the title alone will not support oral language development. Response D is incorrect because a web-based research activity would not directly promote communicative competence.
Competency 004: Listening and speaking proficiency

32.   **(B)**   The correct response is B. Response B reflects the reality that classroom activities sometimes conflict with cultural norms. In some cultures, public speaking conflicts with cultural norms. Teachers need to be aware of this when integrating oral language activities into the classroom. Response A is incorrect because it implies that a goal of ESL instruction is to promote assimilation, which can be seen as diminishing the value of the students' language and culture and suggesting that an L1 background is a deficit. Response C is incorrect because it over-generalizes and stereotypes EL students. Response D is incorrect because the rate of oral language acquisition is not necessarily connected to culture.
Competency 004: Listening and speaking proficiency

33.   **(C)**   The correct response is C. While it could be argued that the sentence makes semantic sense (we can visualize what is going on in the scene), grammatically, the sentence is incorrectly constructed with two prepositional phrases in the subject slot. Response A is incorrect because while the sentence technically starts with a prepositional phrase, this superficial description does not explain the problem. It could be argued that the example is not an actual sentence since there is no grammatical subject. Response B is incorrect because the sentence is not a run-on. Response D is incorrect because the sentence in fact does not have a grammatically correct subject.
Competency 001: Linguistic knowledge

34.   **(C)**   Response C is correct. When a teacher shows students how to complete an academic task, the teacher is *modeling* to create understanding and confidence in learners. Response A is incorrect because scaffolding is a cumulative teaching activity where the teacher creates platforms to build new learning. The modeling activity will serve as scaffolding but in isolation, it is not scaffolding. Response B is incorrect because segmenting means breaking up a longer lesson into smaller chunks of information. Response D is incorrect because while the teacher has created a graphic for the demonstration, the graphic operates as a means to achieve the modeling strategy.
Competency 006: Teaching ESL in content areas

35.   **(B)**   The correct response is B. The teacher has created zone categories that allow students to draw on their life experiences, which is the broad explanation of the *funds of knowledge* construct. Response A is incorrect because the learning zone graphic itself does not represent culturally-relevant pedagogy. Response C is incorrect because we have no information about the teacher's syllabus. Response D is incorrect because filling in the chart is not in itself process writing. Process writing generally refers to multi-step writing that includes prewriting, networking, multiple drafts, feedback, revision, and presentation.
Competency 002: L1 and L2 acquisition

36.   **(A)**   The correct response is A. The think-pair-share activity described in the stem focuses on oral language. Response B is incorrect because while learners collaborate in think-pair-share, the end activity is presentation, which highlights oral language. Response C is incorrect because the activity is not focused on attention to metacognitive strategies; the learners are simply sharing the results of the Learning Zones activity. Response D is incorrect because the assigned task does not include stipulations to use specific vocabulary.
Competency 004: Listening and speaking proficiency

37.   **(C), (D)**   Responses C and D correctly reflect activities designed to promote students' writing proficiency. Response C, the quickwrite, enables students to do a low-stress, short writing on one of the zones. Response D, the word cloud, enables students to start identifying core ideas that could scaffold a full essay. Response A is incorrect because art is not directly a literacy activity in the context of ELPS and ESL pedagogy. The art could be used to derive words for the word cloud or to trigger the quickwrite but the art itself is not a writing activity. Response B is incorrect because internet research is also not directly a writing activity. Response E is incorrect because the questioning is an oral language activity.
       Competency 005: Literacy (reading and writing) proficiency

38.   **(B)**   The correct response is B. Response B correctly explains the source of difficulties that idioms pose for EL students. Response A is incorrect because idioms are not routinely based on allusions. An allusion is a clear reference to a text or event that the creator expects will be recognized by listeners and readers. Response C is incorrect because it suggests that idioms have linguistically logical origins that will make the meaning obvious. Response D is incorrect because the meaning of an idiom is usually relatively clear and direct; the idiom simply allows an edge of creativity in the right register.
       Competency 002: L1 and L2 acquisition

39.   **(A)**   The correct response is A. The examples show consistent use of –*ed* to form past tense, even when there is an irregular past form. So, the writer is *overgeneralizing*. Response B is incorrect because the examples show that the writer has strong knowledge of the rule for forming regular past tense in English as well as knowledge of irregular verb forms. The problem is that the learner is conflating the irregular forms with the rule for regular past forms. Response C is incorrect because the examples show that the writer does know irregular forms; the problem is that the writer is also appending the –*ed* suffix to all the forms. Response D is incorrect because there is no evidence of how the writer responds to hearing the incorrect forms. The student's consistent use of –*ed* forms suggests that the forms seem correct. The error is a problem in morphology, not phonology.
       Competency 001: Linguistic knowledge

40.   **(C)**   The correct response is C. Response C shows correct, and consistent, use of past tense and correct use of the modal *would*. Response A is incorrect because of the present *won't*, the contraction for *will not*. Response B is incorrect because of the present *will not*. Response D is incorrect because *feels* and *writes* show inconsistent use of verb tense as the writer shifts from past to present tense in the short passage.
       Competency 001: Linguistic knowledge

41.   **(B)**   The correct response is B. A false cognate is a word that is spelled similarly in L1 and L2 but that has a different meaning in the two languages and is thus not a true cognate. In Spanish, *asistir* means *to attend*. This confusion in *assist/attend* is a common false cognate problem in EL students with Spanish as L1. Response A is incorrect because usually in approximation, the EL student is aware that he/she doesn't know the exact form and so there is a sort of estimation based on similar forms. In this case, the writer thinks that *assist* means the same thing in L1 and L2, so there is no approximation. Response C is incorrect because we have only one example of the student's writing so we cannot detect a pattern to indicate generalization. Response D is incorrect because the error is clearly a false cognate error which is different from interference caused by relying on L1 structures in L2 environments.
       Competency 002: L1 and L2 acquisition

42.   **(C)**   The correct response is C. The description of the scene indicates that the learner understands and is actively participating. The refusal to read orally is a good indication that the learner is self-checking his readiness to "perform" in oral reading and does not feel ready, which is an indication that his monitor is activated.

Response A is incorrect because the learner is actively participating in an L2 activity; there is no suggestion in the scenario that the student is relying on L1 to understand the reading. Response B is incorrect because the learner's participation and response to the teacher's question indicates that he is getting comprehensible input. Response D is incorrect because the scene does not show the EL student producing L2 discourse, so we cannot determine anything about an interlanguage.

> *Competency 002: L1 and L2 acquisition*

43.   **(C)**   The correct response is C. The structure meets the typical "test" for a simile: a comparison using *like* or *as*. A simile is a type of figurative language used to create a vivid image of an important scene, event, object, or feeling. Response A is incorrect because *hyperbole* is an exaggeration. It could be argued that the phrase is an exaggeration, but it is primarily a simile. Response B is incorrect because the phrase creates an image through the use of a simile. Response D is incorrect because *alliteration* refers to intentional repetition of sounds to create an effect. While the /l/ sound is repeated in the phrase, it is more of a coincidental repetition than the deliberate repetition of alliteration.

> *Competency 001: Linguistic knowledge*

44.   **(B)**   The correct response is B. Janie's output is comprehensible but it clearly suggests that she is relying on her L1 grammar to create her L2 output (using *is* without a subject, appending a vowel sound to the initial sibilant in *study*, using *no* as a generic negative). Response A is incorrect because Janie's L2 performance indicates understanding of fundamental English forms even though her output is rudimentary. Response C is incorrect because there is clear linguistic logic in all of the utterances. Response D is incorrect because the passage reflects that Janie is in fact using L1 to scaffold her L2 performance.

> *Competency 002: L1 and L2 acquisition*

45.   **(A)**   The correct response is (A). The teacher respects Janie's efforts to communicate by focusing on content rather than incorrect forms. By responding in complete sentences that reflect Janie's message, the teacher is promoting Janie's oral language development through modeling and reinforcement. Response B is incorrect because the teacher seems to be using discussion of the assignment to provide scaffolding for the student's L2 development. Response C is incorrect because correcting Janie would be counterproductive in this scenario. Janie's hesitation (the various "uhmmm" utterances) suggest Janie's frustration and self-awareness of her limitations at this point. Furthermore, the teacher's responses indicate that she understands Janie. Response D is incorrect because the teacher's repetition and reconstruction of Janie's basic comments are intended to promote comprehensible input by assuring Janie that her utterances are understandable.

> *Competency 002: L1 and L2 acquisition*

46.   **(C)**   The correct response is C. While the conversation between Janie and her teacher is about incomplete homework, the exchange is focused on communication, on ensuring that the two parties understand what each wants. Basic Interpersonal Communicative Skills reflect everyday language and routine class interactions rather than academic language. Response A is incorrect because this is a conversation about homework completion not about understanding class content. Response B is incorrect because the ease with which Janie converses with the teacher suggests that she is not filtering her output and is interested in trying to communicate. Response D is incorrect because we have only this short snippet of dialogue which does not provide adequate data on Janie's current interlanguage.

> *Competency 002: L1 and L2 acquisition*

47.   **(A)**   The correct response is (A). Janie's mispronunciation of USB demonstrates negative transfer from Spanish phonology. She seems to be appropriating knowledge from L1 to create output in L2. However, fre-

quently such transfer results in L2 errors because of negative transfer. Janie creates an incorrect L2 structure by approximating the long /u/ in USB using a phoneme from her L1. Response B is incorrect because no translation is involved. Response C is incorrect because risk-taking refers to linguistic choices that indicate the learner is applying new but incompletely acquired knowledge. In this dialogue, Janie seems hesitant, which is not a feature of linguistic risk-taking. Response D is incorrect because the conversation suggests that Janie's filter is working—the hesitation, the monosyllabic responses—as she tries to construct meaningful responses.

Competency 002: L1 and L2 acquisition

48.   **(B), (D), (E)**   Response B is correct because the teacher's use of affirmative language and gestures indicates an interest in making the learner feel comfortable during the discussion. Response D is correct because at no point does the teacher suggest that she is not understanding the student; in fact, she repeats Janie's partial or incorrectly worded statements to demonstrate understanding. Response E is correct because the teacher's consistent efforts to sustain the communicative effort clearly show that she understands the way that learners rely on L1 to produce L2 utterances. Response A is incorrect because the teacher is focused on creating comprehensible input for Janie, not on correcting incorrect structures. The teacher's repetition of Janie's comments in correct form indicates that she is trying to show Janie that she understands her. Response C is incorrect because the teacher understands Janie's concern over missing the deadline and even suggests that the assignment can be completed by the end of the day.

Competency 002: L1 and L2 acquisition

49.   **(D)**   The correct response is D. Because this teacher has a wide range of EL levels in his class, he needs an assignment that can be self-adjusted to individual learner levels. This favorite film assignment would create a strong communicative context (authenticity) while providing opportunities for learners to develop writing, reading, speaking, and listening skills. Response A is incorrect because the assignment calls for informal writing that would not require a full-fledged application of writing processes. Response B is incorrect because while students will be doing a short oral presentation, the highly personal nature of the assignment makes this an informal speech situation in which interest in the speaker's opinions and explanations should outweigh concerns about structuring a formal presentation. Response C is incorrect because the set-up does not indicate that the instructor is interested in teaching about film. The film assignment is being used to support a multicultural teaching environment.

Competency 009: Multiculturalism in ESL classrooms

50.   **(D)**   The correct response is D. By stopping at 10- to 15-minute intervals and interacting with his students in the manner described in this response, the teacher is developing his learners' metacognitive strategies for monitoring and boosting their comprehension of content. Response A is incorrect because, while pre-testing and post-testing are traditional assessment tools, the teacher is interested in *developing* knowledge rather than assessment in the scenario described here. Response B is incorrect because simply reading orally from the text (with the teacher interrupting to correct mispronunciations) does not enable learners to glean meaningful content from the lesson. Response C is incorrect because collecting questions at the end of the period provides no opportunity for authentic discussion and clarification of the content covered in the class session.

Competency 003: General pedagogy in ESL context

51.   **(C)**   The correct response is C. This teacher faces the challenge of ensuring that both his native speakers and the ESL students learn literature content and that the ESL learners have appropriate instructional scaffolding to promote language learning. The book talk would provide scaffolding for all learners, including the native speakers. Response A is incorrect because vocabulary lessons would be more effective integrated into class discussion as the class reads the story rather than prior to reading and prior to establishing a context for the words. Response B is incorrect because the goal is to create a learning environment in which students understand the story. Watching

a film about the author's work is a good strategy, but at this point, students need scaffolding to support entry into a literary text such as would be provided by response A. Response D is incorrect because the pedagogical challenge the teacher faces—making the story comprehensible for his students—would not be addressed by having them independently read the story.

Competency 003: General pedagogy in ESL context

52.   **(A)**   The correct response is A. Cloze exams are created from passages in which words are omitted. Usually, the omission formula deletes every fifth or seventh word. However, in this cloze-type passage, the omitted words have been deliberately picked to make the exercise more accessible to EL students whose syntactic proficiency in English is still developing. Cloze exams are intended for practice in syntactic and semantic competence; they are not exclusively used in ESL pedagogy, but they adapt very effectively to ESL teaching situations. Response B is incorrect because DOL exercises are typically one or two sentences that students correct usually working in a whole-class discussion. Response C is incorrect because Sustained Silent Reading is a reading activity that allows students to self-select texts for independent reading. Response D is incorrect because the cloze exam format generally does not involve oral reading since it tests students' cognitive strategies in constructing meaning.

Competency 005: Literacy (reading and writing) proficiency

53.   **(B)**   The correct response is B. The blanks in cloze exams give students an opportunity to determine what word is an appropriate syntactic and semantic fit within the context of the passage. It is important to note that this cloze activity is likely to yield some interesting responses that "fit" into the blanks because they make sense semantically and syntactically. In other words, the teacher would not be looking for a single "right" answer for each blank. Response A is incorrect: the focus is not the student's thinking about his/her own thinking but instead recognizing the syntactic and semantic parameters established by the context. Response C is incorrect because cloze exams do not primarily promote comprehension—too much information is missing and the point of the exercise is to attempt to fill in the blanks with appropriate choices. Response D is incorrect because cloze exams are not focused on knowing meanings but on recognizing what meaning is suggested by the context.

Competency 005: Literacy (reading and writing) proficiency

54.   **(A)**   The correct response is A. An unfortunate side effect of some cloze exams is frustration. Providing a list of possibilities for each blank (with appropriate distractors) is a common strategy for making the activity more accessible to students. Having the students choose from the list will make the activity less challenging, but the instructional goal of developing syntactic and semantic proficiency will still be met. Response B is incorrect because a read aloud should be focused on creating meaning from the text being read; reading it orally should enhance the students' comprehension. Neither of those objectives applies in reading a cloze passage orally. Response C is incorrect because telling students to look up other words in the passage will not address the frustration issue. Response D is incorrect because the cloze activity is not a content-acquisition activity.

Competency 003: General pedagogy in ESL context

55.   **(B)**   The correct response is B. When EL students seek each other out during class activities, it is an indication that they need the support provided by fellow L1 speakers. By putting at least two EL students in each group, the teacher is reducing the anxiety that the students seem to feel. Furthermore, the native speakers can help their EL classmates negotiate the Zone of Proximal Development. Response A is incorrect because restricting EL students' use of their L1 is an inappropriate teaching strategy in this particular scenario because the students are likely to feel isolated and excluded. Response C is incorrect because in providing an L1 translation of the class work, the teacher would not be promoting the students' content-specific language development. Response D is incorrect because reading the instructions orally to each group will not address the underlying problem in this scenario (which is the EL students' apparent discomfort over their limited understanding of science content).

Competency 003: General pedagogy in ESL context

56. **(C)** The correct response is C. Modeling and using visual support will promote this teacher's goal to develop students' Cognitive/Academic Language Proficiency in science. Response A is incorrect because the EL students are at intermediate to advanced levels, indicating that they have substantive proficiency in English, but they need more directive teaching in content. Response B is incorrect because relying on native language descriptions of the science content will not advance the EL students' Cognitive/Academic Language Proficiency. Response D is incorrect because conducting experiments involves hands-on, active learning rather than paper-and-pencil assessment.

Competency 006: Teaching ESL in content areas

57. **(D)** The correct response is D. Conferencing is considered the best method for promoting student competence in writing. As a team, the English teacher and the science teacher could guide the students in using the required written report to reflect their understanding of science content. A good mix of directive conferencing, where the teachers directly explain how to correct errors, and non-directive, where the teachers encourage students to explain their linguistic choices, would help students meet ELPS expectations. Response A is incorrect because marking errors and having students make corrections does not address the level of learner independence suggested in ELPS expectations for writing. Response B is counter to the expectations for a writing workshop environment: peer editing should never be reduced to error hunting. Response C is incorrect because the students in this scenario are at the intermediate and advanced levels, far beyond the proficiency levels where they might have relied on translation from L1 to L2; this approach would be a step back for the learners.

Competency 005: Literacy (reading and writing) proficiency

58. **(C)** The correct response is C. This activity allows the greatest level of collaboration, moves students into higher areas of Bloom's Taxonomy, and actively promotes growth in language proficiency. Response A is incorrect because the identification activity would tell the teacher that students are able to identify prepositions, but it would fail to meet the teacher's goal to encourage them to use a wider variety of prepositions. Response B does not meet the teacher's instructional goal. Searching in the dictionary for words that might be prepositions would probably result in high levels of frustration and limited language growth. Response D would be a good strategy during revision when the teacher could still offer formative comments and students could still make improvements prior to summative assessment.

Competency 005: Literacy (reading and writing) proficiency

59. **(D)** The correct response is D. The teacher seems interested in increasing students' content knowledge by changing her teaching strategy. The collaborative activity she designed will provide opportunities for students to cooperate in completing the task, to forge new understandings of history content, and to operate at higher levels of thinking. Response A misinterprets the teacher's instructional goal: she is not trying to make things more fun; she wants to enhance the students' learning. Response B is incorrect because forced rereading is not the instructional goal. However, students are likely to reread as a manifestation of cognitive strategies for learning new content. Response C is incorrect because it suggests that the teacher has abdicated instructional responsibility by using an alternative to the lecture format.

Competency 003: General pedagogy in ESL context

60. **(B)** The correct response is B. The hallmark of two-way dual immersion approaches is the integration of native speakers and non-native speakers in all areas of instruction. Dual immersion is a bilingual program approach that aims at biliteracy for both native English speakers and non-native English speakers. Response A is incorrect because ESL programs strive to integrate learners rather than to segregate them. Response C is incorrect

because dual immersion programs are not supplementary. Response D is incorrect; it describes the traditional immersion approach that is sometimes referred to as the "sink or swim" approach.

Competency 008: History of ESL instruction

61. **(B)** The correct response is B. The Texas Administrative Code stipulates that in dual immersion programs, both one-way and two-way, at least half of the instruction must be in the non-English language. Response A, Response C, and Response D are incorrect because the L1 to L2 ratio is determined by TAC Title 19, Part 2, Chapter 89 and is correctly represented in Response B.

Competency 008: History of ESL instruction

62. **(C)** The correct response is C. The Texas Education Code (TEC) officially documents all regulations impacting public education in Texas. Information from the TEC is integrated into the Texas Administrative Code (TAC) which is a compilation of all state agency rules in Texas; TEC regulations are integrated into Title 19 of the TAC. Response A is incorrect because TEA facilitates and directs implementation of state and federal requirements for language programs. Response B is incorrect; the U.S. Department of Education impacts education in all states, but specific aspects of Texas public education are managed through the state legislature and TEA. Response D is incorrect; ESSA is the federal legislation for language programs in all states, but the specific Texas applications are implemented by TEA under the direction of state legislative updates in the TEC.

Competency 008: History of ESL instruction

63. **(D)** The correct response is D. The item stem sums up the operational definition of newcomer programs. Response A is incorrect, although many ESL programs, including newcomer programs, are described as "transitional" because the goal is to support students in their L2 literacy and academic development so that they can move to mainstream classes. Response B is incorrect because "initial language program" is not a term used in describing ESL programs. Response C is incorrect because "assimilation program" is not a term used in describing ESL programs.

Competency 008: History of ESL instruction

64. **(A)** The correct response is A. The Elementary and Secondary Education Act (reauthorized in 2015 as the Every Student Succeeds Act) broadly established the need to create equitable educational opportunities for language minority and low income students. Response B is incorrect because federal and state language programs seek proficiency and academic success rather than just fluency in English. Response C is incorrect because establishing an official language is beyond the purview of federal and state regulations that apply to school language programs. Response D is incorrect because it presents a subtractive interpretation of the goals of federally and state-mandated language programs. Response D incorrectly implies that the goal of federal and state regulations for language programs is to eradicate students' first language.

Competency 008: History of ESL instruction

65. **(B)** The correct response is B. This response most effectively reflects the biliteracy goals of two-way dual language/immersion programs, and it is developmentally appropriate for the young learners. Response A is incorrect because it focuses on L2 and thereby fails to capture the intent of the dual language/immersion model. Response C is incorrect because it limits the learners' collaborative efforts and focuses on L2. Response D is incorrect because it focuses on L1; had the assignment gone further, requiring a paragraph written in L2 as well or a translation of the L1 paragraph, this response would be a better fit for the item stem.

Competency 008: History of ESL instruction

66.   **(B)**   The correct response is B. This response offers a concise summary of classroom accommodations designed to promote students' learning in ESL programs. Scaffolding generally refers to instructional activities that offer guidance while learners acquire new knowledge and which are intended to lead the learner toward independence. Response A is incorrect because it describes a traditional classroom activity—testing—without further accommodation for EL students. Response C is incorrect because the film-enriched activity alone does not offer the instructional guidance associated with scaffolding in ESL programs. Response D is incorrect because creating L1 and L2 versions of *every* lesson is not a strategy supported by ESL instructional practices.

Competency 008: History of ESL instruction

67.   **(C)**   The correct response is C. This research activity seems designed to enhance students' understanding of how civil rights struggles are waged throughout the world and throughout history in a variety of cultures and countries. Response A is incorrect because the L1 option seems intended to allow students some choice in how they carry out their research but it does not directly support new content-area learning. Response B is incorrect because the assignment is not described as a means of supplementing or correcting the textbook. Response D is incorrect because technology is not intended to alleviate learner anxiety or reduce the required effort. As presented in the stem, the integration of technology in this assignment will enhance the learners' research efforts.

Competency 009: Multiculturalism in ESL classrooms

68.   **(B)**   The correct response is B. The activity is likely to enhance students' understanding of civil rights advocates throughout history and throughout the world, thereby promoting a multicultural view of this important effort. Response A is incorrect because both the round robin and the letter writing will require critical thinking as learners adjust their language and integrate their new understanding in creating the letter. Response C is incorrect because the activity is not set up as an assessment at this point. Response D is incorrect because the possibility of additional research is not a primary feature of the culminating assignment. As presented in the description, the assignment seems to require only the research that the students have already done.

Competency 009: Multiculturalism in ESL classrooms

69.   **(C)**   The correct response is C. This activity provides a good opportunity to initiate a discussion on childhood universals and their culturally-specific manifestations. Response A is incorrect because the activity in the scenario is not presented as a writing process activity. Response B is incorrect because the integration of the oral language component is secondary to the multicultural focus. Response D is incorrect because it misrepresents the teacher's instructional intent as represented by the item stem. The activity does not promote the use of L1; instead, the activity invites learners to consider similarities in childhood experiences across cultures.

Competency 009: Multiculturalism in ESL classrooms

70.   **(B)**   The correct response is B. Cultural insularity leads students to assume that body language and gestures have universal meaning; this film-viewing activity is designed to extend students' understanding of the importance of nonverbals in conveying meaning in all cultures. Response A is incorrect because this specific, limited outcome is not suggested by the activity description. Response C is incorrect because it misrepresents the activity as a simple film-viewing activity. Response D is incorrect because the scenario specifies that the instructional goal is to explore greeting styles not body language as a whole.

Competency 009: Multiculturalism in ESL classrooms

71.   **(D)**   The correct response is D. The activity is designed to reveal students' preconceived notions of certain *types* of people, which is the core definition of stereotyping. A lesson on stereotyping will move students toward an awareness of the foundations of cultural bias. Response A is incorrect because it oversimplifies the intent of the activity, particularly given the ESL setting, and inappropriately suggests that bias is the result of something as

simple as preference. Response B is incorrect because the assignment focuses not on language but on stereotyping based on preconceived notions about individuals. Response C is incorrect because age differences are irrelevant or at best peripheral to the focus of activity.

Competency 009: Multiculturalism in ESL classrooms

72. **(B)** The correct response is B. In writing paragraphs about themselves and sharing them before the whole class, students will learn quite a bit about each other. In this highly personal writing assignment, students will draw on their cultural background; in listening to each other's paragraphs, they will become more aware of the diversity they all bring to the classroom. Response A is incorrect because collaboration is not the focus of the activity. Response C is incorrect because the sharing activity is not intended to enhance grammar knowledge. Response D is incorrect because this community-building activity is not intended as an assessment baseline.

Competency 009: Multiculturalism in ESL classrooms

73. **(C)** The correct response is C. By integrating parents into classroom scenarios, the teacher is facilitating the ESL students' family involvement in their children's education. Response A is incorrect because it misrepresents the intent of the activity since the classroom is the learning site in this teaching scenario. Response B is incorrect because it suggests parental involvement is a distraction from the rigor of ESL learning rather than an integral part of the students' learning experiences. Response D is incorrect because parental involvement is not a mandated component of TELPAS.

Competency 010: State and federal guidelines, family engagement, and advocacy

74. **(C)** The correct response is C. Student advocacy in ESL programs extends to collaborating with colleagues as described in this response. When ESL teachers share their knowledge with colleagues, both teachers and students benefit. By observing each other, teachers across disciplines would have on-the-spot resources and strategies that they could immediately adapt in their own classrooms. Response A is incorrect because TEA does not offer direct teaching strategies. Simply sharing information about TELPAS will not enable teachers to meet their goal to develop students' listening and speaking skills in the context of content-area instruction. Response B is incorrect because the principal is not likely to be the best resource for specific ESL-related teaching concerns. Response D is incorrect because having students do a multimodal presentation that incorporates a wide variety of communication, content-area skills, and independent work abilities would require competencies that the students may not yet have. The item stem suggests that the teachers are seeking ways to integrate fundamental listening and speaking support into content-area teaching.

Competency 010: State and federal guidelines, family engagement, and advocacy

75. **(A)** The correct response is A. If parents are unsure about how L1 instruction and ESL instruction will benefit their children, a demonstration should ease their concerns much more effectively than simply reading the required consent letter. TEA does not explain why some parents do not provide written approval; this scenario speculates the reluctance might stem from not knowing how ESL education operates on a day-to-day basis. Response B is incorrect because brochures are already available on the TEA website. Simply sending out a brochure that is already available will not address whatever concerns or misunderstandings might keep parents from providing consent. Response C is incorrect because it is unrealistic particularly in schools with a high percentage of EL students. This option would extend the official letter requirement that is already in place, but information about the ESL mandates is not likely to persuade reluctant parents to provide the written approval. Response D is incorrect because if the targeted audience doesn't have sufficient foundational information, they won't be able to ask questions that address their concerns.

Competency 010: State and federal guidelines, family engagement, and advocacy

76.   **(C), (D), (E)**   Responses C, D, and E correctly reflect the membership of the LPAC as stipulated by the Texas Education Code. Response A is incorrect because school board members are not included in the TEC requirements for LPAC members. Response B is incorrect because the TEC does not require a parent-teacher association member on LPAC. Response F is incorrect because the regional service center is not included in the TEC requirements for LPAC membership.

Competency 010: State and federal guidelines, family engagement, and advocacy

77.   **(D)**   The correct response is D. As presented by the TEC and TAC, individual classroom teachers have no direct role in determining students' readiness to exit language programs since the decision is based on students' test scores. Nonetheless, the classroom teacher operates in a powerful advocacy role as the day-to-day director of classroom activities and learner support. Response A is incorrect because informing parents of students' language proficiency progress is an LPAC responsibility. Response B is incorrect because LPAC decision-making does not include classroom performance. The LPAC's annual review *does* include grades in content-area classes, but individual teachers do not have a direct role in the review. Response C is incorrect because the LPAC decisions about placement or reclassification are based on student performance on mandated content-area and language exams.

Competency 010: State and federal guidelines, family engagement, and advocacy

78.   **(A)**   The correct response is A. The Texas Education Code assigns to the LPAC the authority for determining EL status and placement in a specific language program. ESL Exam 154 focuses on ESL program placement. Bilingual programs are available for students whom the LPAC determines would be better served by placement in a bilingual program. Response B is incorrect because language program placement does not involve the language arts teacher. Response C is incorrect because the school principal is not directly involved with student placement in a language program (unless the principal is the school administrator on the LPAC). Response D is incorrect because the district ESL coordinator is not a mandated participant in language program placement decisions.

Competency 010: State and federal guidelines, family engagement, and advocacy

79.   **(B)**   The correct response is B. TEA's Supporting English Learners in Texas web portal assembles a wide variety of state documents, professional resources, and teaching materials. A teacher new to an ESL program would find an abundance of continually updated information on this site. Response A is incorrect because the LPAC framework manual presents the TEC and TAC mandates for the LPAC responsibilities. The manual focuses on procedures and forms rather than teacher responsibilities. Response C is incorrect because the TEC includes official mandates for ESL programs but little information relevant to individual classroom teachers. Response D is incorrect because the English Language Proficiency Standards are presented as student expectations and descriptors of learner performance in the four domains in the four proficiency levels. ELPS does not include explicit information on teacher responsibilities.

Competency 010: State and federal guidelines, family engagement, and advocacy

80.   **(A)**   The correct response is A. Bias generally refers to a view "slanted" toward a preconceived outcome; the bias prohibits fair evaluation of a situation and usually involves overlooking facts that might counter the bias. This teacher's expectation that the ESL students will "fail" the state-mandated exams is an example of bias that interferes with creating an effective multilingual learning environment. Response B is incorrect because the teacher's comments extend far beyond cultural insensitivity. The teacher's comments also demonstrate low expectations for learners on the basis of their cultural, linguistic, and ethnic background. Response C is incorrect because the teacher does not demonstrate an interest in creating pedagogy that leads to good results for all learners. Response D is incorrect because the teacher seems more interested in sustaining the bias that ESL students are doomed to failure on the exams than in helping all students get high scores.

Competency 009: Multiculturalism in ESL classrooms

PRACTICE TEST 2

TExES English as a Second Language Supplemental (154)

Also available at the REA Study Center *(www.rea.com/studycenter)*

This practice test is also offered online at the REA Study Center. We recommend that you take the online version of the test to simulate test-day conditions and to receive these added benefits:

- **Timed testing conditions**—helps you gauge how much time you can spend on each question

- **Automatic scoring**—find out how you did on the test, instantly

- **On-screen detailed explanations of answers**—gives you the correct answer and explains why the other answer choices are wrong

- **Diagnostic score reports**—pinpoint where you're strongest and where you need to focus your study

ANSWER SHEET FOR PRACTICE TEST 2

1. Ⓐ Ⓑ Ⓒ Ⓓ
2. Ⓐ Ⓑ Ⓒ Ⓓ
3. Ⓐ Ⓑ Ⓒ Ⓓ
4. Ⓐ Ⓑ Ⓒ Ⓓ Ⓔ Ⓕ
5. Ⓐ Ⓑ Ⓒ Ⓓ Ⓔ
6. Ⓐ Ⓑ Ⓒ Ⓓ Ⓔ Ⓕ
7. Ⓐ Ⓑ Ⓒ Ⓓ Ⓔ
8. Ⓐ Ⓑ Ⓒ Ⓓ
9. Ⓐ Ⓑ Ⓒ Ⓓ Ⓔ
10. Ⓐ Ⓑ Ⓒ Ⓓ
11. Ⓐ Ⓑ Ⓒ Ⓓ
12. Ⓐ Ⓑ Ⓒ Ⓓ
13. Ⓐ Ⓑ Ⓒ Ⓓ
14. Ⓐ Ⓑ Ⓒ Ⓓ
15. Ⓐ Ⓑ Ⓒ Ⓓ
16. Ⓐ Ⓑ Ⓒ Ⓓ
17. Ⓐ Ⓑ Ⓒ Ⓓ
18. Ⓐ Ⓑ Ⓒ Ⓓ
19. Ⓐ Ⓑ Ⓒ Ⓓ Ⓔ Ⓕ
20. Ⓐ Ⓑ Ⓒ Ⓓ
21. Ⓐ Ⓑ Ⓒ Ⓓ
22. Ⓐ Ⓑ Ⓒ Ⓓ
23. Ⓐ Ⓑ Ⓒ Ⓓ Ⓔ
24. Ⓐ Ⓑ Ⓒ Ⓓ
25. Ⓐ Ⓑ Ⓒ Ⓓ
26. Ⓐ Ⓑ Ⓒ Ⓓ
27. Ⓐ Ⓑ Ⓒ Ⓓ

28. Ⓐ Ⓑ Ⓒ Ⓓ
29. Ⓐ Ⓑ Ⓒ Ⓓ
30. Ⓐ Ⓑ Ⓒ Ⓓ
31. Ⓐ Ⓑ Ⓒ Ⓓ
32. Ⓐ Ⓑ Ⓒ Ⓓ
33. Ⓐ Ⓑ Ⓒ Ⓓ
34. Ⓐ Ⓑ Ⓒ Ⓓ
35. Ⓐ Ⓑ Ⓒ Ⓓ
36. Ⓐ Ⓑ Ⓒ Ⓓ
37. Ⓐ Ⓑ Ⓒ Ⓓ
38. Ⓐ Ⓑ Ⓒ Ⓓ
39. Ⓐ Ⓑ Ⓒ Ⓓ
40. Ⓐ Ⓑ Ⓒ Ⓓ
41. Ⓐ Ⓑ Ⓒ Ⓓ
42. Ⓐ Ⓑ Ⓒ Ⓓ
43. Ⓐ Ⓑ Ⓒ Ⓓ
44. Ⓐ Ⓑ Ⓒ Ⓓ
45. Ⓐ Ⓑ Ⓒ Ⓓ Ⓔ
46. Ⓐ Ⓑ Ⓒ Ⓓ
47. Ⓐ Ⓑ Ⓒ Ⓓ
48. Ⓐ Ⓑ Ⓒ Ⓓ
49. Ⓐ Ⓑ Ⓒ Ⓓ
50. Ⓐ Ⓑ Ⓒ Ⓓ
51. Ⓐ Ⓑ Ⓒ Ⓓ
52. Ⓐ Ⓑ Ⓒ Ⓓ
53. Ⓐ Ⓑ Ⓒ Ⓓ Ⓔ Ⓕ
54. Ⓐ Ⓑ Ⓒ Ⓓ

55. Ⓐ Ⓑ Ⓒ Ⓓ
56. Ⓐ Ⓑ Ⓒ Ⓓ
57. Ⓐ Ⓑ Ⓒ Ⓓ
58. Ⓐ Ⓑ Ⓒ Ⓓ
59. Ⓐ Ⓑ Ⓒ Ⓓ
60. Ⓐ Ⓑ Ⓒ Ⓓ
61. Ⓐ Ⓑ Ⓒ Ⓓ
62. Ⓐ Ⓑ Ⓒ Ⓓ
63. Ⓐ Ⓑ Ⓒ Ⓓ
64. Ⓐ Ⓑ Ⓒ Ⓓ
65. Ⓐ Ⓑ Ⓒ Ⓓ Ⓔ Ⓕ
66. Ⓐ Ⓑ Ⓒ Ⓓ
67. Ⓐ Ⓑ Ⓒ Ⓓ Ⓔ Ⓕ
68. Ⓐ Ⓑ Ⓒ Ⓓ
69. Ⓐ Ⓑ Ⓒ Ⓓ
70. Ⓐ Ⓑ Ⓒ Ⓓ
71. Ⓐ Ⓑ Ⓒ Ⓓ
72. Ⓐ Ⓑ Ⓒ Ⓓ
73. Ⓐ Ⓑ Ⓒ Ⓓ
74. Ⓐ Ⓑ Ⓒ Ⓓ
75. Ⓐ Ⓑ Ⓒ Ⓓ
76. Ⓐ Ⓑ Ⓒ Ⓓ
77. Ⓐ Ⓑ Ⓒ Ⓓ
78. Ⓐ Ⓑ Ⓒ Ⓓ
79. Ⓐ Ⓑ Ⓒ Ⓓ
80. Ⓐ Ⓑ Ⓒ Ⓓ

TIME: 4 hours and 45 minutes
80 multiple-choice questions

> **Directions:** Answer each question by selecting the correct response or responses. Most items on this test require that you provide the one best answer. However, some questions require that you select one or more answers, in which case you will be directed to respond with either a specific number of answers or all answers that apply.

1. Which of the following statements best represents how an ESL teacher can use ELPS to provide instruction that supports EL students' understanding of mechanics, grammar, vocabulary, sentence structure, and word formation?

    A. ELPS identifies specific student expectations in SLA and in the four language domains.
    B. ELPS shows how teachers can use communicative competence as a foundation for higher-level academic skills.
    C. ELPS stipulates specific competencies that EL students should demonstrate at each grade level.
    D. ELPS offers teaching strategies to show EL students how to write grade-level sentences.

2. Which of the following explanations best describes the concept of *interrelatedness of language domains*?

    A. Listening, speaking, reading, and writing are learned sequentially with the simplest—listening—shaping a platform for the more difficult skills.
    B. Listening, speaking, reading, and writing are integrally related, with the learner using skills in a distinct area to support comprehension and output in all other areas.
    C. Listening, speaking, reading, and writing should be taught in isolation to enable learners to concentrate on comprehension and output competencies in each area.
    D. Listening, speaking, reading, and writing in L2 can be fully mastered only when learners develop an expansive vocabulary in L2.

3. Which of the following statements best explains why ESL teachers in all content areas need a strong foundation in linguistics?

    A. Knowing the mechanics and conventions of English enables teachers to identify errors in EL students' speech and writing.
    B. Knowing the structure of English enables teachers to identify linguistic patterns and specialized language that learners need to know in each content area.
    C. Knowing the structure of English enables teachers to create challenging academic lessons to push EL students to higher levels of achievement.
    D. Knowing the mechanics and conventions of English enables teachers to recognize when learners are ready to move to the next level of proficiency.

4. Which THREE of the following explanations correctly describe language programs mandated by the Texas Education Code?

   A. Dual language programs are required for all native speakers and LEP students in Grades 1 through 3.
   B. Bilingual students are automatically placed in language programs so that teachers can determine each student's degree of English proficiency and recommend appropriate mainstream or continued language programs.
   C. Content-based ESL programs are taught in content areas by teachers certified to teach ESL.
   D. Pull-out programs allow EL students to attend mainstream classes with supplementary language instruction provided by specialized language teachers.
   E. Dual language programs promote biliteracy.
   F. ESL programs are available only through Grade 6; after that, LEP students are placed in an English immersion program.

5. Which TWO of the following considerations correctly explain the criteria used to initially identify language learners in Texas?

   A. Limited English Proficiency is the descriptor used for students in state-designated language programs.
   B. Limited English Proficiency is the descriptor used to identify students who are bilingual but are English dominant.
   C. Limited English Proficiency is the descriptor used to identify students whose home language is a language other than English.
   D. Limited English Proficiency is the descriptor used to identify students who need to learn English before they are allowed to enroll in school.
   E. Limited English Proficiency is the descriptor used to designate students whose lack of proficiency in English would inhibit success and understanding in school.

6. Which ONE of the following statements misrepresents the interrelatedness of L1 and L2 in second language acquisition?

   A. Knowledge of L1 supports learning of L2 in both communicative and academic areas.
   B. Cognates can help EL students learn vocabulary in L2.
   C. All languages are fundamentally the same, so there is automatic transfer from L1 to L2.
   D. Knowledge of some aspects of linguistic systems in L1 can be transferred into learning in L2.
   E. Limited formal education in L1 can slow down academic learning in L2.
   F. Many communicative aspects of L1 can be easily transferred into L2 learning.

7. Which THREE of the following types of errors correctly explain sources of difficulties in second language acquisition?

   A. Generalization
   B. False cognates
   C. Approximation
   D. Direct translation
   E. Memorization

8. Which of the following explanations correctly describes code-switching?

   A. Deliberately using words and phrases from L1 in L2 constructions and utterances.
   B. Integrating ideas from L1 in L2 constructions and utterances.
   C. Using pronunciations from L1 in L2 speech.
   D. Directly translating L1 structures into L2 constructions and utterances.

9. Which THREE of the following strategies are typical cognitive processes used in second language acquisition?

   A. Memorization
   B. Repetition
   C. Prior knowledge
   D. Asking questions
   E. Observation

10. In an upper elementary class of intermediate to advanced EL students, the teacher displays the following exercise on the overhead projector.

    Look at this set of sentences. With your group members, come up with a "rule" that explains a sentence structure that you see repeated in all of the sentences.

    1. Growing up, I spent a lot of summers with my grandparents in Mexico.

    2. On my grandparents' ranch, the mesquite trees, dirt piles, and watering holes were my playground.

    3. Almost every day, I would wake up with the first light, gobble my breakfast, and dash outside.

    4. At the end of the summer, it was time to return to my home in Texas.

    This teaching activity is designed to address which of the following cognitive processes in L2 acquisition?

    A. Syntactic variation
    B. Generalization
    C. Transfer
    D. Error analysis

11. Which of the following sentences shows the correct use of an introductory participle phrase?

    A. Looking around, the boys noticed an open window.
    B. Looking around, someone was probably following the boys.
    C. Looking around, the truck seemed too close to the building.
    D. Looking around, it was getting darker and darker.

12. Using prefixes and suffixes effectively to create new forms of words reflects an EL student's knowledge in which of the following areas of linguistics?

    A.   Syntax
    B.   Semantics
    C.   Morphology
    D.   Phonology

13. Which of the following explanations best describes how collaborative activities support EL students' developing English proficiency?

    A.   Simple class activities performed in small group settings allow teachers to assess EL students' language learning in oral language.
    B.   Group activities shift responsibility for L2 learning completely to the EL students through interactive opportunities.
    C.   Using a collaborative approach instead of independent work keeps students from making errors due to limited L2 proficiency because EL students can modulate their participation in group activities.
    D.   Group activities support EL students' social language development by providing opportunities to participate meaningfully with classmates in a variety of learning activities.

14. A middle school history teacher is having a writing workshop while students generate summaries of the current chapter. The class is a mainstream English class with about one-fourth of it made up of pull-out students. On workshop day, the teacher gives each student three colored pencils and gives them the following directions:

    1.   Underline the sentence that you are proudest of having written. This may be a sentence that you are proud of because of how you wrote it (the syntactic structure) or because of what it says (the content).

    2.   With a different color, circle the single word that you are proudest of having included in your essay.

    3.   With the third color, circle one or more words that you are unsure of (you think perhaps you are misusing them or you're not sure about the meaning or you're not sure if they fit the sentence, etc.).

    After the students complete this activity, the teacher has mini-conferences with each student, listening to them as they explain what they underlined and circled in their drafts. This teaching activity reflects the teacher's interest in promoting EL students' language proficiency in which of the following ways?

    A.   The teacher is promoting students' independence as writers.
    B.   The teacher is providing students an opportunity to revise their writing.
    C.   The teacher wants to make sure that students use in-class workshopping to correct their sentences and word choices.
    D.   The teacher wants students to understand that every sentence they write must be correctly structured and effectively worded.

Use this scenario to answer the next two items.

Cindy, a grade 10 EL student, is doing an oral presentation about the animated film *Mulan*. She includes the following statement in her presentation:

The story is based on a sixth century poem.

She pronounces *century* as *senry*.

15. The pronunciation shows which of the following language acquisition strategies?

    A.   Interference
    B.   Transfer
    C.   False cognate
    D.   Translation

16. To help Cindy pronounce *century* correctly, the teacher will apply knowledge from which of the following linguistic systems?

    A.   Phonology
    B.   Morphology
    C.   Pragmatics
    D.   Semantics

17. A student in a high school chemistry class writes the following sentence in a lab report:

    1st i measured the hydrochloric acid & poured it in the beaker because u need exactly the right amount.

    This sentence shows a problem in which of the following areas?

    A.   Syntax
    B.   Pragmatics
    C.   Semantics
    D.   Registers

18. Which of the following sentences demonstrates the use of a subordinating conjunction in a complex sentence?

    A.   Since starting school, I was an average student.
    B.   Since I had started school, I had to give up afternoon backyard dirt wars.
    C.   Since first grade, I have been an average student.
    D.   Since I started attending school because I reached my sixth birthday and had to turn to books instead of playthings.

19. Armando is an EL student in a high school English class. His essay on the importance of his calculator includes the following passage.

    All the school life, I am math whiz. I am figuring out all the problems in the head. But, in the six grade, when I get my calculator, I begin to depend on her in the totality of the times.

    Which THREE of the following L1 to L2 errors are shown in the passage?

    A. Verb tense
    B. Circumlocution
    C. Incorrect use of modals
    D. Code-switching
    E. Pronoun form
    F. Article usage

Use the following scenario to answer the next two items.

> Ms. Sahid teaches at a high school that includes *The Great Gatsby* as mandatory reading in Grade 11 ELA curriculum for all students. Her classes include many intermediate-level EL students.

20. Which of the following accommodations might best help Ms. Sahid's ESL students understand the novel?

    A. Showing a film version of the novel before reading it.
    B. Integrating historical photographs, period music, art, and brief historical overviews to contextualize the themes and events in the novel.
    C. Handing out a chapter-by-chapter summary of the novel.
    D. Listening to a professional recording of the novel as students follow along in their books.

21. To help students appreciate the literary language in *The Great Gatsby*, Ms. Sahid arranges her class into groups and assigns each group an especially vivid passage from the novel. To promote students' understanding of literary language, she asks each group to dramatize the passage they've been given. Which of the following instructional strategies would be most effective in helping students complete this activity meaningfully and effectively?

    A. The teacher models the activity by acting out a passage, explaining how her actions, movements, and gestures reflect the language of the text.
    B. The teacher asks students to underline and label the literary devices they recognize in their passages.
    C. The teacher joins each group and asks group members to read the passage aloud; she corrects all mispronunciations and incorrect intonations.
    D. The teacher asks each group to explain why the passage is important to the reader's understanding of the story.

22. Integrating photographs and visuals, using realia, providing explanations of new content, and breaking up a complex lesson into smaller segments demonstrate which of the following research-based ESL teaching methods?

    A. Cognitive/Academic Language Learning Approach (CALLA)
    B. Content-based instruction
    C. Literacy support for content-area instruction
    D. Sheltered instruction

23. Which THREE of the following explanations correctly connect a teacher's knowledge of language systems to the support of EL students' language learning?

    A. Knowledge of phonology enables teachers to help students with pronunciation.
    B. Knowledge of syntax enables teachers to guide students in writing grammatically correct sentences.
    C. Knowledge of rhetoric enables teachers to help students find errors in their writing.
    D. Knowledge of discourse enables teachers to help students read more effectively.
    E. Knowledge of pragmatics enables teachers to show students how nonverbals contribute to communication.

24. A student in a U.S. history class includes the following sentence in a short essay on early settlements in America:

    The early settlers dominated the land and the indigenous people.

    The wording and structure of this sentence demonstrates which of the following SLA strategies?

    A. The writer is generalizing the meaning of verbs such as *captured*, *conquered*, and *subjugated* into a single verb, *dominated*.
    B. The writer is demonstrating that he/she does not know the meaning of the verb *dominated*.
    C. The writer is showing a limited understanding of this era of U.S. history.
    D. The writer is demonstrating a lack of knowledge of article usage by incorrectly using the definite article, *the*.

Use the passage shown here to answer the next two questions.

Mr. Christopher, a middle school social studies teacher, has a mainstream class that includes a large number of intermediate EL students. His EL students are having trouble understanding the basic information in each chapter. Ms. Caranza, a colleague who teaches ESL classes, suggests breaking up lectures into mini-lessons and allowing time for students to network after each mini-lesson.

25. Ms. Caranza's advice to Mr. Christopher reflects which of the following language learning instructional adjustments?

    A. Scaffolding
    B. Affective support
    C. Segmenting
    D. Authentic assessment

26. Which of the following statements best explains the value of mini-lessons in helping EL learners acquire content knowledge?

   A.   Mini-lessons are short in order to keep EL students from getting bored when they don't understand.
   B.   Mini-lessons enable the teacher to divide a lesson into manageable "chunks" of information to help students receive comprehensible input.
   C.   In mini-lessons, difficult concepts are simplified, so even beginning learners are able to understand.
   D.   Mini-lessons are delivered very quickly so that the teacher is able to cover a lot more information in a class session.

Use the passage below to answer the next three items.

> The passage below is an excerpt from an essay written by Myra, an advanced EL student who is writing practice essays for her college application personal statement.

> During the week, I would give up my afternoons just to go to band practice. Regardless of me having homework. Our paractice would usually last from six to eight. Except for Wensdays. My weekends were never true because I either had a football game to go too. Sometimes it was because I had to show up for practice the next day. It almost got to the point to where I came close to losing some of my friends. Beeing that I had a busy schedule.

27. Which of the following statements offers the best analysis of the writer's syntactic performance in this excerpt?

   A.   The writer treats subordinate structures as independent elements.
   B.   The writer demonstrates spelling difficulties.
   C.   The writer does not seem to have any strategies for varying sentence structure.
   D.   The writer does not know what constitutes a complete sentence.

28. Which of the following strategies should the teacher use to promote Myra's syntactic performance in writing?

   A.   The teacher should mark all the errors in the passage and have Myra rewrite the passage making all the marked corrections.
   B.   The teacher should give Myra grammar worksheets in identifying complete sentences and fragments.
   C.   The teacher should have Myra read the passage aloud, calling Myra's attention to her intonation and inflection as she reads the sentences.
   D.   The teacher should give Myra a new topic and ask her to write a new draft without making all the errors evident in this passage.

29. Which of the following teaching actions would best enable the teacher to be an advocate in Myra's efforts to complete her college application essay?

   A. The teacher can provide models of college application essays for Myra to use as mentor texts.
   B. The teacher can mark all the errors in each essay that Myra writes and ask Myra to rewrite the essay with corrections.
   C. The teacher can have Myra watch an online tutorial on how to write a good college application essay.
   D. The teacher can review each of Myra's drafts and offer formative feedback on how to present her ideas clearly, how to focus on her key points, and how to write strong sentences.

30. In an elementary class that includes beginning-level EL students, which of the following strategies would best promote students' understanding of how the school day is segmented (i.e., reading groups, recess, science time, lunch, etc.)?

   A. The teacher creates a large chart that displays the time each class activity starts and ends.
   B. The teacher creates a poster for each regular class day segment with pictures that clearly illustrate the activity. Each poster is numbered to indicate the place of each activity in the class events sequence.
   C. When it's time for a new activity, the teacher sounds a chime and writes the name and time range of the new activity on the board (for example, 10:00-10:35—READING).
   D. The teacher shows a video of students in reading circles, science centers, recess, art, and other school activities.

31. A Grade 5 teacher wants to promote her intermediate EL students' understanding of content-area lessons. She has a word wall divided into content areas and updates new content vocabulary each week. She also has content cubicles decorated with posters and realia. Which of the following grouping strategies might further promote her students' content-area learning?

   A. The teacher uses a random grouping approach, creating new groups each Monday morning.
   B. The teacher creates two types of groups: one set includes only EL students, the other only native English speakers.
   C. The teacher creates base groups for cooperative learning activities; each group includes native English speakers and EL students.
   D. The teacher allows students to self-select the groups they want to be in.

32. A high school teacher has a class in which almost all the students are intermediate EL students. The teacher presents lessons through lectures followed by an end-of-class quiz each day. The class has a failing quiz average, so the teacher wants to implement an approach that encourages student achievement. Which of the following would be an effective, initial change in this teacher's current approach?

   A. The teacher starts posting the quiz grade average each day and announces that everyone will get a 5-point bonus each time the average goes up by five points.

   B. The teacher starts using a jigsaw approach with each new chapter. Instead of lecturing, he divides the chapter into sections and makes each group responsible for teaching its assigned section to the class.

   C. The teacher chunks the lesson into several 10-minute key point segments. At the end of each segment, the teacher has students engage in a think-pair-share to discuss their understanding of the key point.

   D. The teacher starts making audio tapes of each lesson. He has students listen to each lesson as many times as necessary until they pass the quiz for that lesson.

33. EL students in a Grade 3 class are having trouble learning the names of math figures (hexagon, quadrilateral, pentagon, etc.). Which of the following instructional strategies would most effectively promote students' learning in this area of math?

   A. The teacher devises a quiz in which students have to correctly match the figure to its name. The quiz is administered every day until all the students get 100% correct.

   B. The teacher draws each figure on the board and has students copy the figures into their notebooks. The teacher asks for volunteers to come to the board to label each figure.

   C. The teacher creates a poster for each figure. In addition to an illustration of the figure, the name is written in large letters with the root underlined and the corresponding number of sides written in large print on the poster. The poster includes pictures of words with the same root.

   D. The teacher puts students into groups and assigns a different figure to each group. Their task is to make several models of their figure using a variety of resources such as craft sticks, twigs, pencils, construction paper strips, chenille sticks, and any other materials they can think of.

34. An elementary school teacher gives her beginning EL students the following directions:

   1. Form your reading circles in your usual areas.

   2. Tell your reading circle partners your birth date (month, day, and year).

   3. Talk with your reading circle partners to figure out who has the earliest birthday in the year.

   4. Whoever has the earliest birthday hands out the reading circle books today.

   This classroom interaction activity reflects which of the following EL teaching concepts?

   A. Total Physical Response
   B. Immersion
   C. Classroom community
   D. Pragmatics

Use the following scenario to respond to the next two items.

A high school English teacher is about to start a unit on Jack London's "To Build a Fire" in a sheltered class. The narrative is launched when the main character decides to undertake an on-foot journey through the Yukon in dangerously cold weather.

35. The teacher starts a whole-class discussion by asking, "When the temperature is very high and you feel very hot, what are some things you are supposed to do to stay safe?" She writes their comments on the board and encourages students to follow up on some of the things they say. Then she tells students to work in groups to respond to this question: "When it's very, very cold, what are some things you should do to stay safe?" She gives students five minutes to prepare their group response. Which of the following statements best explains how this activity will address EL students' language development?

   A. The teacher activates prior knowledge to help students connect their real-world experiences to the context of the classroom lesson.
   B. Using the students' group responses, the teacher will be able to create a semantic map to introduce the story.
   C. The teacher knows this story will be challenging for EL students, so she starts with this activity in order to boost their comprehension.
   D. The teacher wants to promote students' active reading skills by showing them how little they know about extreme cold temperatures.

36. As a follow-up, the teacher takes the class to the school library and assigns the following activity:

   1. Work with your group members to find three facts about Alaskan geography, topography, and/or temperatures.

   2. Be ready to do an oral three-minute summary of your findings tomorrow.

   3. Your presentation must include at least one photograph that you found on a State of Alaska website or a group member can draw an illustration that shows your findings.

   Which TWO of the following descriptions best explains how this activity contributes to students' academic skills development?

   A. It allows students to use research-based facts to enhance their understanding of events in the story.
   B. It allows students to apply several learning styles in completing the task.
   C. It integrates technology to reduce the complexity of understanding the events of the story.
   D. It requires cooperative work to simplify the overall challenge of reading the story.

Use the following scenario to respond to the next two items.

A high school social studies teacher has an ESL class made up of beginning and intermediate EL students. To introduce a lesson on different terrains in the United States, the teacher shows slides of deserts, woods, lakes, mountain ranges, river valleys, farmland, mountain valleys, and other topographies.

37. As he shows each scene, the teacher asks students to brainstorm about words suggested by the scene (for example, farmland might elicit words like *rows, neat, planning, harvest*, etc.) and writes the list on the board. Then, he asks for student volunteers to describe each scene orally in a few sentences. This activity primarily supports which of the following ESL instructional goals?

    A. Students share experiences from their homelands.
    B. Students develop communicative competence and learn content concepts in a meaningful context.
    C. Students learn new vocabulary by connecting images to word lists.
    D. Students demonstrate comprehension of important content-area knowledge.

38. As a follow-up activity, students bring photographs or illustrations of a terrain where they have lived or which they have visited. They write short paragraphs describing the area in the photo. Each student is invited to sit in the Author's Chair and briefly talk about his/her picture. Which of the following explanations best describes how this activity supports EL students' language development?

    A. The Author's Chair promotes a comprehensible language environment as students share information with their classmates.
    B. In listening to each other, students recognize the broad parameters of the topic covered in class.
    C. In writing paragraphs about their photographs, students are able to use vocabulary they already know instead of struggling with new content-area vocabulary.
    D. The writing activity prevents learners from relying on L1 words and sentence patterns.

39. A Texas history teacher has assigned an informal speech on important figures in Texas politics. About 50% of the class is made up of EL students. As part of the preparation for this assignment, the teacher shows several videos of famous individuals delivering speeches. The teacher first shows the videos with the sound turned off and then with the sound on. Which of the following rationales best explains how this activity will promote EL students' language development?

    A. Watching film segments with the sound off will provide an opportunity to notice how non-verbal cues, body language, and gestures contribute to communication.
    B. Watching a film prior to a challenging assignment reduces anxiety and helps students perform at a higher level.
    C. Watching film clips will enable students to recognize how important it is to memorize a speech in order to avoid errors in delivery.
    D. Watching film clips will show students how important props are in delivering a good speech performance.

40. An elementary teacher has a class of beginning EL students. During oral reading times, the teacher notices that the students are using many L1 phonemes in pronouncing L2 words. Which of the following strategies would be most effective in helping students develop their L2 phonological knowledge.

    A. The teacher corrects the students each time they mispronounce a word during oral reading.
    B. The teacher has students read along silently as she plays an audio recording of a short book they are familiar with. She plays the recording once more with the students reading along chorally.
    C. The teacher makes a list of all the words the students mispronounced during reading time and gives them a spelling test on this list.
    D. The teacher writes simple sentences using words with the L2 phonemes that the students are having trouble with and has the students copy the sentences into their notebooks.

41. During a writing conference with Ana, an advanced EL student, the teacher asks about a sentence in the draft. The student writer responds, "*Pues* I was reading the sample essay. It had a sentence like this one." The student's utterance is an example of which of the following communicative strategies?

    A. Interference
    B. Transfer
    C. Translation
    D. Code-switching

42. A Grade 11 class made up of intermediate and advanced EL students is completing a unit on the classic film *To Kill a Mockingbird*. The teacher makes the following assignment.

    1. Imagine you and your group members went to the theater to watch this film.

    2. Create a skit in which you have a "walking out of the theater" conversation about this film.

    3. Your skit should sound realistic, but you might include comments such as the following:

        I liked it when. . . .

        One part I didn't like was. . . .

        It was cool when. . . .

        I'm going to tell _____ to watch this movie because. . . .

    Which of the following learning objectives reflects how this activity supports students' language development?

    A. To promote oral language proficiency in an authentic conversational environment
    B. To test students' understanding of the presentation of events in the film
    C. To provide an introduction to reading the novel
    D. To demonstrate the importance of details in movies

43. A Grade 5 ESL teacher has students do short oral reports on their favorite out-of-school activity using appropriate visuals or props. Which of the following represents the most appropriate feedback for students' performance in this oral language activity?

    A. The teacher has students write a summary of each report to determine whether the speakers clearly presented their information.
    B. At the end of each report, the teacher thanks the speaker and leads the class in offering applause. When all the reports are done, the teacher asks students, "Which do you think was the best presentation?"
    C. At the end of each report, the teacher gives each student a detailed, written critique citing all the mispronunciation and language use errors.
    D. The teacher has students write one question they think of during each report. At the end of all the reports, they have a question-and-answer session to ask each other questions and make comments about the reports.

44. An elementary school teacher notices that her beginning and intermediate EL students use constructions such as the following:

    The box for the school things (instead of cubby hole).

    When we go out to play (instead of recess).

    The thing for making circles (instead of compass).

    Which of the following communication strategies best describes these constructions?

    A. Circumlocution
    B. Approximation
    C. Lexical avoidance
    D. Stalling

45. In second language acquisition, EL students rely on linguistic knowledge from L1 to support new learning in L2. Which TWO of the following terms correctly describe this SLA process?

    A. Interference
    B. Interdependence
    C. Translation
    D. Transfer
    E. Approximation

Use the following scenario to respond to the next three items.

In his Grade 9 ESL class, Mr. Elizondo reads aloud a short essay in which the author reminisces about getting his first pen. Students follow along on their own copies of the text. After the oral reading and a short discussion, he gives his students the following assignment:

> Write a short paragraph explaining why the pen was so important to the author. Make sure to use textual evidence to support your points.
>
> This is the essay submitted by Eni.
>
> > Something new, something he have never use is awesome, what can he do with it. A New pen that he can make new thing with it. The pen was cheap, but make him feel good. "Words were hidden–unborn, unwritten–in all that unused ink?" He can write new things, stories, project, whatever he can imagen. He write a story and he can write many more stories with it.

46. This student's writing fits the descriptors for which English Language Proficiency Standards level?

    A. Beginning
    B. Intermediate
    C. Advanced
    D. Advanced high

47. Mr. Elizondo has all the students read their short paragraph orally. After each student reads, he offers a brief comment. In responding to Eni's paragraph, which of the following comments would best target Mr. Elizondo's instructions for this writing assignment?

    A. Mr. Elizondo tells Eni to revise her writing more carefully next time.
    B. Mr. Elizondo tells Eni to reread the passage to make sure she gets the details right.
    C. Mr. Elizondo tells Eni that he noticed that she integrated a direct quotation from the passage.
    D. Mr. Elizondo tells Eni that she has made a lot of errors in verb use.

48. Mr. Elizondo's instructional activity promotes his EL students' literacy development in which of the following ways?

    A. The assignment is simple to enable students with low literacy levels to complete it effectively.
    B. The assignment integrates listening, speaking, reading, and writing in a meaningful classroom activity.
    C. The assignment is short so students will not grow frustrated as they complete it.
    D. The assignment focuses on lower levels of Bloom's Taxonomy increasing students' chances for success in completing it.

49. Ms. Nevarez has a Grade 4 class of beginning and intermediate ESL students. Many of the students are reluctant to read orally during whole-class reading time. She restructures reading time into reading circles and moves from circle to circle making sure to spend time with each group of readers. The change Ms. Nevarez has made will enhance reading instruction in which of the following ways?

   A. The teacher will be able to determine which students do not like reading and move those students to independent reading with easier books.
   B. The teacher will be able to correct students' oral reading more fully in the privacy of the reading circles.
   C. The teacher will be able to eliminate whole-class oral reading since students are now in reading circles.
   D. The teacher will be able to promote students' confidence about reading orally by creating a more limited audience for the oral reading.

50. For a science lesson, an elementary school teacher is planning to read aloud a short storybook about insects to a class of beginning and intermediate EL students. Which of the following prereading strategies would best enable students to understand new vocabulary in the science book?

   A. The teacher posts a list of new words and has students look them up prior to the read aloud.
   B. The teacher posts labeled illustrations of the new words, with each illustration showing the new word in large letters. The teacher explains each new word prior to the read aloud.
   C. Prior to the read aloud, the teacher has students skim through the book and write down all the words they don't know.
   D. The teacher gives the students a short summary of the book prior to the read aloud and tells the students that once she starts the read aloud, they should raise their hands each time they hear a word they don't know.

51. Why is a semantic map considered a good strategy for promoting EL students' content-area learning?

   A. A semantic map allows students to skim through a new text to identify key words that will be important in understanding the content.
   B. A semantic map provides a graphic structure for anticipating and organizing a core concept and associated subpoints.
   C. A semantic map presents all the new vocabulary students will encounter in a content-area lesson.
   D. A semantic map provides a graphic organizer for representing text structures.

52. An elementary school teacher has introduced word problems in his ESL class. The teacher knows that word problems pose conceptual difficulties even for native English speakers, so he wants to provide appropriate instructional support for his EL students' understanding of this math structure. The teacher creates a large graphic showing the parts of a word problem. Which of the following additional strategies would best reinforce the students' understanding of math word problems?

    A. The teacher suggests that students translate the word problems into their L1 before trying to solve them.
    B. The teacher puts the students in a large circle and has each student read a word problem orally.
    C. The teacher organizes students into groups and gives each group 12 pencil cap erasers. Each group writes a short word problem focusing on math operations about the erasers.
    D. The teacher divides the class into two teams. He puts a word problem on the board and gives the teams five minutes to solve the problem. The winning team gets five extra points on their daily math grade.

53. Which THREE of the following prereading strategies promote students' content-area learning when they are assigned a new chapter?

    A. The teacher provides illustrated definitions of new content vocabulary in the chapter.
    B. The teacher does a think aloud of the first few paragraphs of the chapter before having students read on their own.
    C. The teacher creates questions which students answer in short group networking sessions.
    D. The teacher assigns short summaries of the information in each section of the chapter.
    E. The teacher asks students to make a list of new words they encounter in the chapter.
    F. The teacher has students do a concept map based on the title and subheadings in the chapter.

54. A world history teacher whose mainstream class includes intermediate and advanced EL students wants to base an informal class assessment on state standards for world history. The teacher creates a unit focused on the state standard that expects students to identify characteristics of different political systems throughout history. Which of the following instructional activities would most effectively promote students' achievement in meeting this state standard?

    A. Working in groups, students pick a nation and historical period from a list created by the instructor. They are given several class meetings to conduct library and internet research on the nation's political system. They prepare a PowerPoint presentation to share their findings with the class.
    B. The teacher picks four political systems and, over four class periods, presents a detailed lecture on each system. At the end of the four classes, he administers an objective test modeled on the state-mandated exam.
    C. The teacher uses test items from the practice exam provided by the state. Working in groups, students find the correct answers by looking through their history books. They prepare a written report explaining why the incorrect responses are wrong.
    D. The teacher defines the political systems mentioned in the state standard. The teacher gives students two class periods to do internet research to compile a list of countries that have adopted each political system going as far back as 500 BCE. Each group creates a chart of their findings.

55. A middle school math teacher wants to prepare students for success on the Texas English Language Proficiency Assessment System (TELPAS) in oral language proficiency. The teacher plans to incorporate authentic assessment of EL students' oral language proficiency into everyday lessons. Which of the following strategies would enable this teacher to integrate informal assessment in oral language into math content lessons?

   A. The teacher presents the lesson for the day, stopping at the end of each sample problem to ask whether there are any questions.
   B. The teacher appoints an "assistant." As the teacher explains the math lesson on the board, he makes some errors on purpose. Each time he creates an error, he stops and asks the assistant, "What's wrong with my example?"
   C. The teacher distributes cards with math problems to each group. The students work together to solve the problems and then explain the problem, present their work, and explain the solution on the board.
   D. Instead of homework, the teacher cuts back on the day's lesson and allows students to work together on their homework. As they complete the homework problems, students take their assignments to the teacher to be checked.

56. An elementary school teacher has a class of students most of whom are rated at the beginning and intermediate level according to the Texas English Language Proficiency Assessment System (TELPAS). The teacher wants to adjust science instruction to incorporate communicative competence. The teacher plans a new approach for teaching a meteorology lesson. He plans a lecture on major meteorological events and integrates a student participation activity. Which of the following adjustments would best enable this teacher to assess communicative competence as part of the lesson?

   A. After he presents the lesson, the teacher gives each student a card with the name of a weather-related event or phenomenon. He projects pictures of each event and reminds the class of its characteristics. Then he says, "Who has the name of this weather event on your card? Can you tell us the name and post the name on the picture?"
   B. The teacher takes the students outside onto the school grounds. He has students sit on the grass, network with each other about their observations, and write a paragraph about what they think about the day's weather.
   C. The teacher knows that his students come from many different backgrounds, so he assigns a weather story for homework: students are supposed to write a story about the most exciting weather they have ever been in. The next day, the students read their stories to the whole class and the teacher points out the strengths in each presenter's story.
   D. The teacher breaks up the meteorology lesson into several segments. At the end of each segment, students have five minutes to complete a three-question quiz covering the key content of that segment.

Use this scenario to respond to the next two items.

A high school teacher is preparing her EL class for the state-mandated writing exam that is required for all students, including students in language programs. The teacher wants to familiarize students with the format of the writing exam as well as to teach them writing-on-demand strategies.

57. The teacher creates a prompt modeled on the state-mandated writing exam and leads a discussion on how to break down the topic and do quick planning. Which of the following activities would most effectively promote students' initial understanding of the writing task?

    A. The teacher does a think aloud and a demonstration of strategies for thinking about the prompt.
    B. The teacher gives students 15 minutes to write an essay modeled on the format of the state-mandated assessment essay. Then the students read each other's essays and comment on what they like about their peers' essays and what needs to be corrected.
    C. The teacher breaks students into groups and has each group create a collaboratively written essay.
    D. The teacher arranges the class into a large circle. The teacher asks for a volunteer to compose a first sentence for the essay. In a round-robin approach, each student in the circle contributes a sentence to the developing essay.

58. After the introductory activity, the teacher writes a new prompt on the board. Students are given a class period to respond to the prompt. Which of following would be the best *next* step in meeting the teacher's goal?

    A. Students take the drafts home to revise them and submit them for a grade the next day.
    B. The teacher collects the essays written in class, scores them, and returns them to the students the next day.
    C. The teacher collects the essays, covers each name with a label, and distributes the essays for students to score using a rubric based on the state-mandated expectations.
    D. The teacher has students work collaboratively in groups to create a rubric to score the essays. Each group presents its rubric and the class votes on which one to use to score the essays.

Use this scenario to respond to the next two items.

A Grade 4 teacher wants to assess EL students' reading proficiency. The teacher designs several instructional assessment activities.

59. The teacher asks students to select a book they have read more than one time during Sustained Silent Reading. As the student reads, the teacher marks the following checklist.

- Reads with appropriate inflection.

- Voice modulation indicates the reader is engaged in the content.

- Notices miscues and self-corrects.

- Hesitations are infrequent.

This instructional activity will enable the teacher to assess her students' reading proficiency in which of the following areas?

   A.   Comprehension
   B.   Graphophonemic knowledge
   C.   Fluency
   D.   Pronunciation

60. As a follow-up classroom reading assessment, the teacher identifies a paragraph from the science chapter they will cover in two weeks. She gives these instructions to each student when they sit at the reading center in the classroom:

This paragraph is from a chapter we have not read in our science book. I want you to read it orally to me. When you get to a word that is confusing or that you don't understand, I want you to tell me what you are doing to try to figure out the meaning. Okay . . . let's start.

This instructional activity assesses which of the following areas of reading?

   A.   Content-area knowledge
   B.   Metacognition
   C.   Activation of prior knowledge
   D.   Decoding skills

61. During the first week of class, a Grade 6 EL teacher gives her students time to create a "family newspaper" which students put together using class materials like notebook paper, colored paper, and original illustrations and pictures they may have brought from home. Each student will introduce his/her family to the rest of the class through the illustrations and stories in the family newspaper. Which of the following features of effective ESL education does this strategy illustrate?

    A. The teacher is creating an environment where social interaction is a key component of learning.
    B. The teacher is creating a low-stress environment by making sure assignments are easy to complete.
    C. The teacher is demonstrating the centrality of writing in acquiring language proficiency in English.
    D. The teacher is demonstrating that not every activity in the classroom has to have an academic connection.

62. Which of the following features of language education in the U.S. has *not* been addressed by Supreme Court or federal court rulings?

    A. Universal second language instruction for all students in the United States
    B. Undocumented children's right to an education in American schools
    C. The connection between language programs for second language speakers of English and educational equity
    D. Desegregation to prohibit discrimination on grounds of race, color, or national origin

63. A high school teacher is presenting an introductory lesson on cell division to a sheltered science class. His first question is, "When you hear the term *cell*, what do you think of?" Jaime, a student, says, "*La cárcel*." When the class laughs, the teacher says, "That's interesting, Jaime. Can you explain how jail is like the biological cells you read about in the chapter?" The Texas Administrative Code (TAC), Chapter 89, stipulates that ESL programs must address three categories of learner needs. Which of the following descriptions best explains how the teacher's response supports this TAC requirement?

    A. The teacher is creating a content-centered environment that promotes a high level of achievement in academic subjects.
    B. The teacher is creating a low-stress environment by allowing code-switching in an academic discussion.
    C. The teacher is supporting the learner's affective and cognitive needs by valuing the student's contribution to class discussion.
    D. The teacher is supporting the bilingual environment of the class by correcting the student's lapse into Spanish through rephrasing in English.

64. Why was the Bilingual Education Act, Title VII of the Elementary and Secondary Education Act of 1968 significant in the history of ESL education in America?

   A. This act implemented federal guidelines for integrating children of undocumented immigrants into American schools.
   B. This act established the National Center for Bilingual Education as a resource center for teachers and administrators.
   C. This act initiated federal involvement in mandates, funding, rationales, and goals for bilingual/ESL education programs.
   D. This act established the "separate but equal" precedent for implementing bilingual education programs in American schools.

65. Which THREE of the following explanations correctly represent the range of language programs mandated for LEP students in Texas public schools?

   A. ESL programs are mandated only through Grade 8; after that, all students who have not yet exited the designated language program are reclassified as "full immersion" learners because school support is no longer provided.
   B. ESL content-based programs enable LEP students to get instruction in academic content areas with continuing support for developing L2 language proficiency.
   C. Dual immersion two-way programs allow parents to place native English speakers in biliteracy language programs.
   D. ESL and bilingual programs are offered as supplementary linguistic support from instructors who are bilingual and can translate content for LEP students.
   E. Dual immersion one-way programs include only L1 speakers and focus on biliteracy and bilingualism in L1 and L2.
   F. All LEP students are placed in mainstream classes starting in first grade to enable students to receive full instruction from certified content-area teachers.

66. A middle school teacher shows her ESL class film clips from several animated films featuring characters from different cultures. The teacher has zoomed into clips where characters show emotion, such as anger, happiness, confusion, excitement, sadness, or other emotive responses without words. The teacher divides the class into groups and gives the students this task:

   As you watch the clips, pay close attention to how you know what emotion the characters are trying to express. How are you able to figure out each character's emotion?

   This instructional strategy primarily focuses on

   A. showing students that language is not the primary means of communication.
   B. developing students' awareness of the diversity of nonverbals across cultures.
   C. recognizing that animated films are equivalent in narrative value to traditional film.
   D. promoting students' acquisition of a broad range of alternatives to English nonverbals.

67. An elementary school principal has just assigned a new student to a Grade 4 teacher. They have this conversation in the principal's office.

> **Teacher:** Josue Torres. . . . Hmmm. I know exactly what to expect.
>
> **Principal:** Yes . . . a new student. He'll be excited, eager, ready to meet new kids.
>
> **Teacher:** Torres. That says everything. I can expect that he'll never say anything. He'll sit at his desk looking lost all the time. He won't do his homework because he's clueless about English. He won't care when he makes bad grades. I expect all my students to be willing to work hard to make good grades. If they don't want to learn English, I can't help them!

In the context of ESL teaching, the teacher's comments suggest resistance to creating an effective multicultural learning environment. Which THREE of the following attitudes are reflected in the teacher's comments?

A. Instructional autonomy
B. Stereotyping
C. Deficit view
D. Faulty ESL preparation
E. Teaching to the test
F. High expectations

68. Mr. Reyes teaches a math class that includes a large number of EL students. One day, he brings small *piñatas* to the class and distributes them to the groups. He writes math problems such as the following on posters and displays them at the front of the room. Students work in groups to solve the problems and explain their calculations.

Imagine that your *piñata* has to be shipped to Kearney, Nebraska.

1. What size mailing box would have to be used? Report the size in length, height, and width and be ready to explain how you got your answer.

2. Assuming that each piece of candy in the *piñata* is about one cubic inch in size, how many candies will it take to fill your *piñata* half way?

Work with your group members to make sure you can explain how you got your answers to the whole class.

Which of the following explanations best addresses how Mr. Reyes' use of the *piñatas* can facilitate students' cognitive learning and language acquisition in math?

A. The students will work harder because they will understand what Mr. Reyes is talking about.
B. Using the *piñatas* as props, the teacher will be able to create simpler math problems than those in the book.
C. Using a culturally relevant artifact will heighten the students' participation and learning potential in this math lesson.
D. The students will be able to solve the problems because they will not have to use difficult math formulas; instead, they can base their answers on past experience.

69. In their August orientation, teachers at a Central Texas school discuss the following statement from the school's *Handbook of Daily Operating Procedures*:

> The teacher creates an environment that values the beliefs, backgrounds, home learning, home language, and sense of belonging to a group that every learner brings to the classroom and fosters a sense of community that brings diverse learners together.

In the context of ESL teaching, this statement refers to which ONE of the following concepts?

   A. Linguistic diversity
   B. Pedagogical tolerance
   C. Identity preservation
   D. Multiculturalism

70. A high school ESL teacher is having students take turns reading aloud. Every time someone stumbles or hesitates over a word, the students who know the correct pronunciation laugh at the reader. The teacher continues the read aloud, but next time someone laughs at a mispronounced word, she stops and says, "Reading aloud can be scary. You're on the spot; you're sort of performing. Let's listen politely and pay attention to the words we are reading, not to words we're hearing. And if you want to help your classmate, instead of laughing, how about saying the word he or she is trying to pronounce?" The teacher's actions focus on which of the following ESL learner needs?

   A. By choosing to explain instead of rebuke, the teacher is supporting the students' affective learning domain.
   B. By continuing the read aloud, the teacher is demonstrating that linguistic growth occurs by working through a problem independently.
   C. By choosing not to embarrass the students who are laughing, the teacher is promoting a sense of camaraderie among the students.
   D. The teacher is supporting the cognitive domain; instead of focusing on the students who are laughing, the teacher keeps the students' concentration on the content.

71. Which of the following guidelines offers the most research-centered guideline for selecting multicultural literature to teach in an ESL class?

   A. Characters and situations in multicultural literature should help readers create positive self-images of themselves and should reflect national and ethnic groups realistically.
   B. When multicultural literature is integrated into mandated curriculum, the books and stories should have clear connections to themes in the canonical literature.
   C. Multicultural literature should be taught only when a class is made up of 75% or more language minority students.
   D. Language-minority students should be taught only multicultural literature because canonical literature has been shown to be irrelevant to most EL students.

72. A Grade 5 teacher in a dual-immersion program gives each group a picture book with no text (such as David Wiesner's *Tuesday* or *Flotsam*). The teacher makes this assignment:

> Each of the books I handed out tells a story but without words. Work with your group members to tell the story in words. Make a T-chart. On one side of the chart, tell the story in English; on the other side, tell it in Spanish. Be ready to share your stories with the whole class.

This assignment primarily addresses which of the following ESL instructional goals?

    A. The assignment integrates reading, writing, listening, and speaking skills in a meaningful L1 and L2 context.

    B. The assignment introduces students to important authors in children's literature.

    C. The assignment shows students the importance of using complete context (illustrations, nonverbals, and implied meaning) in constructing the meaning of a text.

    D. The assignment creates an opportunity for students to collaborate meaningfully in a content-area assignment.

73. A Grade 3 ESL teacher creates a Home Words Homework Page. The teacher tells the students to have their parents or siblings help them write down 10 words describing their home or objects in their home. The teacher tells the students to put the words in two columns: one column for the English word and one column for the Spanish equivalent. This assignment best addresses which of the following ESL instructional strategies?

    A. The teacher is creating an opportunity for family involvement in the EL students' education.

    B. By having the students ask for help, the teacher is integrating a homework completion check into the assignment.

    C. The teacher knows that students don't like to do homework, so the assignment is designed to be easy and student-friendly.

    D. By having students write the words in English and in Spanish, the teacher is embedding vocabulary and spelling into this assignment.

74. The ESL teachers in a South Texas school district want students and their families to become more familiar with community resources that can promote their students' literacy goals. Which of the following strategies most effectively targets the teachers' goal?

    A. Teachers send home a flyer from the public library explaining how to apply for a library card. If they get a public library card, students are rewarded with bonus points.

    B. The teachers set up a book contribution bin in the main school hallway for teachers and staff members to donate books. Teachers display the donated books under a "Free Books" sign during lunch.

    C. The teachers work with the public library to identify grade-appropriate children's and young adult fiction and nonfiction books. The teachers partner with the library to set up an after-school reading hour for parents and children.

    D. Teachers create a class-specific supplementary reading program. In order to encourage students to patronize the public library, they select books they want students to read but which aren't available at the school library.

75. Homework assignments are sometimes created with the expectation that parents will be able to help students complete the assignment. At a school where the majority of EL students' parents have limited L1 education and no L2 education, which of the following strategies would best promote family involvement in EL students' homework assignments?

A. The teacher sends parents a list of all the homework assignments for the week and asks parents to initial the assignment when the student completes it.

B. The teacher sends parents a video explaining how homework reinforces students' progress in content-area classes.

C. The teacher sends a package of textbooks to each family so that family members can familiarize themselves with the content-area materials their children are covering in class.

D. The teacher invites parents to attend content-area classes and models how they can facilitate their children's homework completion even if they don't understand the subject.

76. What is the LPAC's role in a student's exit from a bilingual or ESL program?

A. When the LPAC identifies a student as an EL, it also sets a minimum time for the student to remain in the ESL program; the student cannot exit before that time period.

B. The LPAC interviews the student at the end of every semester to determine how effectively the student can express him/herself in L2 oral language situations.

C. The LPAC reviews the student's mandated testing scores at the end of the year; if the scores do not meet the state requirement for satisfactory performance, the student is assigned an additional two years in the ESL program.

D. The LPAC reclassifies a student as "language proficient" on the basis of satisfactory scores on TEA-approved tests and a subjective teacher evaluation.

77. Six weeks before the mandated state testing period, a middle school ESL teacher implements a Test Prep Boot Camp Day every week for intensive test preparation strategies. The teacher invites parents to visit the class during these boot camp periods to work with their children during in-class demonstration of the strategies. This activity most effectively addresses which of the following aspects of effective ESL instruction?

A. The teacher is promoting family involvement in EL students' educational success by making parents part of the education team.

B. The teacher is ensuring that families do not unfairly blame the school when their children do not succeed.

C. The teacher enlists the parents in test preparation efforts to make sure that students take the state-mandated test seriously.

D. The teacher is providing an opportunity for parents to recognize the challenges the students will face in taking the state-mandated exams.

78. An elementary teacher in an ESL program is trying to increase students' completion rates on homework assignments. The teacher creates a weekly chart that lists each day's homework assignments. There are four columns for each homework assignment: a three-star column for completing the assignment, two stars for completing most of the assignment, one star for trying, and no stars for no attempt. The students color and decorate the chart in class and take it home. Parents are supposed to check the appropriate column each day. This activity is primarily aimed at promoting EL student achievement by doing which of the following?

   A. Creating a reward system for homework completion.
   B. Providing an opportunity for parents to actively participate in their children's homework responsibilities.
   C. Demonstrating that homework is important and must be completed.
   D. Showing students that homework is a way of extending the learning environment beyond the classroom space.

79. Which of the following statements most accurately presents a research-based summary of the role of parental involvement in EL students' educational achievement?

   A. Parental involvement is considered an important aspect of EL student success, but no mechanisms exist for creating parental involvement programs or for convincing parents to pay attention to their children's day-to-day educational activities.
   B. Fostering parental involvement is not a priority in most ESL programs because of the time and expense involved in educating parents at the same time that children are being educated.
   C. Parental involvement is linked to improved student achievement, student motivation, student attitudes toward language learning, and persistence in the ESL program.
   D. Most teachers and administrators resist parental involvement initiatives because EL students' parents tend to have limited educational background and limited or no proficiency in English.

80. A high school teacher works in a newcomer program in her district. She wants to make sure she integrates all of the Texas Administrative Code (TAC) regulations about meeting learners' needs. She knows newcomer EL students may be shy about asking questions in class so she puts up a poster showing students raising their hands. The dialogue bubbles show some questions in English and some in Spanish. The teacher depicted in the poster has a smile on her face and her thought bubble says, "Great questions!" This classroom strategy is designed to address which of the following learner needs?

   A. Conversational
   B. Understanding of classroom rules
   C. Linguistic
   D. Affective

PRACTICE TEST 2 ANSWER KEY

1.	(A)	21.	(A)	41.	(D)	61.	(A)
2.	(B)	22.	(D)	42.	(A)	62.	(A)
3.	(B)	23.	(A), (B), (E)	43.	(D)	63.	(C)
4.	(C), (D) (E)	24.	(A)	44.	(A)	64.	(C)
5.	(C), (E)	25.	(C)	45.	(B), (D)	65.	(B), (C), (E)
6.	(C)	26.	(B)	46.	(B)	66.	(B)
7.	(B), (C), (D)	27.	(A)	47.	(C)	67.	(B), (C), (D)
8.	(A)	28.	(C)	48.	(B)	68.	(C)
9.	(A), (B), (D)	29.	(D)	49.	(D)	69.	(D)
10.	(B)	30.	(B)	50.	(B)	70.	(A)
11.	(A)	31.	(C)	51.	(B)	71.	(A)
12.	(C)	32.	(C)	52.	(C)	72.	(A)
13.	(D)	33.	(D)	53.	(A), (B), (F)	73.	(A)
14.	(A)	34.	(A)	54.	(A)	74.	(C)
15.	(A)	35.	(A)	55.	(C)	75.	(D)
16.	(A)	36.	(A), (B)	56.	(A)	76.	(D)
17.	(D)	37.	(B)	57.	(A)	77.	(A)
18.	(B)	38.	(A)	58.	(C)	78.	(B)
19.	(A), (E), (F)	39.	(A)	59.	(C)	79.	(C)
20.	(B)	40.	(B)	60.	(D)	80.	(D)

PRACTICE TEST 2 ANSWER EXPLANATIONS

1.   **(A)**   The correct response is A. Response A reflects Competency 001, which connects the teacher's knowledge of linguistics, including language structures and mechanics, to the teacher's ability to use ELPS descriptors to guide classroom instruction for EL students. While ELPS does not suggest specific instructional strategies, teachers with strong ESL pedagogy training can connect the ELPS descriptors to appropriate instructional approaches. Response B is incorrect because ELPS presents communicative competence and academic language proficiency as complementary in EL students' success. Response C is incorrect because ELPS is not aligned to grade levels but instead to developing competencies at four different competency levels in the four language domains. Response D is incorrect because ELPS only describes observable learner performance in the four domains in the four proficiency levels; there is no instructional guidance for teachers in specific areas such as writing "grade-level" sentences.
    Competency 001: Linguistic knowledge

2.   **(B)**   The correct response is B. The *interrelatedness* of the four language domains is a core principle of second language acquisition (SLA). The concept of *interrelatedness* occurs throughout the 10 competencies of ESL exam 154, but it is introduced in Competency 001 as a foundational principle of ESL teaching. To guide students toward proficiency in listening, speaking, reading, and writing, ESL teachers should recognize that language learning seems to happen simultaneously across the four domains, with specific learning in one domain impacting learning in the others. Response A is incorrect because it suggests that listening is the simplest SLA skill, and that is not supported by any theory or practice in language acquisition. Response C is incorrect because it would be impossible to concentrate on only one language domain since comprehension and output rely on holistic, interactive understanding of L2 across the four domains. Response D is incorrect because vocabulary is not a finite learning component of SLA; vocabulary continually develops as an EL student's proficiency in all domains increases.
    Competency 001: Linguistic knowledge

3.   **(B)**   The correct response is B. Competency 001 establishes that ESL instruction occurs not just in ELA classes but also in content-based classes (reading, literature, science, social studies, and math). To guide students toward understanding of specialized concepts in content areas, content-based teachers must be able to analyze the distinct language structures that define the discourse of the discipline. Thus, a strong linguistics background is necessary for effective content-based ESL teaching. Response A is incorrect because identifying errors is not a cornerstone of ESL instruction and, in fact, could inhibit learner progress as the learner creates a hypersensitive filter and may exhibit reluctance to participate in communicative interactions. Response C is incorrect because challenging academic lessons should reflect the instructor's content-area expertise rather than linguistic knowledge. Response D is incorrect because it oversimplifies knowledge of linguistics to mechanics and conventions (which are related to surface errors). A content-based teacher's knowledge of linguistics must be expansive and must extend to solid understanding of phonology, morphology, syntax, and semantics relevant to the content area.
    Competency 001: Linguistic knowledge

4.   **(C), (D), (E)**   Responses C, D, and E correctly represent the structure and expectations of language programs in Texas as mandated by the TEC. Response A is incorrect because dual language programs are not mandated for all learners. Response B is incorrect because decisions about appropriate programs for LEP students are based on students' performance on the state-mandated linguistic proficiency exam and review and recommendation from the LPAC. Furthermore, bilingualism alone is not a factor in channeling students into language programs in Texas. Response F is incorrect because language programs in Texas do not end at Grade 6.
    Competency 008: History of ESL instruction

5.   **(C), (E)**   Responses C and E are correct. As presented in the Texas Education Code, Limited English Proficient (LEP) is the label used to identify students whose home language survey indicates that their dominant home language is a language other than English and whose English proficiency has been determined, by testing data, to be below the level needed to succeed academically. Students' English proficiency is determined by a state-approved language proficiency exam. The LEP designation is defined in the Texas Education Code as follows: "'student of limited English proficiency' means a student whose primary language is other than English and whose English language skills are such that the student has difficulty performing ordinary class work in English" (TEC, 1995). Response A is incorrect because after students are identified as LEP, they are designated as English learners and placed either in an ESL or bilingual language program. Response B is incorrect because English dominance is not a factor in placing students in language programs or in identifying students' English proficiency. Response D is incorrect because students are not prohibited from enrolling in Texas public schools on the basis of their English proficiency.
    Competency 008: History of ESL instruction

6.   **(C)**   Response C, the correct response, stands out as a misrepresentation of the interrelatedness of L1 and L2 in second language acquisition. Transfer is not automatic. Languages are not fundamentally the same, although many linguistic experts suggest that learning L2 activates strategies that were used in L1 acquisition. Responses A, B, D, E, and F present fundamental principles of L1 to L2 interdependence, which is generally defined as the learner's conscious as well as intuitive dependence on L1 knowledge to support L2 learning.
    Competency 002: L1 and L2 acquisition

7.   **(B), (C), (D)**   Responses B, C, and D correctly identify explanations for errors in L2 performance. False cognates, approximation, and direct translation are explanations for mismatches between the learner's intended output and the actual structure or utterance that the learner produces. Response A (generalization) and Response E (memorization) are not associated with *error* but instead with metacognitive strategies that enable EL students to bolster their accurate production of L2 structures and to enhance their meaningful output of L2 utterances.
    Competency 002: L1 and L2 acquisition

8.   **(A)**   Response A is a correct definition of code-switching. Code-switching is sometimes described as an error, but most likely, when code-switching occurs, the EL student is aware that an L1 structure is being deliberately inserted into an L2 utterance. Code-switching may be a way of filling in when the correct L2 structure is still unknown, but it is a deliberate, not accidental choice. Response B is incorrect because code-switching involves actual L1 words and phrases in L2 utterances, not just ideas. Response C is incorrect because L1 pronunciation in L2 speech is usually described as interference. Response D is incorrect because direct translation is a type of error that reflects the learner's attempts to fill in gaps when L2 semantic knowledge does not yet match communicative intentions in L2 and the learner resorts to translating L1 structures into L2 output.
    Competency 002: L1 and L2 acquisition

9.   **(A), (B), (D)**   Responses A, B, and D (memorization, repetition, and asking questions) correctly reflect some of the deliberate, cognitive processes that L2 learners use to promote their learning of new language structures. Response C is incorrect because prior knowledge is not a deliberate cognitive process but instead a reflection of the learner's familiarity with a concept or academic content. Response E is incorrect because observation could be more accurately defined as a stage (the Silent Period) during which the EL is refraining from L2 output because of perceived lack of readiness. The cognitive processes of A, B, and D are strategies that EL students use once they are active participants in L2 discourse.
    Competency 002: L1 and L2 acquisition

10. **(B)** Response B, generalization, is correct because, as presented in the instructions, the teacher expects the learners to recognize the similar structure in all four of the sentences: that each sentence begins with an introductory element marked off with a comma. Generalization means that learners use specific, repeated observations of an L2 occurrence to construct a "rule" that explains a pattern they detect. Generalization is an important part of both first language and second language acquisition. Response A is incorrect because syntactic variation is not a cognitive process. Response C is incorrect because transfer is irrelevant in processing the instructions provided by the teacher. Response D is incorrect because the teacher's instructions do not ask learners to identify errors but instead to look for similarities in the syntactic structure.
   Competency 002: L1 and L2 acquisition

11. **(A)** Response A correctly shows an introductory participle phrase (*looking around*) followed by the noun that it modifies. The "test" for correctness—"who is looking around?"—is correctly answered by "the boys" in the subject position. Responses B, C, and D demonstrate three variations of dangling modifiers, where the adjectival phrase (*looking around*) does not correctly modify the noun or pronoun in the subject position. Participle phrases that are not followed by the noun that the phrase is intended to modify are known as *dangling modifiers*. An interesting thing about dangling modifiers, however, is that even though there is a syntactic error in the sentence, the semantic intention is usually preserved. This is why both native English speakers and EL students have trouble avoiding dangling modifiers.
   Competency 001: Linguistic knowledge

12. **(C)** Response C is correct because morphology, the study of meaningful phonemic clusters used to construct words, explains how prefixes and suffixes can be appended to words to create new words. Response A is incorrect because syntax is the study of how sentence strings are constructed using the sentence-formation rules of the language. Response B is incorrect because although prefixes and suffixes affect the meaning of the original words, knowing how prefixes and suffixes work is part of a learner's morphological knowledge. Response D is incorrect because phonology concerns basic sounds; prefixes and suffixes reflect particles attached to words to change meaning and syntactic function.
   Competency 001: Linguistic knowledge

13. **(D)** Response D correctly describes the connection between collaborative activities and EL students' social needs in developing L2 proficiency. Response A is incorrect because the item stem is not focused on the assessment possibilities provided by group activities. Response B is incorrect because it misrepresents the rationale for group activities; group activities are intended to engage learners actively in learning not to reduce the teacher's instructional burden. Response C is incorrect because well-constructed group activities engage all group members equitably and dynamically, making it difficult if not impossible for any individual learner to recede into nonparticipation.
   Competency 003: General pedagogy in ESL context

14. **(A)** Response A is correct because it explains the literacy-related outcome of this interactive workshop task. By having students tinker with their own drafts in performing specific tasks, the teacher is showing students how to look critically at their writing. Response B is incorrect because the workshop task is not focused on revision at this point. Response C is incorrect because the workshop task includes no instructions on making corrections. Response D is incorrect because the workshop task is focused on having students demonstrate pride in their writing not in identifying problematic structures.
   Competency 005: Literacy (reading and writing) proficiency

15.   **(A)**   Response A correctly explains the probable cause of the mispronunciation of *century*. The /ch/ sound of the /t/ in *century* is likely an unfamiliar sound in Cindy's L1, so she approximates the pronunciation by eliding the /nch/ consonant cluster. The lack of familiarity with the consonant cluster creates *interference* manifested as mispronunciation. Response B is incorrect because there is no phonological transfer involved since the /ch/ is ignored. Had Cindy pronounced the word *sentoory* with the letter *t* pronounced as a /t/ that would have been interference. Response C is incorrect because cognates are not involved in this scenario. Response D is incorrect because Cindy did not translate the sound or the word.
   Competency 002: L1 and L2 acquisition

16.   **(A)**   Response A is correct. The teacher can have a short phonology lesson to explain the variations in sounds represented by the orthographic symbol *t*, explaining to Cindy how sometimes a *t* is pronounced as /ch/. Response B is incorrect because, while the teacher might break the word up into syllables, ultimately the problem centers on matching a letter symbol to the correct sound. Response C is incorrect because pragmatics is irrelevant in this scenario. Response D is incorrect because the student clearly knows the meaning of the word; the problem is the phonological interference from L1.
   Competency 001: Linguistic knowledge

17.   **(D)**   Response D is correct because it identifies the mismatch between the expected academic discourse and the student's choice to use texting language in a lab report. Response A is incorrect because the sentence is correctly constructed, following the rules for English sentence formation. Response B is incorrect because the pragmatics are almost on target as well: the student knows how to demonstrate his competence as a chemist. Response C is incorrect because the student knows the language of chemistry.
   Competency 002: L1 and L2 acquisition

18.   **(B)**   Response B shows a correctly constructed *complex* sentence, a sentence in which *since* is used to construct a *subordinate clause,* a structure that has a subject and a verb but which is dependent on the main clause. Response A is incorrect because *since* is used as a preposition in this sentence. Response C is incorrect because *since* is used as a preposition not a subordinate conjunction. Response D is incorrect because the entire sentence string shows incorrect syntactic construction: there is no subordinate structure because there is no correctly constructed main clause.
   Competency 001: Linguistic knowledge

19.   **(A), (E), (F)**   Responses A, E, and F correctly identify the errors in this passage. Most of the verbs are in present tense even though the writer is recounting a story that occurred in the past. The writer uses *her* to refer to the calculator, a pronoun usage error. In addition, the writer uses *the* with nouns that do not need an article and does not use *a* with *math whiz*. Response B is incorrect because there is no circumlocution: the writer has a strong grasp of the appropriate terms for telling the story. Response C is incorrect because the writer does not use modals in the story. Response D is incorrect because there is no code-switching in the passage.
   Competency 002: L1 and L2 acquisition

20.   **(B)**   Response B is correct because it lists accommodations that are recognized as effective strategies for promoting content-area learning. Response A is incorrect because the film might be significantly different from the novel and because a cinematic presentation might not help students meet the curriculum requirements for the novel. Response C is incorrect because a chapter-by-chapter summary would not promote understanding of the complex elements of the novel. Chapter summaries would be more of a study aid than EL accommodations. Response D is incorrect because simply listening to the novel being read would not promote understanding.
   Competency 003: General pedagogy in ESL context

21.   **(A)**   Response A is correct because the teacher has assigned a challenging task and she is promoting students' ability to complete the task by *modeling* the response to the task and explaining the choices in the response to the learning task. Response B is incorrect because identifying literary language in the task does not help students know how to perform the task. Response C is incorrect because correcting the students' pronunciations as they read aloud does not support their ability to complete the task. Response D is incorrect because analyzing the contribution of the passage to understanding the whole story will not directly address the assigned task.

    Competency 005: Literacy (reading and writing) proficiency

22.   **(D)**   Response D—sheltered instruction—offers a list of accommodations recommended for ESL instruction in content-area classes where there might be a mix of EL students and native speakers. Sheltered instruction integrates teaching strategies that make content-area knowledge accessible to learners who are learning content in L2 while still working on L2 proficiency. Response A is incorrect because CALLA focuses more on the lesson structure rather than the teaching strategies. Response B is incorrect because the stem does not focus on content instruction but on strategies that can be used to make all classroom experiences more meaningful for EL students. Response C is incorrect because the strategies in the stem do not reflect only literacy; the strategies can be used to promote all areas of linguistic proficiency.

    Competency 008: History of ESL instruction

23.   **(A), (B), (E)**   Responses A, B, and E correctly connect knowledge of phonology, syntax, and pragmatics to specific learning support. Competency 001 focuses on the ESL teacher's responsibility to have a firm grounding in phonology, morphology, syntax, semantics, registers, pragmatics, and discourse so as to guide EL students in subtleties and specifics of L2 acquisition. Response C is incorrect because rhetoric, which is not considered one of the basic language systems, is also not typically connected to finding errors in writing. Response D is incorrect because reading support is more likely to be connected to phonology, syntax, and semantics than to discourse knowledge.

    Competency 001: Linguistic knowledge

24.   **(A)**   Response A is correct because it suggests that the writer is conflating semantic knowledge of various verbs that have a similar meaning into a single, generalized verb choice and selecting *dominate* to refer to both *seizing* land and *capturing* or *subjugating* a people. Response B is incorrect because the content of the sentence shows that the writer knows the general, holistic meaning of *dominate*. Response C is incorrect because the item stem directs us to look at linguistic elements of the sentence not content-area representation. Additionally, with only a single sentence shown, we cannot judge the breadth of the writer's knowledge of this topic. Response D is incorrect because the sentence does not include misused articles.

    Competency 002: L1 and L2 acquisition

25.   **(C)**   Response C correctly connects mini-lessons to segmenting, which is a type of linguistic accommodation that involves dividing lessons into smaller chunks to facilitate learner's processing of new information. Response A is incorrect because scaffolding, also a type of linguistic accommodation, involves creating foundations to support subsequent lessons and learning. Response B is incorrect because the suggestions to use mini-lessons and grouping strategies address academic learning not affective support. Response D is incorrect because the teaching suggestions are not related to assessment.

    Competency 003: General pedagogy in ESL context

26.   **(B)**   Response B correctly explains the learning support provided by mini-lessons in the context of SLA. Response A misrepresents the value of mini-lessons; mini-lessons are not intended to keep students from getting bored but instead to increase comprehensible input by segmenting a lesson to optimize student learning of new

knowledge. Response C is incorrect because mini-lessons do not simplify information; the chunking makes it possible to present complex information in segments to support learning. Response D is incorrect because mini-lessons are not presented quickly and are not intended to squeeze more information into a lesson.

Competency 003: General pedagogy in ESL context

27. **(A)** Response A correctly identifies the sentence problems demonstrated in the passage. Several incomplete sentences (fragments) are punctuated as complete sentences. Response B is incorrect because spelling problems are not evidence of syntactic difficulties; spelling is connected to phonology and orthography. Response C is incorrect because the passage shows that the writer is able to use a variety of syntactic structures. Response D is incorrect because it misdiagnoses the problems; the writer demonstrates competence in constructing complete sentences but also demonstrates difficulties in recognizing how to connect subordinate structures to main clauses.

Competency 001: Linguistic knowledge

28. **(C)** Response C correctly identifies a strategy for helping writers identify errors in their writing. Having a student writer read a draft aloud allows the writer to "hear" how subordinate structures are connected to main sentences and the writer is likely to independently make the needed syntactic corrections. Response A is incorrect because marking the errors in student writing and having the writer simply mimic the corrections does not promote writing competence or support the writer's independence. Response B is incorrect because worksheets are not considered an optimal strategy for promoting student competence in writing. Response D is incorrect because a new topic will not address the writing problems shown in the current draft.

Competency 005: Literacy (reading and writing) proficiency

29. **(D)** Response D is correct because providing feedback on how to improve the draft will enable the teacher to actively help the student meet her goal to be accepted into college. The college entrance essay is a high-stakes venture for the student and the teacher as advocate can support the student's efforts by explaining how to improve the draft. Response A is incorrect because simply providing models of college application essays does not put the teacher in an advocacy position. Response B is incorrect because simply marking the errors does not show the student how to improve the essay. Response C is incorrect because having the student watch a video takes the teacher out of the advocacy role.

Competency 010: State and federal guidelines, family engagement, and advocacy

30. **(B)** The correct response is B. The fact that this is a *beginning* level ESL *elementary* class points to the need to reinforce classroom management activities with illustrations and environmental print. The numbered illustrations on the poster will also give students greater understanding about the sequence of class day events. Response A is incorrect because elementary-level, beginning ESL students will not have sufficient L2 reading competence to understand a print chart. Response C is incorrect because it turns class day activities into an arbitrary series of events abruptly announced by a chime. Furthermore, at the elementary level, some learners, both EL and native English speakers, may not have full knowledge of time designations. In combination with the illustrated chart of Response B, the chime would be a good way to mark the segmentation of the day but the chime alone would seem random. Response D is incorrect because the video would not help the learners understand how their own school day is divided. The video, however, would be a good supplementary activity *after* students recognize that the school day is divided into predictable, stable segments.

Competency 003: General pedagogy in ESL context

31. **(C)** The correct response is C. This scenario focuses on cooperative learning as a boost to EL student achievement. Integrating native speakers and ELs in *base* groups—groups that are maintained for a substantive period rather than just for a specific activity—allows students to bond socially. Those social connections, partic-

ularly in an ESL setting, promote learning. Response A is incorrect because random grouping initially inhibits the camaraderie that is at the heart of effective cooperative learning. Response B isolates and marks EL students as different and possibly deficient. Response D is discouraged for almost any cooperative learning scenario, the assumption being that students self-select groups of friends. Additionally, self-selected grouping encourages exclusionary practices that teachers should strive to avoid in any teaching situation but particularly where EL students are involved.

Competency 003: General pedagogy in ESL context

32. **(C)** The correct response is C. Breaking up the lesson into shorter segments and then reinforcing the information by focusing on key points are strategies likely to help intermediate EL students master the content and thereby reach higher achievement levels. Furthermore, the think-pair-share allows learners to process the new knowledge and the teacher to quickly assess whether the learners have understood the new information. Response A is incorrect because it does not take into account strategies for helping students boost the quiz average. Response B is incorrect because it overlooks the core problem: the failing quiz average suggests that students are having trouble mastering the new information. Asking students to teach each other information that they don't understand will not address the teacher's instructional goal. Response D is incorrect because it includes no strategies for promoting the learner's achievement through greater understanding of course content. Audio recordings *are* considered a good instructional strategy in EL settings; however, simply listening to incomprehensible input over and over will not make it comprehensible. Response D does not address the teacher's goal.

Competency 003: General pedagogy in ESL context

33. **(D)** The correct response is D. This is the most learner-centered response and most appropriate for the targeted age and EL level. Working with manipulatives in a math class is considered a learning-inducing strategy: hands-on strategies create engagement and promote understanding. Response A is incorrect because it would force the students to guess rather than to demonstrate competence in learning to identify the math figures. The scenario specifies that the students are having trouble learning the names of the figures; a quiz will not promote learning in this scenario. Response B is incorrect because it does not initially create understanding of the differences or distinctiveness of the figures. Drawing and labeling the figures would be a good way to reinforce students' understanding after students learn the names and shapes of the math figures. Response C is incorrect because it does not actively engage learners in the activity; furthermore, a poster does not address the teacher's goal to have students learn the shapes and names of the math figures.

Competency 006: Teaching ESL in content areas

34. **(A)** The correct response is (A). The teaching activity focuses on following simple directions, which is the hallmark of TPR. Furthermore, the directions call for the learners to respond physically by forming a reading circle, briefly talking to each other and then doing the distribution activity. Response B is incorrect because this isolated activity does not offer sufficient context to classify the approach as immersion (which is characterized by minimal L1-L2 scaffolding). Furthermore, *immersion* is a holistic approach; the scenario focuses on a specific, distinct classroom activity, not on a whole program approach. Response C is incorrect because the activity is focused on organization and following instructions rather than shaping community. Response D is an area of linguistics (see Competency 001), not a teaching strategy.

Competency 004: Listening and speaking proficiency

35. **(A)** The correct response is A. The scenario describes a prereading activity to provide scaffolding for meaningful discussion and to activate prior knowledge as students prepare to read a story. In discussing cold-weather extremes, students will be ready to process the character's decisions once he starts his journey. Response B is incorrect because creating a semantic map is not mentioned in the scenario. However, the semantic

map follow-up might reinforce the learners' understanding of the impact of extreme cold which will support their comprehension of the story. Response C is incorrect because the prereading activity does not directly support comprehension. Prereading activities prime learners to initially enter the text; comprehension activities occur later in the reading process. Response D is incorrect because the prereading activity should not demonstrate deficiencies or lapses in knowledge but should help learners discover what they already know about something relevant to an upcoming reading.

Competency 006: Teaching ESL in content areas

36. **(A), (B)** The correct responses are A and B. Research on the setting will allow learners to envision the conflicts the character faces as he conducts his journey through the Yukon. The teacher has set up a short research assignment that integrates a variety of ways to learn the assigned material: cognitive engagement through research, creative opportunities through the illustrations, and group participation through the oral presentation. Response C is incorrect because technology is integrated to bolster students' participation in the experience of reading the story not to simplify the learning task. Response D is incorrect because cooperative activities are not intended as a way to simplify a learning task but as a means to use socialization and collaboration to enhance learning.

Competency 006: Teaching ESL in content areas

37. **(B)** The correct response is B. The scenario creates a meaningful learning experience for students by integrating listening and speaking proficiencies in the context of prior knowledge. Response A is incorrect because the scenario focuses on presentation of content knowledge, not on sharing homeland experiences. Response C is incorrect because new vocabulary is not the focus of this activity. The activity is an introductory, oral language activity. Response D is incorrect because the activity is not focused on comprehension; it is more of a prereading strategy carried out in a communicative language context.

Competency 004: Listening and speaking proficiency

38. **(A)** The correct response is A. The Author's Chair activity will allow students to develop both listening and speaking skills. Response B is incorrect because the initial impact of the Author's Chair is simply active listening. Response C is incorrect because the scenario is focused on a funds-of-knowledge approach not on vocabulary development. Response D is incorrect because L1 support is a normal part of writing in SLA contexts; the teacher should expect EL students to rely on their L1 knowledge to support their L2 writing.

Competency 004: Listening and speaking proficiency

39. **(A)** The correct response is A. Response A describes a prolific strategy for helping EL students recognize how nonverbal and body language enhance oral communication. Response B is incorrect because the teaching activity is focused on constructing meaning from a visual text, not on reducing anxiety. Response C is incorrect because the scenario explains that students will be delivering an *informal* speech, not one that needs to be memorized. Response D is incorrect because the scenario does not specifically mention ancillary materials in the speech.

Competency 004: Listening and speaking proficiency

40. **(B)** The correct response is B. The teacher needs to promote students' ability to *hear* the phonemes in L2 contexts. Thus, the audio exercise followed by choral reading of a familiar text would contribute both to comprehensible input and to meaningful output. Response A is incorrect because oral reading is a social activity; correcting students during oral reading would embarrass the speaker and thwart the intent of the oral reading activity. Response C is incorrect because it misconstrues the learning objective to help students improve their pronunciation. A spelling test would focus on orthography not on pronunciation. Response D is incorrect because writing sentences does not address the phonological problem that the teacher is targeting.

Competency 004: Listening and speaking proficiency

41.   **(D)**   The correct response is D. The student's use of *pues*, a Spanish word, in the context of an English conversation is a classic example of code-switching. Code-switching occurs when EL speakers insert an L1 word or phrase into an L2 string, using syntax and meaning that reflects L2 structures. Code-switching is deliberate and reflects the speaker's adept blending of L1 structures in L2 utterances. Response A is incorrect because there is no interference involved from L1 to L2; instead, a distinct word from L1 occurs in logical syntactic and semantic use in L2. Response B is incorrect because the speaker is not transferring L1 knowledge directly; instead, she is using an L1 phrase in an L2 context. Response C is incorrect because the example does not show that the student is translating an L1 word into L2 context.
   Competency 004: Listening and speaking proficiency

42.   **(A)**   The correct response is A. This activity capitalizes on the urge to talk about a movie when we walk out of a theater. The teacher's suggested questions prompt the students to create a skit that replicates "walking out of the theater" conversations. Creating the skit will promote language proficiency in a cooperative setting. Presenting the skit will promote presentational language skills including nonverbals, intonation, and context-specific word choice. Response B is incorrect because the intent of the activity is to create an authentic conversational environment, not to assess students' understanding of events or details of the film. Response C is incorrect because the talking-about-the film activity is focused on promoting communicative competence not on introducing the novel. Response D is incorrect because the activity focuses on the students' affective response, not on noticing details.
   Competency 004: Listening and speaking proficiency

43.   **(D)**   The correct response is D because a planned Q & A on the reports enables students to be active listeners and then to use their oral language skills to pose questions to their classmates. The questions from classmates would provide authentic feedback on how effectively the speaker presented his/her out-of-school activity. Response A is incorrect because writing a summary of each report is not focused on listening and speaking skills and would not provide feedback to the learner. Response B is incorrect because the applause does not provide meaningful feedback to the presenter. The best speech question would be inappropriate since the class has not been given criteria for selecting the best presentation. Response C is incorrect because the focus on pronunciation and usage errors would compromise the communicative intent of the activity.
   Competency 004: Listening and speaking proficiency

44.   **(A)**   The correct response is A. Circumlocution is a communicative strategy used by EL speakers when there is a mismatch between semantic and lexical knowledge: the speaker knows the meaning he/she wants to convey but not the corresponding L2 word, so the speaker *describes* the object or circumstance. Response B is incorrect because approximation means that the speaker substitutes a word semantically or lexically similar to the intended word. Response C is incorrect because lexical avoidance refers to a strategy whereby the learner figures out a way to state the meaning by avoiding the intended term, usually because the speaker realizes he/she has L2 grammatical deficiencies in that area, possibly pronunciation, possibly inexact understanding of the targeted word. Response D is incorrect because stalling is a communicative filler used to gain time while the learner tries to remember the needed term.
   Competency 002: L1 and L2 acquisition

45.   **(B), (D)**   The correct responses are B and D. Interdependence and transfer explain how EL students strengthen their learning in L2 by relying on their knowledge and experience in L1. For example, an EL student's knowledge of grammar structures in L1 will support their learning of L2 grammar, even when the languages are markedly different. Similarly, literacy development in L2 is supported by reading and writing competence in L1. Even if the learner does not know how to read in L1, knowledge of sounds in L1 can be transferred into L2 learning. Response A is incorrect because interference generally creates errors in L2 when the learner relies on

L1 knowledge that does not match the communicative or the linguistic context. Response C is incorrect because translation is a deliberate strategy in which EL students attempt to understand L2 strings by relying fully on the L1 version of the utterance. Translation can also occur when an EL speaker inserts an L1 word or phrase not in deliberate code-switching but as a way to fill in when the L2 expression is not yet in the speaker's L2 knowledge. Response E is incorrect because approximation is considered an error that occurs when the learner doesn't quite know the right word or structure and approximates a similar structure from L1 in an L2 utterance.

Competency 002: L1 and L2 acquisition

46. **(B)** The correct response is B. The example fits ELPS descriptors for intermediate proficiency in writing. The passage shows numerous, frequent errors associated with L2 writing and shows "emergent forms of writing." Response A is incorrect because ELPS descriptors for beginning level writing focus on deficiencies and limitations that demonstrate "little or no ability" in writing. Despite the numerous errors, the sample shows far more than beginning writing skills. Response C is incorrect because the sample does not quite show grade-level appropriate writing. A lot of the errors suggest writing that might be appropriate for an elementary-level writer, not a Grade 9 writer. Response D is incorrect because the writer does not show writing competence "nearly comparable to native English-speaking peers."

Competency 005: Literacy (reading and writing) proficiency

47. **(C)** The correct response is C. Despite the numerous errors in this passage, the writer does effectively address a key requirement of the assignment: using textual evidence. In a public discussion of each student's effort, recognizing the effective features is a better writing feedback strategy than calling attention to the errors. Responses A, B, and D show the teacher making critical comments about the writing and pointing out problems. These should not be feedback strategies for short oral presentations that are most likely designed to promote class community. Learners, particularly EL students who are already insecure about their language competence, are likely to be embarrassed by having their language lapses pointed out publicly. Thus, the focus on what the writer did effectively (Response C) is the best oral feedback choice.

Competency 005: Literacy (reading and writing) proficiency

48. **(B)** The correct response is B. This assignment effectively integrates the four language domains in a meaningful class activity. Response A is incorrect because there is no indication that the teacher is targeting students with low literacy levels. Response C is incorrect because the scenario does not suggest that the teacher is trying to avoid student frustration by making a short assignment. In actuality, the response involves significant effort: reading, writing, presentation, and processing feedback. Response D is incorrect because the assignment is based on higher cognitive levels of Bloom's Taxonomy: analysis and creation.

Competency 005: Literacy (reading and writing) proficiency

49. **(D)** The correct response is D. If the teacher wants to reduce students' discomfort over reading orally, establishing reading circles is a good strategy. Students are able to read independently but also help each other in the less public environment of the small circle. Additionally, sometimes the reading circle format allows each circle to pick the book they want to read. Response A is incorrect because identifying reluctant readers is not the primary rationale for creating reading circles. Reading circles may show that some students are reluctant to read but they also create enthusiasm for reading as students share their responses to the texts they selected for their group. Response B is incorrect because it misconstrues the purpose of reading circles—reading circles are supposed to encourage students to want to read in a non-threatening situation, but if they associate reading circles with the teacher's criticism, their engagement in reading may diminish. Response C is incorrect because reading circles are not replacements for whole-class oral reading.

Competency 005: Literacy (reading and writing) proficiency

50.   **(B)**   The correct response is B. In a class of beginning and intermediate EL students, using visual support to present new content-area vocabulary is a good prereading strategy. Furthermore, with the teacher defining the words prior to the read aloud, the students' attention is focused on seeing how the new words fit into the lesson. Response A is incorrect because looking up words prior to reading does not contextualize the words within the new content. Response C is incorrect because the students might overlook words that are relevant to the new content. Response D is incorrect because the interruptions to define words during the read aloud will interfere with the coherence of the reading.

   Competency 005: Literacy (reading and writing) proficiency

51.   **(B)**   The correct response is B. A semantic map is considered a robust strategy for preparing learners for new content. By focusing on a core content term and considering related concepts, learners are primed for processing new knowledge. Response A is incorrect because semantic maps should be created prior to reading as a way of helping learners anticipate new information. Response C is incorrect because, while a semantic map *may* include new vocabulary, the purpose of the semantic map is to introduce concepts that will show up in new content material. Response D is incorrect because semantic maps are not designed to show text structures.

   Competency 006: Teaching ESL in content areas

52.   **(C)**   The correct response is C. Having students create their own word problems will give them insider knowledge on the structure and rationale of word problems. Notably, the students have the teacher-created graphic that explains the structure of word problems, so creating their own problem will give students a chance to demonstrate their understanding. Response A is incorrect because it does not address the teacher's objective to promote students' understanding of math content. The students are young (elementary level), so the word problems are new knowledge even for students with past schooling in L1. Response B is incorrect because it includes no indication of how reading word problems will promote students' math knowledge. Response D is incorrect not because it is not a good teaching strategy but because it doesn't fit the teacher's objective at this point. Later, when students demonstrate comprehensive understanding of word problems, the contest would be a good strategy for reinforcing that math content proficiency.

   Competency 006: Teaching ESL in content areas

53.   **(A), (B), (F)**   Response A is correct because it shows a linguistic accommodation recommended for sheltered instruction: reinforcing content area vocabulary with illustrations or realia. Response B is correct because a short think aloud will enable the teacher to show learners how to process the new information, perhaps connecting it to prior chapters, perhaps raising questions that might be answered in the chapter. Think alouds are considered excellent strategies for showing learners how to use metacognitive strategies in reading. Response F is correct because it offers an opportunity for learners to use textual organization markers to support their learning and anticipate chapter content. Response C is incorrect because the scenario focuses on prereading strategies. Answering questions would be a better post-reading activity. Response D is incorrect because it reduces learner participation in the reading activity. Furthermore, summaries are generally used as post-reading checks on comprehension. Response E is incorrect because the stem focuses on prereading. Generating a list of new vocabulary words would be something that happens as learners are reading the chapter.

   Competency 006: Teaching ESL in content areas

54.   **(A)**   The correct response is A. This activity provides the highest level of student choice, engagement, and collaboration in an assessment activity. Additionally, it integrates technology and creates opportunities to take individual learner's abilities into account as students in each group pool their academic resources and strengths in preparing the slide presentation. Response B is incorrect because the lectures and testing approach does not include strategies for improving student achievement, which is the teacher's objective. Response C is incorrect

because it does not address the teacher's goal to prepare students for a specific state standard. Knowing the answers to the sample questions will not help students acquire the knowledge called for by the state standard on political systems. Response D is incorrect because the task is too complex for the time period the teacher is allowing. Additionally, the task does not effectively address the state standard that the teacher is targeting.

Competency 007: Assessment in ESL contexts

55. **(C)** The correct response is C. Asking students to solve problems and then explain the process to the whole class provides an authentic oral language experience with an opportunity for the teacher to informally assess the learner's understanding of the math task. Response A is incorrect because asking if students have questions does not directly promote oral language proficiency; this response does not encourage students to use oral language to promote their content area learning. Response B is incorrect because making an error on purpose and expecting students to detect the error is a counterproductive teaching strategy. The instruction is focused on the error, not on genuine understanding. Furthermore, the student assistant strategy creates oral language opportunities for only one student. Response D is incorrect because the students are more likely to concentrate on completing the homework assignment (so they don't have to do it at home) than on talking and listening to each other in meaningful oral language interactions during this activity. Additionally, "checking" homework is not meaningful assessment.

Competency 007: Assessment in ESL contexts

56. **(A)** The correct response is A. The card and picture recognition activity is well suited for the EL proficiency levels of this young class. Additionally, the students' responses will provide feedback on how students are using listening and speaking skills. Responses B is incorrect because it focuses on affective response to the environment not on demonstration of science knowledge. Response C is incorrect because it focuses on construction of a narrative based on personal experience rather than on science content. Furthermore, the narrative assignment does not provide opportunities for informal assessment of students' understanding of science content. Response D is incorrect because a lecture followed by a quiz does not meet the teacher's goal to adjust assessment opportunities to integrate oral language.

Competency 007: Assessment in ESL contexts

57. **(A)** The correct response is A. Figuring out what the prompt is asking for is a key aspect of the state-mandated writing exam. The think aloud of the prompt would meet the teacher's goals to familiarize students with the exam format as well as to teach them how to negotiate the expectations of writing on demand (high-stakes writing done in a limited time frame on an unfamiliar topic). Response B is incorrect because this 15-minute writing assignment focuses on students' affective response to each other's writing rather than on the criteria for the state-mandated writing exam. Response C is incorrect because collaborative writing will not effectively prepare individual learners for managing writing on demand. Response D is incorrect because the round-robin approach may be a "fun" class activity but it does not prepare students for the experience of writing on demand.

Competency 007: Assessment in ESL contexts

58. **(C)** The correct response is C. Training materials for the state-mandated writing exams in Texas encourage teachers to create classroom rubrics to give students feedback on exam-like essays. Having the students use the rubrics to assess their own and their classmates' essays would provide an "insider's view" into the state writing requirements. Response A does not address the writing-on-demand environment. In the testing, students will not have time for reflective revision. Response B is incorrect because it does not indicate what criteria the teacher is using to score the essays. Students need "insider information" on what is needed for a satisfactory score on the state-mandated writing exam. The rubric mentioned in Response C would provide the state exam expectations. Response D is incorrect because while creating a rubric is a good writing instruction strategy, in the context of the

teacher's goal to prepare students for the state-mandated writing exam, the teacher should use the rubric provided by the state to give students a strong sense of expectations.

Competency 007: Assessment in ESL contexts

59. **(C)** The correct response is C. Although Sustained Silent Reading is not supposed to be used in assessment, the scenario explains that the teacher wants to use SSR scaffolding for an informal assessment activity. The teacher's checklist indicates that the assessment is focused on fluency. Thus, using a book that the student is familiar with will allow a fair assessment of the reader's fluency. Response A is incorrect because the teacher's checklist does not address comprehension. Response B is incorrect because the ability to connect sounds and symbols is suggested in the recognition of miscues and self-correction but is only part of what the teacher is assessing. Response D is incorrect because the teacher's checklist does not focus on pronunciation.

Competency 007: Assessment in ESL contexts

60. **(D)** The correct response is D. The teacher's instructions indicate that she is trying to assess the learners' use of strategies for constructing meaning of new words or content-area vocabulary by decoding the words on the page. Decoding can involve phonological strategies or semantic cues and clues from the passage. Response A is incorrect because the teacher's instructions do not focus on determining what content knowledge the learner is taking away from the reading. Response B is incorrect because metacognition is a broader concept than the decoding focus that the teacher presents in the instructions. Response C is incorrect because the teacher has not done anything to activate prior knowledge and is presenting the selected passage as a new text that the students are reading "cold" with no preparation.

Competency 007: Assessment in ESL contexts

61. **(A)** The correct response is A. The family newspaper activity contextualizes language learning within a highly social activity, which is a pillar of effective ESL education. Response B is incorrect because the assignment is actually quite challenging; students will have to make decisions about content, layout, illustrations, and then presentation. Response C is incorrect because although they are creating a newspaper, the activity will integrate several types of learning activities and learning styles: content, art, and layout. Response D is incorrect because this activity is in fact highly academic since it combines several performance outcomes.

Competency 008: History of ESL instruction

62. **(A)** The correct response is A. To date, court rulings have addressed inequities in educational opportunities for students whose native language is not English and who need language support; however, no rulings exist on making all students in America proficient in a second language, which is what "universal second language instruction" would implement. Response B is incorrect because undocumented children's rights to public education was addressed by Supreme Court case *Plyler v. Doe* in 1982. Response C is incorrect because the connection between language programs and educational equity has been addressed by numerous U.S. Supreme Court and federal court decisions. Response D is incorrect because desegregation has been addressed by numerous court cases beginning with *Brown v. Board of Education* (1954).

Competency 008: History of ESL instruction

63. **(C)** The correct response is (C). By not criticizing the student's "wrong" response, the teacher is reinforcing the learner's affective needs, the need to be recognized and valued as a member of the class community. By linking the student's apparent incorrect response to the chapters, the teacher is integrating content-area knowledge into the discussion while valuing the student's contribution. Response A is incorrect because it does not take into account the teacher's student-centered response to what might be considered an inappropriate student response followed by being laughed at by the class. Response B is incorrect because the focus of the class event is not the

student's use of code-switching but the teacher's careful response to an apparently incorrect answer. Response D is incorrect because it reflects a small component of the teacher's behavior, but it does not address the TAC requirement that is the focus of the item stem.

Competency 008: History of ESL instruction

64. **(C)** The correct response is C. By recognizing the inherent inequity in educational opportunities for language-minority students, the Bilingual Education Act created the foundation for bilingual and ESL programs in schools throughout America. However, the BEA did *not* mandate bilingual education. Response A is incorrect because rights of undocumented children were addressed in *Plyler v. Doe* in 1982. Response B is incorrect because the BEA did not establish a center for bilingual education. Response D is incorrect because this term is not used in describing or implementing bilingual programs in the U.S.; in fact, several court cases have addressed the problems with programs that segregate linguistic majority and linguistic minority students into environments that claim to offer equal education to both sets of students.

Competency 008: History of ESL instruction

65. **(B), (C), (E)** Responses B, C, and E correctly reflect some of the components of language programs in Texas. Response B correctly identifies content-based classes as one of the options for LEP students. Response C correctly notes that parents of native speakers of English can opt to have their children placed in two-way bilingual programs. Response E correctly identifies dual immersion one-way programs as special programs that include only non-native speakers of English. Response A is incorrect because ESL programs in Texas do not end at Grade 8. Response D is incorrect because it states that translating content into L1 is the primary task of language teachers. Certified ESL and bilingual teachers offer content area instruction with well-constructed support for language learning. Response F is incorrect because LEP students are evaluated by the LPAC to determine which language program best meets their language learning needs.

Competency 008: History of ESL instruction

66. **(B)** The correct response is (B). Watching the exaggerated gestures of animated characters in scenes with no dialogue would enable learners to evaluate how emotive response can be expressed through facial expression, body language, gestures, and physical reaction. The teacher's choice to focus on characters that represent a variety of cultures seems clearly intended to heighten students' awareness of the variance of non-verbal meaning across cultures. Response A is incorrect because the activity is not intended to create a hierarchy in language options. Nonverbals are a vital part of cultural communication. Nonverbals do not take primacy over verbal language. Response C is incorrect because the scenario does not suggest that the teacher is attempting to demonstrate equivalence between animated and live action film. Response D is incorrect because the item scenario does not indicate that the teacher wants students to learn non-English gestures.

Competency 009: Multiculturalism in ESL classrooms

67. **(B), (C), (D)** The correct responses are B, C, and D, all of which reflect attitudes counter to good ESL teaching practice. Response B is correct because the teacher's comments reflect preconceived notions about the student's performance based not on first-hand knowledge but on stereotypes founded on the learner's ethnicity. Response C is correct because the teacher's comments reflect the attitude that second language learners are deficient cognitively and lack motivation to succeed. Response D is correct because a good ESL teacher preparation program would have included training in maintaining high expectations for all learners, in seeing difference as an asset, and in shaping instruction to meet the needs of all learners. Response A is incorrect because it misrepresents the spirit of the comments; generally, *autonomy* is a positive term. Privileging this teacher's attitude as an example of instructional autonomy violates the principles of effective multicultural education. Response E is

incorrect because the teacher does not indicate an interest in teaching to the test. Response F is incorrect because the teacher's comments reflect a resistance to high expectations for all learners.

Competency 009: Multiculturalism in ESL classrooms

68. **(C)** The correct response is C. Culturally relevant artifacts help students connect meaningfully with classroom experiences by mirroring real-world experience, thereby creating an effective multicultural learning environment. Even if students have never had experience with a real *piñata*, they are likely to know about it as an artifact of Mexican culture. Response A is incorrect because it presents a deficit view of ESL students by suggesting that unless a cultural connection is made, students will not work hard or will not understand course content. Response B is incorrect because using realia does not simplify academic content. Using realia enables students to find real-world connections in course content. Response D is incorrect because manipulatives are intended to provide students hands-on experiences to illuminate content-area concepts, making content knowledge accessible not easier.

Competency 009: Multiculturalism in ESL classrooms

69. **(D)** The correct response is D. The statement encompasses key aspects of multiculturalism: cultural awareness, respect, and inclusion. Response A is incorrect because it presents a limited view of the statement. Response B is incorrect because it suggests that cultural and individual differences are aberrations that need to be "tolerated." Response C is incorrect because it implies a negative view of the school experience suggesting that being in school is a threat to one's identity.

Competency 009: Multiculturalism in ESL classrooms

70. **(A)** The correct response is A. The teacher supports all learners' affective needs through her response; significantly, she avoids embarrassing anyone and instead makes comments designed to promote confidence and self-assurance in all learners. Response B is incorrect because it does not reflect the core problem presented in the scenario. The classroom event is not about working through a linguistic problem but about respecting each other's rights as learners. Response C is incorrect because it minimizes lack of respect shown by the students who are laughing. Response D is incorrect because it ignores both the holistic problem (the students' lack of respect for classmates) and the immediate impact (distraction from the content of the lesson).

Competency 009: Multiculturalism in ESL classrooms

71. **(A)** The correct response is A. A key tenet of literature pedagogy is the belief that readers should see themselves reflected in characters and situations in novels. In creating an effective multicultural learning environment, teachers need to ensure that multicultural literature does not stereotype or offer negative views of the culture it claims to represent. Response B is incorrect because it misrepresents the rationale for introducing multicultural literature into an ESL curriculum. Nonetheless, research and practice shows that multicultural literature is thematically consistent with themes in canonical literature. Response C is incorrect because it presents a false "standard" for integrating multicultural literature. Response D is incorrect because it erroneously singles out EL students as incapable of making meaningful connections to canonical literature.

Competency 009: Multiculturalism in ESL classrooms

72. **(A)** The correct response is A. This response offers a strong explanation of how this assignment supports the goals of two-way dual language immersion teaching by giving students an opportunity to broadly showcase L1 and L2 competencies. Response B is incorrect because the goal of the activity is to focus on students' biliteracy skills, not on learning about an important author. Response C is incorrect because, with a picture book, the students are having to construct their own story to showcase their biliteracy; the collaborative assignment actually shows that you can start with an apparently "incomplete" text and still construct meaningful output. Response D

is incorrect because collaboration is not the focus of the task described in the scenario; instead, collaboration is the means by which the students address the task.

Competency 009: Multiculturalism in ESL classrooms

73. **(A)** The correct response is A. The teacher has created an assignment designed to elicit family participation. The targeted students are young and likely to need help completing the assignment. Even if parents cannot help for various reasons, the children could ask an older sibling for help. Response B is incorrect because it misinterprets the intent of the assignment as presented by the teacher's instructions, placing parents in the role of checkers of homework. Response C is incorrect because there is no suggestion in the assignment that it is simplified to encourage students to complete it. It is age appropriate rather than simplified to a lower level. Response D is incorrect because creating a vocabulary list is not the primary purpose of the assignment; as a follow-up activity, the teacher could move to a vocabulary activity, but that extension is not reflected in the item stem.

Competency 010: State and federal guidelines, family engagement, and advocacy

74. **(C)** The correct response is C. Inviting parents to the library with their children is a proactive method of encouraging parents to take advantage of community resources for promoting their children's literacy development. Response A is incorrect because a flyer offers information but does not show parents the actual library experience, which is the intent presented in the item stem. Response B is incorrect because it focuses on teacher efforts, not on encouraging families to make use of community resources. Response D is incorrect because it turns the library experience into a class assignment, not a family and community resources opportunity.

Competency 010: State and federal guidelines, family engagement, and advocacy

75. **(D)** The correct response is D. This response fully involves parents in their children's homework responsibilities. With the awareness that the parents do not have the necessary academic or language background to help their children with homework in traditional ways, the modeling would show parents other ways to participate in their children's homework completion. Response A is incorrect because it puts the parent in the role of administrator rather than homework coach. Response B is incorrect because it does not show parents how to participate in helping their children complete homework assignments. Response C is incorrect because it overlooks the parents' limited L2 literacy and limited academic proficiency described in the item stem.

Competency 010: State and federal guidelines, family engagement, and advocacy

76. **(D)** The correct response is D. The LPAC is the body responsible for making decisions about the admission and reclassification of ELs. This is the process described in the *LPAC Framework Manual*, which reflects TEC and TAC mandates. Response A is incorrect because LPAC does not set a minimum time limit for students to be in designated language programs. Response B is incorrect because student linguistic proficiency is not based on LPAC interviews. Response C is incorrect because learner participation in language programs continues year by year until the learner meets the criteria described in Response D. The LPAC does not set minimum participation times based on test scores.

Competency 010: State and federal guidelines, family engagement, and advocacy

77. **(A)** The correct response is A. Mandated tests create stress for both teachers and students. Inviting parents to a test prep boot camp brings in parents as partners in helping EL students feel confident about the approaching tests. Response B is incorrect because it suggests that inviting the parents is a preventative strategy rather than a team-building effort. Additionally, this response presupposes that learners will not succeed on the exams. Response C is incorrect because it is asking parents to perform a task that is appropriately the teacher's and the school's responsibility. Response D is incorrect because it implies that the teacher sees the tests as an obstacle that students and parents face.

Competency 010: State and federal guidelines, family engagement, and advocacy

78.   **(B)**   The correct response is B. For numerous reasons, parents cannot always participate fully in their children's homework assignments. This chart places the responsibility in the student's hands but the recognition in the parent's hands, creating a viable opportunity for parental involvement and partnering with their children in supporting homework completion. Response A is incorrect because no rewards are mentioned in the item stem. Response C is incorrect because the chart does not include a mechanism for ensuring that students complete the tasks. Response D is incorrect because the chart does not integrate a proactive attempt to see homework as an extension of classroom learning.

Competency 010: State and federal guidelines, family engagement, and advocacy

79.   **(C)**   The correct response is C. Parental involvement is widely recognized as a critical component of EL students' success. A problematic aspect of parental involvement, however, is the reality that the teacher has to take the initiative and integrate opportunities for such involvement; nonetheless, the difficulties do not detract from the recognized importance of parental involvement. Response A is incorrect because ESL teaching materials include many suggestions for involving parents. Response B is incorrect because it misrepresents the attitudes and practices exemplified by most ESL educators. Response D is incorrect because it suggests that school personnel do not want to work with parents to promote EL students' success. This response in some ways explains the exigencies of working actively to involve parents. Parents with limited educational backgrounds need guidance in learning how to support their children's educational success.

Competency 010: State and federal guidelines, family engagement, and advocacy

80.   **(D)**   The correct response is D. The teacher's visuals are focused on easing students' concerns about asking questions, a problem that persists even in mainstream classes made up only of native speakers. The poster might diffuse cultural conflicts in learners whose cultures value quiet participation instead of interactive participation through questioning and class discussion. The strategy addresses learners' affective needs by promoting confidence and self-assurance about asking questions. Response A is incorrect because "conversational" suggests that the activity is a social activity. Asking questions in class is generally considered an academic activity. Response B is incorrect because the poster does not present classroom rules but instead seems to invite all learners to participate in class discussion. Response C is incorrect. While the teacher's poster strategy may promote students' speaking proficiency, that is a side effect of the targeted goal to meet TAC regulations on social, cognitive, and affective needs.

Competency 009: Multiculturalism in ESL classrooms

Glossary

Accommodations—adjustments made to allow learners equitable access to learning situations. Accommodations can be *linguistic accommodations* made in classroom instruction to support EL students' full participation in learning activities. Accommodations also refers to adjustments and supports in testing and other output situations to increase accessibility for learners with special needs.

Advocacy—serving as a supporter of EL student and family needs by knowing resources, programs, and options available to students and their families.

Assessment—measurement of student achievement. Assessment should include means for reporting student strengths and weaknesses in performance of tasks related to specific learning outcomes. Assessment should reflect a mindset of continual improvement; in other words, assessments should provide opportunities to improve performance. Lessons should initially be constructed with awareness of how learning outcomes will be assessed.

Authentic assessment—promotes the mindset that assessment is ongoing, success-driven, and student-centered. Authentic assessment often occurs on-the-spot during lessons when teachers realize that an instructional strategy needs to be tweaked to promote student learning. Authentic assessment reflects well-constructed assessments and assessment instruments that allow learners to showcase their achievement and that allow teachers to offer fair, meaningful commentary on learner accomplishments.

Basic Interpersonal Communicative Skills (BICS)—One strand of a dichotomy that describes types of L2 acquisition: basic interpersonal communicative skills and cognitive/academic language proficiency. Jim Cummins proposed that basic interpersonal communicative skills, which EL students need in order to participate in meaningful speaking and listening interactions with L2 speakers, develop much more quickly than higher-level cognitive skills (Cognitive/Academic Language Proficiency).

Behavioral outcomes—instruction should be guided by learning outcomes that reflect what the learner should know and be able to do at the end of the instructional period. Behavioral outcomes are *measurable*.

Bilingual programs—Bilingual programs are one of two broad language programs implemented in Texas public schools to develop the language and academic proficiency of students who have been designated LEP on the basis of their performance on the state-approved English proficiency exam. In bilingual programs, instruction is delivered in English and another language. In Texas, there are four types of bilingual programs: two transitional programs (early exit and late exit) and two dual language programs (immersion/one way and immersion/two way).

Bloom's Taxonomy—a classic system of hierarchical cognitive tasks that teachers use to construct developmentally appropriate instructional activities and assessments. Bloom's Taxonomy includes six levels of cognitive tasks: remembering, understanding, applying, analyzing, evaluating, and creating. The verbs in learning objectives should match the cognitive task reflected by the objective in order to ensure coherence in instruction, activities, and assessments related to the objective.

Code-switching—a deliberate integration of a structure from L1 into an L2 structure. Real code-switching is intentional, either to fill a gap in current L2 proficiency, in which case it is more of a translation or transfer strategy, or to enact a rhetorical, political, or social motive.

Cognitive processes—In the context of the ESL exam's competencies, cognitive processes refer to the deliberate or unconscious thinking processes that modulate an EL student's learning. SLA requires that learners be aware of what they can do cognitively to enhance their L2 learning.

Cognitive/Academic Language Proficiency—One strand of a dichotomy that describes types of L2 acquisition: basic interpersonal communicative skills and cognitive academic language proficiency. Jim Cummins proposed that basic interpersonal communicative skills, which EL students need in order to participate in meaningful speaking and listening interactions with L2 speakers, develop much more quickly than higher-level cognitive skills (Cognitive/Academic Language Proficiency). CALP is what is taught in schools in content areas and it takes much longer to develop than BICS because it is so much more cognitively demanding. Cummins warned that looking only at surface proficiency in L2 could result in early exit from language programs before learners are truly adept in cognitive language skills.

Collaborative learning—Involving learners in activities that call for cooperation and interaction. Most group activities are collaborative because learners are usually given a task that must be performed by working together toward the assigned outcome.

Communication with families—It is the teacher's responsibility to initiate and maintain fruitful communication with families. Communications sent to families should express openness to involve the families in the learner's school world. Communication with families from different cultures should take into account possibilities for miscommunication and should factor in cultural norms that impact how families interact with schools. In ESL settings, teachers may need to seek campus assistance in translating communication into the learner's family's primary language.

Communication—a vital part of L2 learning. Communication is the generic term used to refer to social, pragmatic, and functional uses of language.

Communicative competence—The ability to interact meaningfully in social situations using basic linguistic skills, nonverbals, and appropriate registers. Communicative competence is acquired relatively quickly; researchers estimate that most EL students can learn basic communicative skills in about two years whereas academic skills take up to seven years or longer. Researchers also believe that EL students rely on fundamental communicative skills that transfer across languages, which explains the rapid development of communicative competence.

Community resources—A variety of community resources can help learners meet their academic and personal goals. Teachers can inform both learners and their families of community organizations and services that target specific needs. A teacher's awareness of learner needs contributes to knowing what community services and organizations might best suit the learner and/or the family. In ESL settings, teachers can help learners and families acculturate by being aware of resources that can provide academic, personal, financial, political, and health services.

Competencies—the English as a Second Language framework is presented in 10 competencies in three domains. The competencies are statements of the general knowledge that beginning teachers should have in pivotal areas of ESL teaching content, with each competency subdivided into descriptive statements that offer details on expected ESL certification knowledge and skills.

Comprehensible input—A term coined by Stephen D. Krashen to describe the catalyst for successful SLA. Krashen explained that individuals learn L1 via ongoing meaningful, context-related input, and while L1 learning processes cannot be replicated in SLA, Krashen contended that L2 learning could be enhanced by ensuring that learners receive constant comprehensible input in authentic communicative and cognitive interactions.

Comprehension—a term associated with reading. Comprehension refers to the holistic construction of meaning when we read a text. Readers use many cognitive, linguistic, and reading skills to shape meaning as they read and then holistically at the end of a reading segment.

Computer-administered tests (CATs)—All TExES exams are administered online in a designated testing center. Logistical information about registering for any TExES exam is available through a link to the current exam vendor provided in the Texas Educators tab on the TEA website.

Content-area teaching—In teaching ESL, we often create a dichotomy between supporting English proficiency and teaching discipline-relevant subject matter. Content-area teaching refers to teaching math, science, social science, literature, and reading, subject areas that call for specialized knowledge but that require strong proficiency in English to support learning in those subjects. Realistically, ESL teachers teach both proficiency and subject area content.

Content-based instruction—A type of ESL program in which EL students are placed in content-area classes (science, social studies, literature, math, reading) taught by an ESL-certified teacher. Instruction is in English but with appropriate accommodations to address the linguistic and cognitive needs of EL students.

Conventions—expectations that influence written and spoken output. These aren't "rules" in the sense that word order in sentences is a rule of grammar. Instead, conventions are guidelines about when to make choices: for example, the choice to use *-er* vs. *more* in a comparative structure or *-est* vs. *most* in creating a superlative. Conventions are also relevant in major language decisions, like adding new words to the language through increased usage of invented forms or through the need of a word to represent a new phenomenon.

Cross-curricular ELPS—student expectations for content-area performance. Cross-curricular ELPS focus on cognitive and practical language skills that EL students need in order to learn disciplinary content while also learning English. ELPS stipulates that teachers must provide linguistic accommodations to support content-area learning.

Culturally relevant pedagogy—teaching approaches that aim to create inclusion for all learners from all ethnic, national, or social groups. Cultural relevance can be integrated into lessons that include circumstances, situations, and scenarios that reflect multiple cultures.

Descriptive statements—Each of the 10 ESL competencies is broken down into specific knowledge that the beginning teacher should demonstrate in the broad area of the competency. Descriptive statements begin with active verbs: *knows, analyzes, recognizes, understands, uses, accepts, plans, enhances, stimulates, teaches, provides, presents, creates, works, organizes, applies, engages, communicates, practices, employs, develops, responds, conducts.*

Developmental characteristics—the cognitive, social, affective, and physical characteristics that learners exhibit at various stages in their educational progress. Developmental characteristics significantly impact learner readiness to engage in the cognitive demands of content-area work, but they also determine how a learner participates in the class community. Instructional choices should reflect the learners' developmental characteristics. Usually, developmental characteristics are broadly labeled using chronological categories: early childhood, elementary, middle school, and adolescent. However, learner characteristics are not homogeneous; teachers need to make individual, differentiated instructional choices in order to meet all learners' needs.

Developmentally appropriate—knowing learners' characteristics enables teachers to construct lessons and activities that reflect learners cognitive, social, affective, and (if appropriate) physical readiness to attempt the tasks. Developmentally appropriate tasks should enable learners to progress in their learning by attempting and completing tasks that reflect what they are able to do on their own and what they can do with appropriate assistance and mentorship from the teacher. Learning tasks should challenge the learner in a way that creates learner satisfaction but not frustration. Tasks that are consistently too simple for learners may be aimed at developmental levels below the learners' current level and may consequently lead to learner disinterest.

Differentiated instruction—Instruction that takes into account individual learners' needs. It may be impractical to create designated lessons for individual students, but differentiation suggests that teachers can tailor general instruction to address specific learner's needs so as to pull the learner into the holistic learning experience.

Discourse—the distinct linguistic and cognitive expectations for communication in a specific setting. Discourse is bound and defined by the parameters of the setting in which the output and input are produced. Specific discourses are associated with distinct social groups, academic groups, political groups, or any group in which members share ways of thinking, acting, and believing.

Discussion—discussions can be whole-group discussions involving the entire class or small group discussions. In ESL settings, it is vital that teachers modulate whole-group discussions so that all learners participate even if they do not contribute comments or questions. Teachers need to factor in appropriate wait time to allow EL students time to construct responses. Small group discussions can be facilitated if the teacher assigns specific tasks and sets time limits for discussion. Whether whole class or small group, discussions should aim for inclusivity and equitable participation of all learners.

Diversity—the differences that learners bring to a class community. Differences may be attitudinal, ethnic, national, gender-based, disability-based, linguistic, physical, social, economic, or any number of other distinctions. Differences should be used to create a cohesive class community of distinct learners with individual as well as holistic needs.

Domains—the content of the TExES ESL (154) Supplemental exam is presented in three *domains* which represent broad areas of knowledge: Domain I—the teacher's knowledge of linguistics; Domain II—the teacher's ability to construct effective ESL instruction; Domain III—the teacher's ability to contextualize ESL within historical frameworks and social aspects of language instruction. Each domain is further divided into competencies and descriptive statements.

Dual language programs—a type of bilingual education program in which instruction is delivered in L1 and L2 with a goal of biliteracy for all learners. Two-way dual language programs include native speakers of English as well as language learners; one-way dual language programs are focused on EL students.

Elementary and Secondary Education Act (ESEA)—Passed in 1965, this act was aimed at general improvement in the educational circumstances of young learners in the U.S. Although the 1965 act was intended to achieve equity for low-income students, in subsequent revisions and reauthorizations, ESEA has been instrumental in implementing language programs to support the needs of students for whom English is not a first language.

English as a Second Language (ESL)—ESL programs are one of two broad language programs implemented in Texas public schools to develop the language and academic proficiency of students who have been designated LEP on the basis of their performance on the state-approved English proficiency exam. In ESL programs, instruction is delivered in English although teachers are expected to make linguistic accommodations to support learners' ability to learn English while they are learning content-area material in English.

English Learners—students whose home language is a language other than English and are working toward proficiency in English. EL students are designated EL through testing and are placed in ESL or bilingual education programs on the basis of their proficiency in English as determined by a state-approved test.

English Language Proficiency Standards (ELPS)—a section of the Texas Essential Knowledge and Skills (TEKS) curriculum that includes categories of proficiency for EL students: beginning, intermediate, advanced, and advanced high in listening and speaking and in reading and writing. ESL and bilingual education teachers are responsible for knowing the characteristics of each proficiency level to ensure that instruction is appropriately adjusted to meet EL students' academic and linguistic needs.

Every Student Succeeds Act (ESSA)—the 2015 reauthorization of the 1965 Elementary and Secondary Education Act which focused on improving the quality of elementary and secondary education by emphasizing equity and access. ESSA is the updating of No Child Left Behind which was characterized by the average yearly progress requirement. ESSA focuses on providing appropriate language support to enable EL students to reach high levels of achievement in the same academic subjects and opportunities as native speakers.

Family involvement—ESL teachers must engage families in striving for the success of EL students in school. Family involvement is fostered through communication, through on-going contact with parents, and through invitations for parental participation. A teacher can serve as an intermediary or liaison in official communication from LPAC, especially when parents may not understand what testing data or language program status information means specifically for their children. Teachers can also direct parents to state and national websites aimed at helping parents of English learners participate in their children's education.

Feedback—comments a teacher offers in response to an in-progress or completed learning task. Feedback should clearly identify what the learner has done effectively and what the learner needs to do to improve. Feedback can be immediate in class, as during a class activity, or deferred, as in the formal commentary or scoring of a learning product. Feedback is a component of assessment.

First language acquisition—the processes of becoming fluent in one's native or first language. First languages are acquired intuitively, naturally, and quickly without instruction. First language acquisition processes cannot be realistically replicated in SLA, but the comprehensible, meaningful input hypothesis is an attempt to establish that if first language acquisition occurs through meaningful communicative interactions, then we should be able to carry that learning platform into ESL instruction.

Fishbowl—a prolific classroom strategy for demonstrating learning activities. Fishbowl relies on the metaphor of a fish in a bowl that can be viewed swimming around and doing fish activities. In the classroom, students volunteer to be the fish by demonstrating an activity while everyone else watches, comments, and asks questions. The fishbowl is considered a robust strategy for fostering learner engagement.

Formative feedback—responding to student learning products in a way that identifies strengths and offers guidance for specific improvement. Formative assessment should include opportunities to revise based on the comments for needed improvement. Formative feedback is offered while a learning task is still in progress and students have the opportunity to revise what they have done to demonstrate higher levels of achievement.

Grouping strategies—collaborative activities call for decisions about grouping. The teacher's choices for arranging students into groups significantly impact the classroom environment. A teacher can promote diversity by creating random groups. Base groups, which are more or less permanent, however, contribute to learners' feelings of responsibility to classmates. Self-selected groups allow learners to assemble themselves in comfortable social groups. The grouping strategy should reflect the learning objectives for the specific collaborative learning task.

High expectations—a teacher attitude that reflects the belief that all learners can achieve their goals. A mindset of high expectations creates a learning community where learners feel they have every chance to succeed. High expectations eliminate stereotyping based on past learner failure or subpar performance.

Higher-order thinking—learning tasks that promote evaluation of ideas, exploration of multiple perspectives, problem-solving, inquiry, critical exploration of ideas, abstract thinking, reflection, and other cognitive tasks that challenge learners to look beyond the surface level of a topic. Higher-order thinking tasks should reflect learner readiness based on developmental levels.

Inclusion—a pedagogical attitude that emphasizes access and opportunity for all learners. Inclusion is usually used to describe how difference is dealt with in classrooms. Federal laws dealing with linguistic difference or disabilities aim to create equity of access for all learners. Ideally, a class community should embrace difference, recognizing that individual distinctiveness enriches the community as a whole.

Input hypothesis—Stephen D. Krashen contended that for language learning to happen, the learner must be in an environment of meaningful intake of language, which he labeled "comprehensible input." According to Krashen, learners acquire L2 only if they are immersed in an environment of comprehensible input.

Instructional goals—what the teacher hopes to accomplish in a lesson or set of lessons (as in a unit). Goals are generally subdivided into measurable learning objectives which articulate what the learner should know and be able to do at the end of a lesson or set of lessons.

Instructional techniques—the actual choices a teacher makes for delivering instruction. Instructional techniques should reflect learning outcomes and should enable learners to participate fully and meaningfully in their learning. Instructional techniques may start out as a generic technique (like an activity for activating prior knowledge) but the actual technique can reflect teacher creativity and innovation.

Interlanguage—A coherent intervening stage in a learner's trajectory toward L2 proficiency. Interlanguages are systematic, showing the learner's current holistic competence in L2. Interlanguages are idiosyncratic, with each learner moving through numerous interlanguage stages on the path toward L2 proficiency.

Interrelatedness—the connectivity among listening, speaking, reading, and writing. While we analyze language acquisition in these four language areas, learning a language past the first, or native language, occurs with almost simultaneous learning in all of the domains. In ESL instruction, interrelatedness means that teachers need to integrate all the domains as they support students' development in communicative and academic proficiency.

L1—A learner's first or native language.

L2—A learner's second or additional language.

Language acquisition—the process of learning a language. Learning a language is such a complex process that language specialists distinguish between *learning* and *acquisition*. In this distinction, *learning* is almost a superficial process where the learner can participate in the discourse of L2 but lacks full involvement, engagement, and/or motivation. *Acquisition*, on the other hand, is a deeper process in which the learner strives to join the full discourses of L2, demonstrates a high level of engagement, and feels confident and competent in joining into L2 communities. Acquiring a second language requires conscious learning processes, metacognitive attention to those processes, and transfer of L1 structures.

Language Proficiency Assessment Committee (LPAC)—Mandated by the Texas Education Code, an LPAC is formed on each campus to oversee the implementation of federal and state regulations regarding education of EL students. Membership includes a parent of an EL student, language teachers, and appropriate administrators. The LPAC initially evaluates proficiency test results to determine the best language program for each student who has been designated LEP. The committee also sends out the required parent approval letters and provides detailed, annual progress reports showing EL students' performance on required tests. Based on test results, this committee determines when students can exit the language program or can be reclassified as fluent English speakers.

Learning styles—Learners process new information in a variety of ways. Some researchers suggest that each learner has a preferred way of learning, with some learners preferring text, others visual stimuli, some kinesthetic activities. Other researchers point out that because of the complexity and interrelatedness of our cerebral activity, learning occurs in all ways. When instruction reflects a variety of learning styles, the teacher is able to provide learners with diverse platforms for constructing new understandings.

Lexicon—the collection of words and associated semantic understandings in a specific language. However, lexicon can also refer to the body of words that an individual learner knows. A lexicon is like the learner's individually-constructed dictionary of words that he/she knows either fully and operationally (words that the learner can actually use to construct meaningful utterances) or words that are known to a limited extent but are recognized in appropriate contexts. Learners construct lexicons for individualized circumstances that require environment-specific knowledge of specialized terms, as in sports, special activities, and content areas.

Limited English Proficient (LEP)—This is the official label used by Texas to designate students in need of language support: "'Student of limited English proficiency' means a student whose primary language is other than English and whose English language skills are such that the student has difficulty performing ordinary class work in English" (TEC, 1995).

Linguistic accommodations—Teachers who have EL students in their classes must provide adaptations that enable all learners to participate equitably in all classroom activities and learning. Accommodations should not call attention to the learner; instead, accommodations should be integrated holistically into teaching to promote inclusion.

Linguistic knowledge—in the context of teaching ESL, linguistic knowledge allows the teacher to identify structures that the EL student is attempting in speaking or writing. Linguistic knowledge is the full understanding of the systems of English: phonology, morphology, semantics, and syntax. The specific student expectations presented in ELPS are based on demonstration of specific linguistic performances, so teachers need a strong background in linguistics to connect learner output to elements of linguistic systems.

Literacy—the ability to use linguistic, rhetorical, and discourse systems to construct meaning from a text and to participate in meaningful use of these systems to generate meaningful utterances. Literacy often refers simply to the ability to read, but increasingly, literacy explains more expansive abilities to use a variety of linguistic systems to meet communicative, personal, social, political, or economic goals.

Mechanics—these are rule-like expectations in writing, like capitalizing the first word of a sentence, spacing after a period, using a hyphen between some compound words. "Mechanical" aspects of writing don't necessarily impact meaning but they affect the way writing is perceived by a reader. Mechanics are not grammar rules.

Modeling—demonstrating how a learning task is to be performed. In ESL instruction, modeling is a valuable teaching strategy for guiding EL students toward growing understanding of specialized content-area knowledge. Modeling can be done by the instructor or by students.

Morphology—the word construction system of a language. Morphemes are meaningful linguistic units that are used in constructing words. Morphemes can be bound (must be attached to other morphemes to create meaningful words) or free (can exist as a meaningful word without being attached to other morphemes). The word *geography* is made up of two bound morphemes which both have distinct meaning: *geo* and *graphy*. Both of these bound morphemes can be combined to form other words such as *geologist* or *biography*. Morphemes are *not* the same thing as syllables because morphemes have distinct meaning while syllables represent sound combinations distinct to a specific language.

Multiculturalism—both a mindset and an actual approach to teaching that integrates diverse ways of thinking, multiple sources of culturally-diverse resources, and strategies for pulling learners into cohesive, egalitarian class community activities. The goal of multiculturalism is to foster community based on celebration of diversity.

Orthography—the spelling system of a language. Orthography determines how letters combine to represent sounds and form words in graphophonemic form.

Phonology—the sound system of a language. The phonological system identifies distinct, meaning-making sounds (phonemes), and creates alphabetic representations for those sounds. Phonemes are combined to create syllables and then whole words. Knowing how sounds are produced enables ESL teachers to help EL students modify their sound production to create English utterances.

Pragmatics—knowing how to use language to act upon the world, to get things done. Pragmatics involves extra-linguistic factors such as tonality, inflections, circumstance-specific variations, irony, sarcasm, humor, gestures, body language, and other choices in performative speech acts. EL students may not fully understand pragmatics until they have interacted significantly and meaningfully in L2 environments.

Prior knowledge—what the learner already knows about a new learning topic either from past academic experience or life experience. Prior knowledge is considered essential for engaging learners in a new learning task. Learning tasks should include activities for activating prior knowledge.

Proficiency levels—ELPS identifies four proficiency levels: beginning, intermediate, advanced, and advanced high. Each level has specific descriptors for performance in listening, speaking, reading, and writing. ESL teachers are expected to recognize student performance levels in order to shape instruction to support student advancement to higher levels of proficiency.

Proficiency—in the context of ESL usually refers to English Learners' growing linguistic abilities in English. State of Texas guidelines and statutes charge content-area as well as specialist teachers with the responsibility for promoting EL students' proficiency in speaking, listening, reading, and writing in English.

Pull-out programs—a type of ESL program in which EL students participate in mainstream content-area classes with specialized instruction in language and literacy delivered by an ESL teacher. In this system, an ESL-certified teacher provides instruction to ELs in an inclusionary model within the confines of the classroom or by removing the learner from it by "pulling" the learner out of the class for targeted language instruction.

Read aloud—a teaching strategy in which the teacher reads a core text aloud to demonstrate effective reading strategies and/or to enable learners to hear the rhythms of the text. Read alouds are considered highly effective teaching strategies in ESL content and literacy instruction.

Realia—props, objects, items, or manipulatives that teachers integrate into lessons to support learners' understanding of content. Realia allow learners to use concrete objects connected to actual experiences to construct meaning. For example, a teacher starting a unit on recycling might want to bring in the following realia: an empty tissue box, an empty plastic water bottle, and a clean, empty aluminum can.

Recursiveness—the loop-like quality of learning. As we try to master new knowledge, we find ourselves backtracking in order to move forward. A learner's understanding that learning is recursive is a valuable cognitive strategy for mastering all types of content.

Registers—Registers are systems of variable language uses. Simply stated, registers are the "way" we interact linguistically in different discourse settings with different people. Registers reflect social groupings and social settings. Registers are marked by setting-specific word choices, attitudes, discourse expectations, and user groupings. Registers generally refer to communicative (listening and speaking) interactions. In early stages of second language acquisition, EL students are likely to have difficulty recognizing the nuances of output expectations in different registers.

Responsive teaching—a teacher's ability to recognize learners' needs and to make adaptations so that the learner is able to participate fully and meaningfully in instructional activities. A responsive teacher is attuned to learner reactions to classroom events, to specific instruction, to classmates, to the classroom climate, and to all the generalized transactions of the classroom.

Rubric—criteria for scoring presented in performance levels and criteria for each level. When rubrics are distributed as the learners work on a learning task, the rubric allows for self-evaluation and contributes powerfully to self-directed learning. Rubrics should be task-specific rather than generic in order to show learners exactly what is required for a distinct learning task.

Scaffolding—Presenting new information in segmented, incrementally complex stages. Scaffolding allows learners to support increasing understanding with platforms of established knowledge and comprehension.

Second language acquisition (SLA)—the processes of learning and acquiring a language other than the first or native language. SLA occurs through conscious application of learning strategies, application of L1 support, transfer of L1 knowledge, and direct learning of L2 content. SLA is quite different from first language acquisition which many researchers and theorists say occurs intuitively and naturally as individuals interact with experienced speakers in communicatively-significant settings, like home and family settings, and without direct instruction. SLA, in contrast, is often triggered by pragmatic logistics such as having to learn an additional language to participate in school or in a job. In ESL settings, teachers facilitate learners' SLA processes through research-based applications of learning strategies.

Segmenting—dividing a learning task into smaller units to facilitate learner understanding and to allow teachers to assess learners' incremental mastery of complex tasks.

Semantics—the system of meaning in a language. Semantics involves knowing how and why words carry meaning. At the simplest level, semantics can be thought of as the vocabulary or lexicon of a language, but once we start using words of a language, we discover that meaning can be constructed, manipulated, implied, or deflected on the basis of the way we use words.

Sheltered instruction—an approach to ESL instruction that calls for adaptations and accommodations to promote inclusion of EL students in meaningful learning. Instruction is modified by integrating such supports as visuals, more explanation of content-area terms, presentation of content-area information in accessible language, interaction among learners, and demonstrations. Many teachers point out that sheltered instruction embraces principles and practices found in *all* teaching; the difference, however, is that ESL teachers who use sheltered instruction consistently integrate these practices in order to support continual language, cognitive, and academic growth of language learners.

Silent period—a stage of second language acquisition in which the learner is mostly observing and taking in L2 information. The learner may be reluctant or unready to actually talk in L2 circumstances, hence the "silent" label.

State of Texas Assessments of Academic Readiness (STAAR)—the state assessment system. STAAR exams are administered in core areas starting in Grade 3 and continue through end-of-course exams in high school. The exams are based on selected TEKS for the content area being tested. EL students must take STAAR exams as part of ESSA expectations for demonstrating academic proficiency. Accommodations may be requested to create equity and access for EL students in mandated testing situations.

Student diversity—the individual qualities that create a heterogeneous community marked by differences among learners. Diversity should be celebrated as an indicator of individuality among learners. In class communities, diversity should be valued, with difference seen as distinctiveness not as deficit.

Student expectations—ELPS cross-curricular essential knowledge and skills are presented as lists of performances and abilities that students are expected to demonstrate in listening, speaking, reading, and writing.

Summative assessment—a final assessment that includes summaries of learner performance but with no opportunity for redoing the assessed work. Ideally, summative assessments come at the end of a learning cycle that has included formative assessment and that has allowed multiple opportunities for learners to apply feedback to improve their performance.

Syntax—the system of "rules" for constructing sentences in a language. Syntactic "rules" are acquired intuitively by learners. They refer not to the grammar rules taught in school but to the way that words are put together to form meaningful utterances in a language.

Target language—the language that an EL student is learning through ESL or bilingual instruction. The term is sometimes seen as politically incorrect because it can imply a diminishment of the importance of the native language. The term is used infrequently in discussions of ESL instruction; instead the term L2 is used to identify the language being acquired.

Teacher talk—a generic term for the talk initiated by teachers in classrooms. Teacher talk includes activities such as greeting students, modulating transitions among class activities, answering questions, delivering instruction, giving directions, and all the phatic communication that occurs in classrooms. Researchers and practitioners generally advocate that teachers work at cutting down teacher talk to increase learners' meaningful interactions with each other.

Technology—electronic and digital enhancements for teaching. Technology in teaching now involves far more than computer-assisted instruction. Instead, technology should transform traditional teaching by creating new ways to present new knowledge and to involve learners in their learning. In ESL instruction, technology is seen as a way to allow EL students to practice language structures, to construct background knowledge, and to adjust learning processes to a pace that allows them to review and repeat instruction.

Texas Administrative Code—a compilation of all state agency rules in Texas. Title 19 of the TAC includes chapters on the Texas Education Agency and the State Board for Educator Certification. TEKS are included in the section on TEA.

Texas Education Agency (TEA)—the state organization that oversees public education in Texas. TEA offers information, guidance, leadership, and direction to public school teachers and administrators in all areas of public school education. TEA is a prime resource in issues related to mandated state or federal requirements for language programs in Texas. TEA headquarters are in Austin.

Texas Education Code—a compilation of education-related laws and statutes passed by the Texas state legislature.

Texas Essential Knowledge and Skills (TEKS)—the state-approved curriculum standards in basic content areas and several specialized areas. TEKS are statements of what students should know about the content area at grade levels from kindergarten through high school. ELPS is a component of TEKS.

Texas English Language Proficiency Assessment System (TELPAS)—the state system of assessment of English learners. Administered annually, TELPAS exams are used to assess EL students' performance and achievement in listening, speaking, reading, and writing.

TExES English as a Second Language (ESL) Supplemental (154)—"Supplemental" means that you attempt this exam after you have achieved full certification by passing a content area or all-level exam and the Pedagogy and Professional Responsibilities exam. Exam 154 certifies you can teach English as a Second language in the ESL program in Texas public schools. Exam 154 is not equivalent to certification in bilingual education. There is a separate supplemental exam for that.

Thematic units—clusters of lessons that focus on a theme or broad topic rather than a specific curricular element. Thematic units may be interdisciplinary and are considered highly effective instructional tools for creating and sustaining student engagement.

Total Physical Response—a learning strategy that includes kinesthetic activities to promote learners' comprehension of L2 vocabulary, commands, directions, and activities. While TPR may seem to engage learners in rudimentary learning of limited L2 phrases, TPR can actually promote learners' multimodal engagement by linking language to physical response, thereby activating a higher level of cognitive engagement.

Transfer—a prolific, natural strategy in SLA. Individuals with strong first language systems naturally rely on linguistic knowledge in L1 as they work on L2 proficiency. Transfer can occur in all language domains. Transfer can be productive and accurate, but it can also lead to L2 errors when learners approximate structures in L2 by using structures from L1 that do not correctly fit in the intended L2 output.

Transitional programs—a type of bilingual program in which substantive support for L2 learning is provided in L1. The goal of transitional programs is to move students into mainstream classrooms as soon as they acquire sufficient proficiency in English to function effectively in regular classrooms. Transitional programs can be early exit, which means that learners may spend as little as two years in the program, or late exit, which means that learners are in the program for six or more years.

Translingualism—an increasing number of language specialists contend that knowledge of multiple languages results not in bilingualism (literacy and fluency in two separate languages) but instead in a merging of the language systems in an idiosyncratic, learner-specific hybrid. Translingualism is *not* something as simple as code-switiching. True translingualism shows learners appropriating linguistic and rhetorical patterns across the multiple language systems to create utterances that demonstrate evidence of effective, creative crossings in linguistic systems.

Wait time—the time that a teacher allows for learners to process a question during class discussion. Wait time should allow learners to think about the question and formulate a response. Higher-order thinking questions require more wait time. Teachers should not see silence during the interval between the question and the student response as idle time. In classes that include EL students, wait time should be extended so that second language learners can fully process the question.

Zone of proximal development (ZPD)—a construct attributed to Lev Vygotsky. ZPD is the hypothetical "area" or "zone" between what a learner currently knows and what the learner is capable of doing with the guidance or mentoring of a knowledgeable individual.

References

A&E Television Networks. (2020a). *Brown v. Board of Education.* History.com. https://www.history.com/topics/black-history/brown-v-board-of-education-of-topeka

A&E Television Networks. (2020b). Civil Rights Act of 1964. History.com. *https://www.history.com/topics/black-history/civil-rights-act*

A&E Television Networks. (2020c). *Plessy v. Ferguson.* History.com. https://www.history.com/topics/black-history/plessy-v-ferguson

A&E Television Networks. (2020d). *U.S. immigration since 1965.* History.com. https://www.history.com/topics/immigration/us-immigration-since-1965

American Immigration Council. (2016). *Public education for immigrant students: Understanding Plyler v. Doe.* https://www.americanimmigrationcouncil.org/research/plyler-v-doe-public-education-immigrant-students

Anderson, L.W., & Krathwohl, D.R. (Eds.) (2001). *A taxonomy for learning, teaching, and assessing: A revision of Bloom's taxonomy of educational objectives.* New York: Longman.

ASCD. (2010). Differentiated with technology for ELs. [Video]. http://www.ascd.org/ascd-express/vol9/918-video.aspx

Atwell, N. (1998). *In the middle: New understandings about writing, reading, and learning,* 2nd ed. Portsmouth, NH: Heinemann.

Banks, J.A. (2019). *An introduction to multicultural education* (6th ed.) [Kindle book]. New York: Pearson.

Bartholomae, D. (1980). The study of error. *College Composition and Communication, 31*(3), 253–269.

Bergmann, J. and Sams, A. (2012). *Flip your classroom: Reach every student in every class every day.* International Society for Technology in Education. http://www.ascd.org/publications/books/112060.aspx

Bialystok, E. (2007). Acquisition of literacy in bilingual children: A framework for research. *Language Learning, 57*(1), 45–77.

Brock, C.H., Pennington, J.L., Oikonomidoy, E., & Townsend, D.R. (2010). "It's just like telling them they will never be scientists": A white teacher's journey transforming linguistic and racial categories. In G. Li & P.A. Edwards (Eds.), *Best Practices in ELL instruction* (pp. 328–352). New York: The Guilford Press.

Brock, C., Lapp, D., Salas, R., & Townsend, D. (2009). *Academic literacy for English learners: High-quality instruction across content areas.* New York: Teachers College Press.

Brown, H.D. (2014). *Principles of language learning and teaching: A course in second language acquisition* (6th ed.). White Plains, NY: Pearson.

Burden, P., & Byrd, D.M. (2013). *Methods for effective teaching methods: Meeting the needs of all students* (6th ed.). Boston, MA: Pearson.

Burke, J. (2013). *The English teacher's companion* (4th ed.). Portsmouth, NH Heinemann.

Caruso, C. (2008). Bringing online learning to life. *Educational Leadership, 65*(8), 70–72. http://www.ascd.org/publications/educational-leadership/may08/vol65/num08/Bringing-Online-Learning-to-Life.aspx

Castañeda v. Pickard. (1981). No. 79–2253. United States Court of Appeals, Fifth Circuit. www.casetext.com

Chamot, A.U., & O'Malley, J.M. (1989). The cognitive academic language approach. In P. Rigg & V.G. Allen (Eds.), *When they don't all speak English: Integrating the ESL student into the regular classroom* (pp. 108–125). Urbana, IL: National Council of Teachers of English.

Chamot, A.U., & O'Malley, J.M. (1994). *The CALLA handbook: Implementing the cognitive academic language learning approach.* Reading, MA: Addison-Wesley Publishing Co.

Chomsky, N. (1957; 2002). *Syntactic structures* (2nd ed.). Berlin: Mouton de Gruyter. https://ebookcentral-proquest-com.ezhost.utrgv.edu

Corder, S.P. (1974; 1967). The significance of learners' errors. In J.C. Richards (Ed.), *Error analysis: Perspectives on second language acquisition* (pp. 19–27). Essex: Longman. (Reprinted from *International Review of Applied Linguistics in Language Teaching, 5*(4), 1967).

Crovitz, D., & Devereaux, M.D. (2017). *Grammar to get things done: A practical guide for teachers anchored in real-world usage* [Kindle version]. New York: Routledge.

Crovitz, D., & Devereaux, M.D. (2019). *More grammar to get things done: Daily lessons for teaching grammar in context.* New York, NY: Routledge and the National Council of Teachers of English.

Cummins, J. (1979). Cognitive/academic language proficiency, linguistic interdependence, the optimum age question and some other matters. *Working Papers on Bilingualism*, 19, 198–205.

Cummins, J. (2000). *Language, power, and pedagogy: Bilingual children in the crossfire.* Clevedon, England: Multilingual Matters, LTD.

Data Recognition Corporation [DRC]. (2019). *LAS links first edition (Forms A, B, Español A). Connecting assessment, language, and learning.* https://laslinks.com/las-links-english/

Del Valle, S. (2003). *Language rights and the law in the United States* [Ebsco host ebook]. Clevedon, UK: Multilingual Matters Press.

Denstaedt, L., Roop, L.J., & Best, S. (2014). *Doing and making authentic literacies* [ebook]. Urbana, IL: National Council of Teachers of English.

Díaz-Rico, L.T. (2013). *Strategies for teaching English learners* (3rd ed.) [Kindle version]. Boston, MA: Pearson.

Echevarriá, J., & Graves, A. (2010). *Sheltered content instruction: Teaching English Learners with diverse abilities* (5th ed.) [Kindle version]. Boston, MA: Pearson.

Elbow, P. (1973). *Writing without teachers.* Oxford: Oxford University Press.

Elledge, S. (1984). *E.B. White: A biography.* New York: W. W. Norton.

Freeman, D. (2003). Struggling English Language Learners: Keys for academic success. *TESOL Journal, 12*(3), 5–10.

Freeman, Y.S., Freeman, D.E., Soto, M., & Ebe, A. (2016). *ESL teaching: Principles for success.* [ebook]. Portsmouth, NH: Heinemann.

Fromkin, V., Rodman, R., & Hyams, N. (2017). *An introduction to language* (11th ed.) [ebook]. Boston, MA: Cengage.

Gallagher, K. (2006). *Teaching adolescent writers*. Portland, ME: Stenhouse Publishers.

Gass, S. (2009). Second language acquisition. In S. Foster-Cohen (Ed.), *Language acquisition* (pp. 109–139). Basingstoke: Palgrave Macmillan.

Gass, S. (2013). *Second language acquisition: An introductory course* (4th ed.) [Kindle version]. New York: Routledge.

Gee, J.P. (2001). Reading as situated language: A sociocognitive perspective. *Journal of Adolescent and Adult Literacy, 44*(8), 714–725.

Goldenberg, C., Rueda, R.S., & August, D. (2006). Synthesis: Sociocultural contexts and literacy development. In D. August & T. Shanahan (Eds.), *Developing literacy in second-language learners: Report of the National Literacy Panel on Language-Minority Children and Youth* (pp. 249–268). Mahwah, NJ: Lawrence Erlbaum.

Gonzalez, V., Yawkey, T., & Minaya-Rowe, L. (2006). *English-as-a-second-language (ESL) teaching and learning: Pre-K–12 classroom applications for students' academic achievement and development*. Boston: Allyn and Bacon.

Gottlieb, M. (2016). *Assessing English Language Learners: Bridges to educational equity*. Thousand Oaks, CA: Corwin.

Gregory, G.H., & Burkman, A. (2012). *Differentiated literacy strategies for English Language Learners grades 7–12*. Thousand Oaks, CA: Corwin.

Guild, P. (1994). The culture/learning style connection. *Educational Leadership*, 51(8), 16–21. http://www.ascd.org/publications/educational-leadership/may94/vol51/num08/The-Culture~Learning-Style-Connection.aspx

Gunderson, L., D'Silva, R.A., & Odo, D.M. (2014). *ESL (ELL) literacy instruction: A guidebook to theory and practice* (3rd ed.). New York: Taylor & Francis.

Haas, E.M. (2019). *Equal Educational Opportunity Act*. U.S.A. Education Law. https://usedulaw.com/279-equal-educational-opportunity-act.html

Haines, R. (Director). (2006). *The Ron Clark Story*. [DVD]. Calgary, Alberta, Canada: Alberta Film Development Program of the Alberta Foundation for the Arts.

Hanson, M.B. (2003). Mrs. Hanks' wink: Early lessons in being and becoming a teacher. *English Journal, 93*(2), 32–35.

Herrell, A., & Jordan, M. (2020). *50 strategies for teaching English Language Learners* (6th ed.) [Kindle version]. Hoboken, NJ: Pearson.

Himmele, P., & Himmele, W. (2009). *The language-rich classroom: A research-based framework for teaching English language learners* [ebook]. Alexandria, VA: ASCD. http://www.ascd.org/publications/books/108037.aspx

Hudelson, S. (1989). "Teaching" English through content-area activities. In P. Rigg & V.G. Allen (Eds.), *When they don't all speak English: Integrating the ESL student into the regular classroom* (pp. 139–151). Urbana, IL: National Council of Teachers of English.

International Literacy Association [ILA]. (2019). *Literacy Glossary*. https://literacyworldwide.org/get-resources/literacy-glossary

International Phonetic Alphabet. (2020). *IPA Chart with Sounds*. IPA The Phonetic Representation of Language. http://www.internationalphoneticalphabet.org/ipa-sounds/ipa-chart-with-sounds/

International Phonetic Association. (2015). *Full IPA Chart*. https://www.internationalphonetic association.org/content/full-ipa-chart

Kemerer, F.R. (2017). United States v. Texas. In *Handbook of Texas Online*. Texas State Historical Association [TSHA]. http://www.tshaonline.org/handbook/online/articles/jru02

Krashen, S.D. (1985). *Inquiries & insights: Second language teaching immersion & bilingual education literacy*. Englewood Cliffs, NJ: Alemany Press.

Krashen, S.D. (1985). *The input hypothesis: Issues and implications*. London: Longman.

Krashen, S.D. (2000). What does it take to acquire language? *ESL Magazine, 3*(3), 22–23.

Krashen, S.D., & Terrell, T.D. (1983). *The natural approach: Language acquisition in the classroom*. Oxford: Pergamon Press.

Layne, S.L. (2015). *In defense of read-aloud: Sustaining best practice*. Portland, ME: Stenhouse Publishers.

Loomis, K. (2020, April 2). *Lesson planning with balance in mind during the troubled times of COVID-19*. SoftChalk. Innovators in Online Learning—Webinar. https://players.brightcove.net/1204622959001/default_default/index.html?videoId=6146822281001

McGee, L.M., & Richgels, D.J. (2012). *Literacy's beginnings: Supporting young readers and writers* (6th ed.). Boston, MA: Allyn & Bacon.

McGroarty, M. (1984). Some meanings of communicative competence for second language students. *TESOL Quarterly, 18*(2), 257–272.

Moll, L.C., Amanti, C., Neff, D., & Gonzalez, N. (1992). Funds of knowledge for teaching: Using a qualitative approach to connect homes and classrooms. *Theory into Practice, 31*(2), 132–141.

National Science Teaching Association (NSTA). (2014). *Case study 4: English Language Learners and the next generation science standards*. https://ngss.nsta.org/case-study-4.aspx

Newman, B.M. (2019). *TExES PPR EC-12 (160)*. Cranbury, NJ: Research & Education Association.

Newman, B.M., & Garcia, R. (2019). Teaching with bordered writers: Reconstructing narratives of difference, mobility, and translingualism. In I. Baca, Y.I. Hinojosa, & S.W. Murphy (Eds.), *Bordered writers: Latinx identities and literacy practices at Hispanic-Serving Institutions* (pp. 125–146). Albany, NY: SUNY Press.

No Child Left Behind Act of 2001 [NCLB]. (2002). Public Law 107–110. https://www.congress.gov/bill/107th-congress/house-bill/1/text

O'Malley, J.M., Russo, R.P., Chamot, A.U., & Stewner-Manzanares, G. (1988). Applications of learning strategies by students learning English as a second language. In Weinstein, C.E., Goetz, E.T., & Alexander P.A. (Eds.), *Learning and study strategies: Issues in assessment, instruction, and evaluation* (pp. 215–231). San Diego, CA: Academic Press.

Parker, F., & Riley, K.L. (2010). *Linguistics for non-linguists: A primer with exercises* (5th ed.). Boston, MA: Allyn & Bacon.

Pearson Education, Inc. (2019a). *English as a Second Language Supplemental (154) Preparation Materials*. https://www.tx.nesinc.com/Content/StudyGuide/TX_SG_obj_154.htm

Pearson Education, Inc. (2019b). Texas Educator Certification Examination Program. http://www.tx.nesinc.com/

Pei, M.A., & Gaynor, F. (1954). *A dictionary of linguistics*. New York: Philosophical Library.

Peregoy, S.F., & Boyle, O.F. (2017). *Reading, writing, & learning in ESL: A resource book for teaching K–12 English Learners*. Boston: Pearson.

Poetry Foundation. (2020). Jabberwocky by Lewis Carroll. https://www.poetryfoundation.org/poems/42916/jabberwocky

Risko, V.J., & Walker-Dalhouse, D. (2007). Tapping students' cultural funds of knowledge to address the achievement gap. *The Reading Teacher, 61*(1), 98–100.

Selinker, L. (1974). Interlanguage. In J.C. Richards (Ed.), *Error analysis: Perspectives on second language acquisition* (pp. 31–54). Essex: Longman.

Short, D., & Echevarría, J. (2004/2005). Teacher skills to support English Language Learners. *Educational Leadership, 62*(4), 8–13. http://www.ascd.org/publications/educational-leadership/dec04/vol62/num04/Teacher-Skills-to-Support-English-Language-Learners.aspx

Snelling, J., & Fingal, D. (2020, March 16). *10 strategies for online learning during a coronavirus outbreak*. International Society for Technology in Education. https://www.iste.org/explore/10-strategies-online-learning-during-coronavirus-outbreak

State Board for Educator Certification [SBEC]. 2001. English as a Second Language (ESL) Standards. FINAL. https://tea.texas.gov/sites/default/files/FN_TX_ ESL.pdf

Texas Administrative Code [TAC]. (1996). Chapter 110. Texas Essential Knowledge and Skills for English Language Arts and Reading. Subchapter A. Elementary. §110.7 English Language Arts and Reading, Grade 5, Adopted 2017. https://texreg.sos.state.tx.us/public/readtac$ext.ViewTAC?tac_view=5&ti=19&pt=2&ch=110&sch=A&rl=Y

Texas Administrative Code [TAC]. (1996). Chapter 89. Adaptations for Special Populations. Subchapter BB. Commissioner's rules concerning state plan for educating English Language Learners. https://texreg.sos.state.tx.us/public/readtac$ext.ViewTAC?tac_view=5&ti=19&pt=2&ch=89&sch=BB&rl=Y

Texas Administrative Code [TAC]. (1996). Chapter 74. Curriculum Requirements. Subchapter A. Required Curriculum. Title 19. Education. Part 2. Texas Education Agency. https://texreg.sos.state.tx.us/public/readtac$ext.TacPage?sl=R&app=9&p_dir=&p_rloc=&p_tloc=&p_ploc=&pg=1&p_tac=&ti=19&pt=2&ch=74&rl=1

Texas Administrative Code [TAC]. (2007). §74.4. English Language Proficiency Standards [ELPS]. Chapter 74. Subchapter A. Required Curriculum. Title 19—Education. Part 2. Texas Education Agency. http://ritter.tea.state.tx.us/rules/tac/chapter074/ch074a.html#74.4

Texas Administrative Code [TAC]. (2008). Chapter 128. Texas Essential Knowledge and Skills for Spanish Language Arts and Reading and English as a Second Language. Subchapter C. High School. Title 19. Education. Part 2. Texas Education Agency. http://ritter.tea.state.tx.us/rules/tac/chapter128/ch128c.html

Texas Administrative Code [TAC]. (2017). Chapter 128. Texas Essential Knowledge and Skills for Spanish Language Arts and Reading and English as a Second Language. Subchapter B. Middle School. Title 19. Education. Part 2. Texas Education Agency. http://ritter.tea.state.tx.us/rules/tac/chapter128/ch128b.html

Texas Administrative Code [TAC]. (2017). Chapter 128.36. English Language Development and Acquisition (ELDA) (One Credit), Adopted 2017. Subchapter C. High School. Title 19. Education. Part 2. Texas Education Agency. http://ritter.tea.state.tx.us/rules/tac/chapter128/ch128c.html

Texas Association for Bilingual Education [TABE]. (2005). *The Texas bilingual story: Celebrating our legacy.* [Video]. https://www.youtube.com/watch?v=AWbN_Y8aa5k&feature=youtu.be

Texas Education Agency [TEA]. (2012). *ELPS instructional tool: A language development process for beginning and intermediate English Language Learners.* [PowerPoint]. https://projects.esc20.net/upload/page/0070/docs/ELPS-InstToolTrainingSlides.pdf

Texas Education Agency [TEA]. (2017). *Every Student Succeeds Act-State overview.* [Video]. https://tea.texas.gov/About_TEA/Laws_and_Rules/ESSA/Every_Student_Succeeds_Act

Texas Education Agency [TEA]. (2017). *Pocket Edition 2016–2017 Texas Public School Statistics.* 2017. https://tea.texas.gov/communications/pocket-edition/

Texas Education Agency [TEA]. (2018). 2018–2019 LPAC STAAR decision-making guide. https://tea.texas.gov/Student_Testing_and_Accountability/Testing/State_of_Texas_Assessments_of_Academic_Readiness/STAAR_Spanish_Resources

Texas Education Agency [TEA]. (2018). *Supporting English Learners in Texas.* http://ELtx.org/index.html

Texas Education Agency [TEA]. (2019 Aug. 8). Update on the single statewide assessment for identification of English Learners, effective 2019–2020 school year. *h*ttps://tea.texas.gov/About_TEA/News_and_Multimedia/Correspondence/TAA_Letters/Update_on_the_Single%2C_Statewide_Assessment_for_Identification_of_English_Learners%2C_Effective_2019–2020_School_Year

Texas Education Agency [TEA]. (2019). 2019–2020 accessibility features. https://tea.texas.gov/sites/default/files/Accessibility%20Features_tagged.pdf

Texas Education Agency [TEA]. (2019). 2019–2020 Accommodation Resources. https://tea.texas.gov/Student_Testing_and_Accountability/Testing/Student_Assessment_Overview/Accommodation_Resources

Texas Education Agency [TEA]. (2019). Civil Action 5281. Government Relations and Legal. About TEA. https://tea.texas.gov/About_TEA/Government_Relations_and_Legal/Civil_Action_5281

Texas Education Agency [TEA]. (2019). *Learning Proficiency Assessment Committee [LPAC] framework manual.* https://projects.esc20.net/page/lpac.framework-documents

Texas Education Agency [TEA]. (2019). Limited English Proficient (LEP) / English Learner (EL) Decision Chart for the Language Proficiency Assessment Committee (LPAC). Special Student Populations. Bilingual Education and English as a Second Language Instruction https://tea.texas.gov/Academics/Special_Student_Populations/Bilingual_ESL_education

Texas Education Agency [TEA]. (2019). Making the ELPS-TELPAS Connection Grades K–12 Overview. [Powerpoint]. Produced by TEA Student Assessment Division. https://tea.texas.gov/Student_Testing_and_Accountability/Testing/Texas_English_Language_Proficiency_Assessment_System_%28TELPAS%29/TELPAS_Resources

Texas Education Agency [TEA]. (2019). STAAR Resources. https://tea.texas.gov/Student_Testing_and_Accountability/Testing/State_of_Texas_Assessments_of_Academic_Readiness

Texas Education Code [TEC]. (1995). Subchapter B. Bilingual Education and Special Language Programs. Chapter 29. Educational Programs. Subtitle F. Curriculum, Programs, and Services. Title 2. Public Education. https://statutes.capitol.texas.gov/Index.aspx

U.S. Congress (1965, April 11). *Elementary and Secondary Education Act of 1965*. Public Law 89–10-Apr. 11, 1965. *h*ttps://www.govinfo.gov/content/pkg/STATUTE-79/pdf/STATUTE-79-Pg27.pdf#page=1

U.S. Congress. (1968, Jan. 2). *Bilingual education act*. Public Law 90–247-Jan. 2, 1968. Title VII of the Elementary and Secondary Education Amendments of 1967. https://www.govinfo.gov/content/pkg/STATUTE-81/pdf/STATUTE-81-Pg783.pdf#page=32

U.S. Congress. (2015, Dec. 10). *Every student succeeds act*. Public Law 114–95. 114th Congress. https://www.congress.gov/114/plaws/publ95/PLAW-114publ95.pdf

U.S. Department of Education. (2017). Every Student Succeeds Act (ESSA). https://www.ed.gov/essa?src=policy

U.S. Department of Education. (2019). *Developing programs for English Language Learners: Lau v. Nichols*. Office for Civil Rights. https://www2.ed.gov/about/offices/list/ocr/EL/lau.html

U.S. Department of Education. (2019). Elementary and Secondary Education Act, as amended by the Every Student Succeeds Act. https://legcounsel.house.gov/Comps/Elementary%20And%20Secondary%20Education%20Act%20Of%201965.pdf

United States Code. (1974, Aug. 21). Equal Educational Opportunities Act of 1974. U.S. Code. Title 20. Education. Chapter 39. Equal Educational Opportunities and Transportation of Students. Subchapter 1. Equal Educational Opportunities. https://uscode.house.gov/view.xhtml?path=/prelim@title20/chapter39&edition=prelim

United States v. State of Texas, No. 71–1061. (1971). United States Court of Appeals, Fifth Circuit. https://casetext.com/case/united-states-v-state-of-texas-10

WETA Public Broadcasting. (2019). ¡*Colorín Colorado!* A bilingual site for educators and families of English language learners. www.colorincolorado.org

Wright, W.E. (2015). *Foundations for teaching English Language Learners: Research, theory, policy, and practice* (2nd ed.). Philadelphia, PA: Caslon Publishing.

Yang, A. (2020, March 11). *Online teaching: Do this, not that*. Alison Yang blog. https://alisonyang.weebly.com/blog/oreo-online-learning-guidelines

Yang, A. (2020, March 2). *OREO online learning guidelines*. OREO Online Learning. Creative Commons. https://alisonyang.weebly.com/blog/oreo-online-learning-guidelines

Zemelman, S., & Daniels, H. (1988). *A community of writers: Teaching writing in the junior and senior high school*. Portsmouth, NH: Heinemann.

Index